PENGUIN BOOKS

IN FLANDERS FIELDS

Leon Wolff, an American, served in the US Air Force during the Second World War. *In Flanders Fields* was his second book, the first being *Low Level Mission*, which dealt with the raids on the Ploesti oilfields in 1943. His third book, *Little Brown Brother*, won the Francis Parkman Prize from the Society of American Historians.

IN FLANDERS FIELDS

The 1917 Campaign

By
LEON WOLFF

PENGUIN BOOKS

PENGUIN BOOKS

Published by the Penguin Group
Penguin Books Ltd, 80 Strand, London WC2R ORL, England
Penguin Putnam Inc., 375 Hudson Street, New York, New York 10014, USA
Penguin Books Australia Ltd, Ringwood, Victoria, Australia
Penguin Books Canada Ltd, 10 Alcorn Avenue, Toronto, Ontario, Canada M4V 3B2
Penguin Books India (P) Ltd, 11 Community Centre, Panchsheel Park, New Delhi – 110 017, India
Penguin Books (NZ) Ltd, Cnr Rosedale and Airborne Roads, Albany, Auckland, New Zealand
Penguin Books (South Africa) (Pty) Ltd, 24 Sturdee Avenue, Rosebank 2196, South Africa

Penguin Books Ltd, Registered Offices: 80 Strand, London WC2R ORL, England

www.penguin.com

First published by Longmans, Green and Co. 1959
Published in Penguin Books 1979
Reprinted as a Classic Penguin 2001

3 .

Printed and bound in Great Britain by Cox & Wyman Ltd, Reading, Berkshire

To Lillian

In Flanders fields the poppies blow
Between the crosses, row on row,
   That mark our place; and in the sky
   The larks, still bravely singing, fly
Scarce heard amid the guns below.

We are the Dead. Short days ago
We lived, felt dawn, saw sunset glow,
   Loved and were loved, and now we lie
   In Flanders fields.
Take up our quarrel with the foe:
To you from failing hands we throw
   The torch; be yours to hold it high.
   If ye break faith with us who die
We shall not sleep, though poppies grow
   In Flanders fields.

JOHN McCRAE

Contents

Introduction   xi
Preface   xxi

1. The Deadlock   1
2. The Home Front   13
3. The Overture   30
4. L'Affaire Nivelle   52
5. The Interlude   68
6. Triumph at Messines   87
7. The Signed Contract   104
8. On the Brink   124
9. The Opening Phase   140
10. The Intermission   163
11. The Menin Road   177
12. Haig's Decision   194
13. The Slough of Despond   209
14. Journey's End   232
15. War and Peace   254
Sequel   274
Reference Notes   282
Bibliography   297
Index   301

Plates

Field-Marshal Sir Douglas Haig   40

General Sir William Robertson and Field-Marshal Ferdinand Foch   41

Marshal Joseph Joffre, Raymond Poincaré, King George V, Foch and Haig   41

Albert Thomas, Haig, Joffre and David Lloyd George   56

General Sir Herbert Plumer, Major-General H. A. Lawrence and Haig   57

Crown Prince Rupprecht of Bavaria   72

Field-Marshal Paul von Hindenburg, Kaiser Wilhelm II and General Erich von Ludendorff   72

General Robert Nivelle   73

General Sir Hubert Gough   73

Stretcher-bearers in action following the Battle of Pilckem Ridge, 1 August, 1917   88

Field gun bogged: Pilckem Ridge, 2 August, 1917   88

Near Zillebeke: 9 August, 1917   89

After the battle   89

Walking on tracks over the Zonnebeke Marshes: October 1917   200

A trench near Westhoek: 17 October, 1917   200

Bogged down: October 1917   201

Near Pilckem: 10 October, 1917   201

A Mark IV tank: 12 October, 1917   216

Plates

Ypres: 27 October, 1917   216

Polygon Wood: November 1917   217

Remus Wood: November 1917   217

All photographs are reproduced by permission of the Imperial War Museum except that of General Robert Nivelle which is reproduced by permission of E.N.A.

Maps

The Flanders Front: 6 June, 1917   70

Messines: 6 June, 1917   98

General Plan: July 1917   125

The Attack: 31 July, 1917   128

Allied Front Line: 9 October, 1917   211

The Passchendaele Salient: 11 November, 1917   255

The Western Front   257

Introduction

By Major-General J. F. C. Fuller, C.B., C.B.E., D.S.O.

THIS is an outstanding book, the most fascinating I have read on the period reviewed. It is much more than a military history, rather an invocation which summons from out the depths of the past the catastrophic year 1917—the progenitor of the age in which we live. Here are brought to light again all its many facets, its antagonisms, its blunders, its horrors and its heroism, also their repercussions on politics and social life.

The sources drawn upon are multitudinous and varied, ranging from official histories and the memoirs of statesmen and generals to obscure articles and long-forgotten newspaper reports. The participants come strikingly to life: Lloyd George, the mercurial, who says one thing one day and another thing the next; Haig, the man of gun-metal, who says nothing and does the same thing day after day; Nivelle, the cocksure; Pétain, the cautious; Foch, the oracle of the offensive; Henry Wilson, the military harlequin; Robertson, the baiter of politicians; and Repington, the curtained intriguer. These and a host of others play their parts, and as the author says—although he tried to avoid saying it—the play itself unrolls before the reader 'with the inevitability of a Greek tragedy'.

During this 'carnival of death', as Chief of the Tank Corps General Staff, I met most of the leading participants, and took part in all the British battles mentioned in this book; and what astonishes me is not so much the author's insight and devotion to facts but the extraordinary way in which he has recaptured the atmosphere of forty-one years ago, and made facts live again as they were then lived. Two are outstanding: the inability of the politicians to win a profitable peace, and the incapacity of the generals to win profitable battles.

As regards the first, the author writes: 'Early 1917 would have been a splendid time to stop the war.' With this I full-heartedly agree, and it was the only time. Until then the fighting had been largely experimental; the battles of Verdun and the Somme, in which 1,800,000 men of both sides were killed and wounded, had exhausted the belligerents, and had shown that frontal assaults on entrenched positions were unable to solve the stalemate. These massacres and the famous Lansdowne peace proposal of 14 November, 1916, led to the fall of the Asquith administration, and Lloyd George, who succeeded Asquith, was pledged to a more vigorous prosecution of the war. His policy, as the author points out, was to hit and hit again with all our strength until the Germans cracked, and although later he anathematized Haig's Flanders campaign as 'this insane enterprise', politically he was responsible for it.

Early in 1917, the sole sane alternative to a negotiated peace—the only type of peace which, as history has again and again shown, can lead to profit—was to put great battles into cold storage, and rely on the blockade to starve Germany into submission—that is, to win the war by sea power instead of land power. Three months later America entered the war, and a negotiated peace became impossible. April 6 was the black day in European history.

As regards the incapacity of the generals to win profitable battles, because the author—perhaps wisely—does not discuss tactical developments prior to the war, I think it is of importance for the reader that I should make clear what was at the bottom of their failures.

It was the rifle bullet, which had rendered the defence stronger than the attack: it begot the rifle-pit and the trench, it sheathed the bayonet, it blunted the sword, it drove back the cannon, and it dismounted the horseman. Fifty years before 1914, in the American Civil War, when the muzzle-loading rifle prevailed, a participant wrote: 'Our infantry were tired of charging earthworks. The ordinary enlisted men assert that one good man behind an earthwork was equal to three good men outside of it.' Summed up, the rifle bullet was lord of the battlefield.

Although between then and 1914 the breach-loading magazine rifle and the machine-gun had been introduced, with fire power a hundred-fold greater than in 1861–65, so conservative were armies that all—there are no exceptions—adhered in essentials to the tactics of the flintlock musket, which took a minute to load, and had an effective range of less than 100 yards. It may astonish the reader to learn that the only man who accurately forecast what happened in 1914 was a Polish banker, M. Bloch of Warsaw, who in 1899, in his book *Is War Impossible?*, wrote:

The war, instead of being a hand-to-hand contest . . . will become a kind of stalemate. . . . Everybody will be entrenched in the next war. It will be a great war of entrenchments. The spade will be as indispensable to the soldier as his rifle. . . . All wars will of necessity partake of the character of siege operations. . . . Your soldiers may fight as they please; the ultimate decision is in the hands of famine. . . . That is the future of war . . . the bankruptcy of nations and the break up of the whole social organization.

And in 1918 it was famine, the dividend of the blockade, more so than battles, which brought the Central Powers to ruin.

All this was miles beyond Haig's mental horizon, and the author's estimate of him closely tallies with my own. He lived and worked like a clock, every day he did the same kind of thing at the same moment, his routine never varied. In character he was stubborn and intolerant, in speech inarticulate, in argument dumb. But he was not an uneducated soldier. Unlike so many cavalrymen of his day, he had studied war, and, strange to say, this was to be his undoing, because he was so unimaginative that he could not see that the tactics of the past were as dead as mutton. We are told he held that the 'role of cavalry on the battlefield will always go on increasing', and that he believed bullets had 'little stopping power against the horse'. This was never true, as an intelligent glance at past battles would have made clear to him. Yet it had to be true, otherwise how could he employ his cavalry? Thus, in spite of fire, wire and mire, cavalry figured in all his battles, and to the detriment of the other arms, because they and their enormous forage trains blocked communications. Further, General Charteris, his Chief of Intelligence, tells us he considered himself 'the predestined instrument of Providence for the achievement of victory for the British Armies'—'British' should be noted, because he was congenitally anti-French.

His Chief of Staff, General Kiggell, a tall, gloomy and erudite soldier, was Commandant of the Staff College when I was a student there in 1914, and the only thing I distinctly remember him saying was: 'In the next war we must be prepared for very heavy casualties.' His theory of war was to mass every available man, horse and gun on a single battlefield, and by the process of slow attrition wear down the enemy until his last reserves were exhausted, and then annihilate him.

Within the walls of the old Vauban fortress of Montreuil, where G.H.Q. were established, Kiggell meditated like a Buddhist bhikku; revolved the prayer-wheel of his doctrines, and out of them concocted Napoleonic battles on paper, which on the ground turned out to be slaughter-house dramas. He was essentially a cloistered soldier; he never went near a battle, and—if correctly reported—only once visited a battlefield, and then long after the battle had been fought. Spiritually he was the twin brother of Flecker's Mandarin general in the 'Golden Journey to Samarkand',

> Who never left his palace gates before,
> But hath grown blind reading great books on war.

The remaining members of G.H.Q. General Staff were non-entities; but they should not altogether be blamed for being so, for to serve a projection of the deity is apt to make the most prominent feel small. All were, as they had to be, yes-men, and the only one who had any influence with Haig was General Charteris, a hale and hearty back-slapping fellow, as optimistic as Candide, who conjured forth resounding victories from each bloody hundred yards' advance like rabbits from a hat; he fed Haig on false news—anyhow false to the men at the front—and completely misled the Press and British public. It was he who, to pep up the troops, invented the German corpse factory, which, although it did not add to the prestige of his office, certainly made the front line rock with laughter.

The battles examined in this book form two pairs of Siamese twins; the one, those of Arras and Aisne II in the spring, and the other, those of Messines and Ypres III in the summer and autumn; and their origins and the politico-military wranglings which shaped them will greatly intrigue the reader. He should, however, bear in mind that the first two coincided with the entrance of America into the war and the outbreak of revolution in Russia; the one meant enormous eventual additional strength for Great Britain and France, and the other pointed to the release of a large number of German divisions on the eastern front and their transference to the western.

The battle of Arras, which opened on 9 April, led to an advance of 7,000 yards at the cost of 160,000 casualties. That of Aisne II, under Nivelle—of whom the author has much to say—was begun eight days later. It resulted in a severe French repulse and the loss of 180,000 in killed, wounded and missing; worse still—in mutinies in the French army. These prohibited a resumption of a French offensive for several months.

Haig had objected to both these battles, for ever since he succeeded Sir John French in December 1915, his eyes had been glued on Flanders, and with him a battle in that region had become an obsession.

Next, on 7 June, came the battle of Messines, which is particularly well described. Its aim was to flatten out the salient south of Ypres, so as to facilitate the launching of Haig's master battle eastward of that city. It came as a tactical surprise—a novelty in this war—and because of this and because its objective was a limited one it was a great but costly success.

Meanwhile, from the battle of Arras onward, an acrimonious wrangle between Lloyd George and Haig had been going on. The former, in spite of his hit-and-hit-again policy, was violently opposed to the latter's stubborn adherence to a battle in the Ypres area. At length, to force the Prime Minister's hand, Admiral

Jellicoe was roped in to say that, because of the U-boat menace, 'if the Army cannot get the Belgian ports, the Navy cannot hold the Channel and the war is as good as lost'. Haig knew this to be bunkum. Charteris has a note on what he said about it: 'No one really believed this rather amazing view, but it had sufficient weight to make the Cabinet agree to our attack.' Later, the plea put forward that, in order to reduce pressure on the French, Haig was compelled to attack, was a post-war afterthought to justify his battle. He did not fight at Ypres for submarine bases or for the French; he fought because he was confident of victory. He did what Napoleon said was the worst thing a general could do—paint an imaginary picture of a situation and accept it as real.

Haig knew the Ypres area well; he had fought over it in 1914 and, although the mud had not then been excessive, he must have known that the level of the surface water was so high that in many places parapets had to replace trenches—incidentally, the original tank was designed to surmount them. This should have made it clear to him that were the ground and its drainage dikes heavily shelled, irrespective of rain, the battlefield would become a bog; this had actually happened during the battle of Messines.

As more than half this book is devoted to the Third Battle of Ypres, all that space allows me is to reinforce the author's illuminating analysis with a few observations of my own.

In the preparatory bombardment 4,283,550 shells, weighing 107,000 tons, were hurled on to the reclaimed bog-land of Ypres, and in the opinion of the official historian 'the British Army . . . by its own bombardment and barrages created in front of itself its own obstacle'. This I can vouch for, because on 2 August, the third day of the battle, I went forward to look at the battlefield. The ground was shattered beyond recognition, and in many places slush was two feet deep. On my return, my general, Hugh Elles, asked me: 'How are things going?', to which I replied, 'Look at me!'—I was plastered with mud from head to foot. The next day I put in a report, a line or two of which the author quotes in Chapter 9; in it I suggested that the Tank Corps be withdrawn from the battle and, in order to distract the enemy, be employed in the French St. Quentin area. After reading it, Elles remarked that Haig would never co-operate with the French; thereon I suggested instead the British Front facing Cambrai—we little suspected at the time, this was the seed which was to sprout into the first great tank battle in history.

By the night of 31 July, the first day of the battle—heavy rain was then falling—Haig's project of massed infantry assaults followed by massed cavalry pursuits had foundered in the slough created by his massed artillery bombardments, and automatically Kiggell's theory of attrition came into play.

It led to such slaughter that G.H.Q. calculated that by October reinforcements would be 100,000 men short. On 21 August a conference was assembled to discuss what could be done to keep the battle going until November. Every department was to be depleted of men; work on roads, railways and hutting was to cease, and the Director-General of Medical Services considered it would be possible to get a certain number of men from the venereal class, though this might spread infection.

Reader, note the date—only three weeks after the battle had opened. Next, note another date. On 2 October, by when pack-mules were being used to supply the forward guns, and it was taking fourteen hours to bring a wounded man back from the front line, Haig assembled another conference to set before it his views on how the successes gained could be exploited. Preparations were to be made to launch a general offensive on the heels of the retreating enemy. Behind it the Cavalry Corps was to advance, and when the moment was favourable the enemy was to be pursued and annihilated. Yet, in actual fact, had the entire German Army volatilized, it would have been impossible for troops to pursue, because on account of the mud it would have been impossible to have supplied and fed them.

On 10 November the battle ended four and a half miles from its starting line. Ten days later came the battle of Cambrai. There was no preparatory bombardment, instead 376 tanks led the infantry assault over unbroken ground and through the toughest trench system in France at negligible cost. Although lack of reserves led to failure, the battle proved to all who could see that the stalemate was not an unsolvable problem, and that the answer to the bullet was a sheet of half-inch armour plate—the solution was as simple as that!

With a brief mention of this revolutionary battle, except for the author's final comments, this remarkable book on 1917 ends.

Acknowledgements

We are indebted to the following for permission to quote copyright material:

Messrs. George Allen & Unwin Ltd. for extracts from *Britain Holds On*, by Caroline Playne; the Australian War Memorial Committee for extracts from *Official History of Australia in the War*, Volume 4, published by Messrs. Angus & Robertson Ltd.; Lord Beaverbrook for a passage from a letter from Andrew Bonar Law to Lloyd George dated 18 September, 1917; Messrs. Ernest Benn Ltd. for extracts from *Chauffeur to Brigadier*, by C. D. Baker-Carr; Messrs. Cassell & Company Ltd. for extracts from *Soldiers and Statemen*, by W. Robertson; *Sir Henry Wilson*, by C. E. Caldwell; *Field-Marshal Earl Haig*, by Brigadier-General John Charteris; *Life of Lord Rawlinson*, by F. Maurice; and *The Red Knight of Germany*, by F. Gibbons; Messrs. Chatto & Windus Ltd. for an extract from *Unknown Warriors*, by K. E. Luard; The executors of the late Mr. H. G. Wells for an extract from *Outline of History*; Lord Haig and Messrs. Eyre & Spottiswoode (Publishers) Ltd. for extracts from *The Private Papers of Douglas Haig*, edited by Robert Blake; Sir Philip Gibbs for extracts from *The Struggle in Flanders*; Messrs. John Lane, The Bodley Head Ltd., for an extract from *How We Lived Then*, by C. S. Peel; Mr. B. H. Liddell Hart for an extract from *Through the Fog of War*; Lord Norwich for an extract from *Haig*, by Duff Cooper; Messrs. Odhams Press Ltd. for extracts from *The World Crisis*, by Sir Winston Churchill; the Oxford University Press, Inc., New York, for an extract from *Battlefields and the World War*, by Douglas Wilson Johnson; The Public Trustees and the Society of Authors for extracts from *What I Really Wrote About the War*, by Bernard Shaw; *Punch* for 'In Flanders Fields', by John McCrae; and Messrs. Putnam & Co. Ltd. for extracts from *The Winding Road Unfolds*, by Thomas Hope.

Preface

IN the beginning, Neolithic intertribal rivalries had gradually blended into coherent European history. Thousands of years came and went. The people, the kingdoms, the quarrels, the modes of conflict changed; but the causes of the wars remained as irrational as ever. In 1871 a routine incident took place: Alsace and part of Lorraine were annexed by Germany as part of her price for having won the Franco-Prussian war. While this technical transfer caused little change in the lives of the inhabitants of the area (except possibly for the better), they became properly incensed none-the-less, and their former French compatriots promised revenge.

German military power continued to grow, though now Bismarck took care to inform the world that his country's conscription system, broadened militarism and accentuated naval power were only defensive. 'Germany is surfeited,' he insisted, and was only arming to withstand evil powers which might try to deprive her of legal rights and possessions.

But other nations did not understand this, and considered the increasing strength of the *Reich* a threat to their own security. The two giants, Russia and France, drew even closer together when Germany and Austria (in reflexive fear of the Russian-French friendship) banded together in their military alliance of 1879. This was expanded into the Triple Alliance a few years later when Italy joined it. Its purpose was at least frank; it was directed flatly and by name against the defensive Franco-Russian coalition, which in turn was directed against the defensive Austro-German combination.

Thus far, all the alarums and excursions caused primarily by Bismarck's attempts to keep Germany supreme on the Continent had at least been confined to Europe. But now a new and more ambitious personality entered the scene—Emperor William II of Germany. He had a larger axe to grind; for it was his youthful dream to expand German trade, colonies and prestige throughout the world. While the blessings of such a programme, even if successful, might have trickled down only microscopically to the more humble occupants of his realm, they reacted to it with such enthusiasm as to suggest that they envisioned heaven on earth thereby. But in commencing to build the necessary navy the Germans brought forth a new and formerly aloof antagonist —Great Britain.

The watchful English had no intention of being pre-empted, and began to lay down an even bigger and better navy. Secondly they entered into defensive combination with France and Russia. Thus was born the Triple Entente.

Now the Germans in great indignation accused Edward VII of 'encirclement', and proceeded to strengthen their ties not only with Austria-Hungary and Italy but with Turkey. All of the last-named three had designs, meanwhile, on the Balkans, for ponderous reasons having to do with Serbian designs on Austria and Bulgarian designs on Turkey, to name only two such designs. There was a great Balkan crisis in 1908, followed by a sudden, nasty squabble in 1912, in which all the small countries ganged up on the helpless remnant of the Ottoman Empire and swallowed its European portion. Italy, Bulgaria, Serbia, Greece, Rumania and Turkey were involved in this affair, which came and went with such callousness as to bring a twinge of fear to the Great Powers. However, instead of trying to remove the basic causes of tension they proceeded to intensify them by still more desperate military measures.

A last-minute arms and naval race followed—'militarism run wild'—and in their fear the people, statesmen and kings turned to their generals and admirals for protection. The power of the military clique became enormous in all nations balancing on the brink. The symbols used to justify the drive to war grew apace, and were exaggerated into quasi-religious articles of unquestionable faith.

Austria-Hungary furnished a classic example of such phobias and slogans. She was determined to maintain the Dual Monarchy. She was provoked over losses of political power and prestige in the Balkan cockpit. She was hateful of the gains won by her Serbian rival. She was determined to expand her sphere of influence eastward. And when Archduke Francis Ferdinand, heir to the Austro-Hungarian throne, was killed at Sarajevo by Serb patriots as bemused as those of other lands, Vienna found a pretext for crushing her rival once and for all. Germany reluctantly backed Austria.

What followed was as swift, as purposeful, as inevitable, as though it made sense. For when Austria attacked Serbia, Russia (protector of the Slavic States) could not stand by. And Germany had to support her main ally in deeds as well as words. Yet France was committed to Russia on the basis of the Triple Entente, for tangible reasons of economics, and by a Premier who welcomed war. For similar reasons Britain had to support France and Russia. On the other side, Italy was theoretically obliged to fight beside Germany and Austria. Within a week almost everybody in Europe was fighting, and in time practically the whole world joined in.

In the fourth year of this war there occurred one of many military cataclysms: the Third Battle of Ypres, often referred to as the Passchendaele campaign or the 1917 Flanders offensive. While its importance was no greater than several others, it did possess, as we shall see, certain unique features which have set it somewhat apart in drama and interest. My aim has been to examine this fearsome and controversial episode in general terms rather than from a military standpoint alone. I have tried, but without avail, to avoid saying that it unrolled with the inevitability of a Greek tragedy. It did; and the problem in writing of it was not to trace the familiar sequence of events but to throw light on them from an embarrassing richness of source material. Thus the book is an essay in interpretation, with whatever defects must flow therefrom. Its perspective is British (and I am not), and here again distortions may have arisen. Finally, I found almost all reference sources more or less inclined against the military strategy which was adopted. These factors should be borne in mind in evaluating the narrative that follows, as well as my admission that I found it impossible to escape the point of view which probably colours much too plainly the telling of the story. Once I had hoped to relate it with such inhuman neutrality as would arouse the wonder and admiration of all shades of critical readership. I soon found that I could not believe what I was writing. The situation was most distressing, and I therefore decided to set down the facts and to comment upon them in the way which seemed to me inescapably logical. Yet I will never cease to suspect that I may be wrong, nor should the reader fail to do the same. All shades of opinion, however, are represented in the Bibliography which follows the narrative; and I have also consulted many periodicals of the day, especially the London *Times*, but since these are referred to by name throughout the book they are not listed here.

Other than these sources (and others used too meagrely or obliquely to require formal credit) I am in debt to my wife, who brought about changes in certain chapters, and to my publishers in New York and London, who uncovered many small blunders and who suggested ways of reorganizing and rephrasing portions of the manuscript. They did not concern themselves with my interpretations and attitudes; and the usual formality concerning the sole responsibility of the author is perhaps more meaningful in this case than most. The argument about Passchendaele continues with unabated bitterness. Haig and his campaign have been seized upon as ideal targets by those who abhor the military mind and its works, while their opponents defend their own way of life and thought with equal vigour. Thus the conflict now seems to be running deeper than its origin. I hope this book will contribute a trifle to the understanding at both levels.

L. W.

1

The Deadlock

SOMEWHERE in the limitless darkness a man coughed, a bird twittered an isolated phrase, a muffled voice spoke up. Many miles behind the front, thousands of lorries, wagons, gun limbers, horses and men moving endlessly along the Belgian roads furnished a soft, pulsating background, like that of a kettle-drum stirred by felt hammers while the orchestra rests and watches its score. Here in the advance zone of the dread Salient around Ypres hardly a man moved, nor did many even know or care that the old year was dying.

The officer standing beside the field piece watched the glowing second hand of his wrist watch. At the stroke of midnight he said 'Fire!' The gun roared, and a shell was lobbed somewhere into the German positions. A few seconds later there was a single, distinct, far-off explosion, following which a strained silence hung in the air. Then the enemy threw up anxious flares, ghastly green but of great beauty. These illuminated No-Man's-Land linger-ingly, froze it briefly into the aspect of a charcoal sketch, and then faded away. The British battery fired nine rounds in erratic succession, paused, and then seven more. Thus the new year, 1917, was advertised by seventeen shells, to which the Germans did not respond; and the rest of the evening passed in relative peace there and elsewhere on the Western Front.

A cheerless morning dawned some hours later. In Belgium there were snow and sleet flurries beneath a steel-grey sky, in France temperatures below freezing and strong damp winds that chilled the men in their icy entrenchments; and only near the French-Swiss Alps did the sun appear elusively, though here the

cold was even greater. Most of the front from Switzerland to the
English Channel was a black snake writhing through white snow
that covered the hills, plains and woodlands of belligerent Europe.

As the skies lightened the great armies stirred. The big guns
boomed their required number of rounds at registered targets in a
lacklustre way. Men filtered sleepily into the forward trenches
and took up their arms, groaning and cursing in the way of early
risers. To revive their spirits, snipers fired a few careless rounds at
the enemy sandbags. Machine-gunners cut loose and swept
No-Man's-Land for a minute or two, to clear the area of spooks
and enemy prowlers. The British troops yawned and stretched,
were issued their daily ration of rum, replied with age-old
complaints as to quantity and quality, and sipped it meditatively.
Through peep-holes and periscopes they scanned the enemy
parapets, about 100 yards away.

Blue smoke arose where the enemy was frying bacon. As the
snipers watched through their tiny loopholes, blackish-brown
heads and shoulders occasionally hurried past narrow gaps in his
parapets. These blurred fragments were actual enemy soldiers,
briefly visible against the misty sunlight and under the star shells
that now blazed whitely. Still the countless wheels, hooves and
boots rumbled like faraway thunder, and could clearly be heard
between the pounding of machine-guns, rifle fire, mortar explosions and the roar of artillery.

For the first time the soldiers were no longer betting that the
war would be over by next year. They had begun to whisper that
'it might last a lifetime', usually followed by the mocking:
'They say the first seven years will be the worst.' Nobody sang
'Tipperary' any more—that dashing, inspiring tune of earlier
days. It had been replaced by 'Take Me Back to Dear Old Blighty'.
And hopelessly, sardonically they hummed to the tune of 'Auld
Lang Syne':

> We're here because we're here,
> Because we're here, because we're here;
> We're here because we're here,
> Because we're here, because we're here.

The third New Year's Day of the first Great War had arrived on the Western Front.

The conflict which had exploded in 1914 was, it was felt at the time, fortunately going to be a short one. All the generals on both sides (as in the paradox of conflicting prayer) stated that they would prevail in a short time; and even among the few pessimists there was a feeling that military operations of such impending magnitude had to end in a rapid decision one way or the other. The German and French General Staffs had been especially sanguine. The latter, under the influence of General Foch, felt that any morally righteous offensive had to triumph if pursued with sufficient zeal. Thus, the French were bound to triumph by merely undertaking their plainly righteous offensive with the zeal to triumph. That there might be a flaw in this gem-like reasoning escaped them. And the Germans were also caught in their own trap of rapid conquest. For, in the event, the unexpected power of the defensive (though it should not really have been so surprising in view of lessons taught in the American Civil War and the Franco-Prussian War) brusquely smashed the respective military schemes of the equally aggressive and confident Great Powers.

For the first two months events had seemed to bear out the German warlords. They had counted on a speedy war of movement against the French through Belgium, while holding off the slow-moving Russian bear. Thus they expected to win before either Britain or Russia could effectively join in the fray. At first all went well. Liège was captured; the German armies swept through Belgium; soon Paris itself was in sight. But then the German goose-step was stopped at the Marne. Both sides now tried to outflank each other to the west. Each easily parried the other's slow, courtly counter-motions, and the so-called 'race to the sea' continued until the front rested on the Channel coast. For all practical purposes the war of movement was now dead, two months after birth. The Germans sensed the futility of attempting to revive it; it would be more than three years before they would again go over to the offensive.

The French were slower to learn. General Foch had insisted that 'any improvement in firearms is bound to strengthen the offensive'. Napoleon had stated that victory was certain to be won by the 'big battalions', and the revered Clausewitz had told of the invincibility of great masses of troops. The French and Russians alone, not to mention the British troops gradually being fed into the fight, drastically outnumbered the Central Powers. The mobile, rapid-firing 75-mm. French field gun was the greatest of its type in the world, and the French had thousands of them. The French, having recovered from their initial shock, found the hated Germans deep inside their borders and determined to drive them out and go forward to inevitable victory, muttering Napoleon's plausible axiom: 'The moral is to the physical as three to one.'

How this would apply to pious, moralistic Mother Russia was another story, short as she was of rifles, railroads, cannon, machine-guns, foodstuffs, roads, motor transport—even uniforms. Only in men did the Czar possess an abundance of riches. With this flood of brave, blindly obedient manpower (plus her French and British allies) Russia too felt certain of winning, despite early setbacks.

As for Great Britain, though the home islands entered the conflict with a mere 160,000 expeditionary troops, they were the acknowledged cream of the world's striking forces on land. Her navy, of course, was unparalleled and in itself would certainly strangle the enemy coalition, if the war lasted any great length of time. The trend of thought among British military planners was as bullish as that of their counterparts. Britain—like France, like Russia, like Germany, like Austria—expected successfully to solve by one surgical excision the political ills of the Western world. Never before had a war started with such grim confidence on the part of all concerned.

But after the opponents had met head-on like two mountain goats that first summer of the war, and were halted dazedly by each other, a rigid front was formed that defied all efforts of the French and British to break through. Under the command of

'Papa' Joffre, dull battering-ram efforts took place that only served to demonstrate the incapacity of this general and of others whose mental processes were confounded by the deadlock and the impossibility of turning manœuvres. All they could think of was a policy of attrition and frontal attacks.

In 1916 Foch, under his continuing delusion that sheer will-power could break through barbed wire and machine-guns, further drained the life blood of France in vast, notorious battles, the worst of all (during 1916) being the one fought on the Somme. The disaster here sealed the fate of his army, and perhaps of France herself as a world power, for ever.

By this time the British under Sir Douglas Haig were fighting in numbers equal to those of their ally; and at the Somme they were similarly cut down. They lost 60,000 men the first day alone; and when the offensive had dragged to its weary end in November 1916 only a few square miles of worthless tortured ground had been captured, while the losses of 538,000 troops on the part of the Central Powers compared to 794,000 of the Allied attackers. After this blood-bath a plaintive cry went up: 'No more Sommes!'

When the year ended a few weeks later, it was clear to all observers who still respected the meaning of human life—even soldiers' lives—that some kind of cross-roads had been reached, and that this state of affairs could continue no longer.

From the northern border of Switzerland to the Belgian coastline near Ostend a scribbled line of entrenchments stretched south-east to north-west for 350 miles, dividing the French, Belgians and British from the Germans and Austrians in opposition. This complex system of trenches and dug-outs, behind which were more trenches and dug-outs, existed in combination with dense whorls and loops of barbed wire, thousands of armoured machine-guns (that new and utterly frustrating 'concentrated essence of infantry'), and various other new and old methods of defensive warfare.

Now there was little scope for the brilliant commander, for

the Hannibal-like manœuvre, for the cut and thrust of traditional warfare waged by artful foot soldiers and speedy cavalry. There was no flank to be turned, unless by some miracle the mountains and the sea could be mastered by forces of decisive size. With no way to go around, with no way of crashing through, with no generals or statesmen sufficiently subtle to find another key that might turn, both sides settled down in despair and frustration to a mutual siege. Neither could enforce its will upon the other; and since the folklore of the times excluded any settlement other than military the war went on, in its fashion.

In and near the front several millions of men lived like moles, fearing even to show their steel helmets above the sandbagged parapets. Front-line trenches were the dominating feature of the stalemate. In time, after they had been fought over a good deal, almost all sense and direction were lost to them and they became murderously confused, interconnected in haphazard new ways, astounding labyrinths in which the men moved warily and felt little security. Sometimes British and German troops occupied what was in effect the same trench, only separated from each other by a bomb barrier and an unspoken agreement. Sandbags, boards, mud and tree branches were used as supporting revetments, and the job of keeping the trenches deep and erect never ended. To avoid being taken in enfilade, they were dug with sharp kinks every few yards, called traverses, in which swearing, squeezing traffic-jams were chronic.

Perpendicular to the front-lines were communication trenches —poor, shallow affairs, usually wet and crumbling, that weaved as much as five miles rearward to the reserve areas. It was through these, as a rule, and not 'overland', that troops travelled to and from the front during daytime.

And finally in the intricate, mole-like maze of the Western Front were the dug-outs, in their most primitive form merely extra-large holes scooped into the side of a trench for the personal use of one man. But many caverns were minor marvels of crude engineering ingenuity that housed dozens of troops. Here in the fetid smell of unwashed bodies and dank earth the men lived

when not on active duty, made coffee in brown pots, dried their
stockings, played chess, warmed potatoes, dozed, argued, cleaned
their rifles, wrote letters, waited for morning, or guard duty, or a
bit of action, and shuddered peaceably under the pounding of
enemy artillery exploding overhead with dull, harmless thuds.
Candles flickered (far back in the dugout the air was so bad they
often went out), the rats prowled, but there was little peril even
from the direct hit of a 15-inch railway shell. The sound of war
was muffled almost to extinction and the men enjoyed some of
the comforts of home. They were going nowhere; they were
there to stay; and this they did as best they could. They sang:

> I love the ladies,
> I love to be among the girls . . .

and on the slimy walls they hung mirrors, clocks, even electric
bulbs, pin-up pictures that showed daringly trim ankles and saucy
smiles. Life was almost comfortably lazy. There were tooth-
brushes, magazines, sometimes even straw floors, and stoves that
heated the clammy interiors sporadically, if not well. In the midst
of desultory bedlam the men smoked their pipes, came down with
boils, shored up the sides of their trenches and dug-outs, munched
bully-beef in tins and Belgian cheese, and waited to be put back
into reserve.

On both sides were the card players—German, English,
French, Austrian, Canadian, Welsh, Australian; the mania cut
across all national lines. Not even the war could interrupt their
gambling and never did they seem to sleep. Day and night the
card players, a race apart, continued their relentless games.

Between the lines was No-Man's-Land, above which nightly
hung the star shells thrown up to probe the stripped, blasted
wasteland with a nightmarish glare. Machine-guns in set patterns
raked the desolate ground searching for enemy patrols. The
snipers aimed at gaps in the sandbags, the communication-trench
entries, the mess areas further back; and every man knew the
whiplash crack of a rifle bullet near the direct line of fire, and the
melancholy whine of a ricochet.

As for men, they were seldom to be seen. For this was the peculiarity of the Western Front: the uproar seldom ceased and the number of men involved was countless, but the terrain seemed deserted. Nothing moved in the lethal zone where the great armies brushed against each other. Nobody appeared to be fighting. Here and there somebody stared through a loop-hole. Occasionally a man actually fired a gun of some size, seemingly at random. It seemed impossible that anyone could be hit by it. Yet the casualties went on—about seven thousand each day, except when serious fighting occurred.

The enemy was remote. It was difficult to hate him. All the usual procedures were reversed, and the hero of last century charging forward with a shout, his rifle at the 'engage', was no longer brave but a fool. Religion and chaplains were tolerated sourly, even by men of real faith, and patriotism was something of a joke. After years of stalemate there had been heavy losses not only in men but in normal standards of belief and behaviour. Militarily, morale was neither good nor bad. In a war where the individual counted even less than in any other war before or since, the men merely stuck it out and did their best, up to a point. The solemn axiom was, 'Never obey orders—they're already cancelled.'

No decisive warfare was attempted along the Western Front during the long intervals between vast, convulsive campaigns. Mostly there were mere trench raids with the object of capturing the trench or dug-out directly in front, or to kill some of the enemy, or to take prisoners. From a company point of view, in fact, the entire war sometimes seemed to be nothing but a series of trench raids—hysterical mêlées in which hundreds of opposing troops often occupied the invaded trench along with the original inhabitants. What with clumsy Smith-Wesson revolvers, armoured machine-guns, Lugers, Lewis guns, rifle fire, Mills grenades, bayonets, flame-throwers—all of these at close range— the casualties were enormous by the standards of later wars. By 1917 thousands of these routine, unknown, forgotten trench raids had taken place, and many had cost more lives than famous

battles of a later generation. When they were over, the trenches
were left piled with dead and wounded; and, if it became necessary
for the visitors to leave hurriedly, they could scarcely be blamed
for trampling friend and foe underfoot with their hobnailed
boots.

And during the lulls the wounded called and groaned in
No-Man's-Land, lingered for as much as a week, and usually died
there, and sometimes screamed in their incoherent agony; while
above them sounded the joyous songs of the birds. The thrushes,
especially, twittered wildly each morning, for they were used to
the guns. During the height of battle the wounded begged their
friends to save them, but the latter rushing from shell-hole to
shell-hole were usually too distracted to be of service. A German
poem ran:

> I can't give you a hand;
> You're for the Promised Land,
> My Comrade, good and true.

Except during trench raids the stagnation of siege warfare gave
the illusion of peace. For weeks and months on end nothing
happened of any importance, and the daily communiqués
reported, 'On the Western Front small-scale infantry actions took
place west of Lens . . .' and '*Im Westen nichts neues*', leaving the
usual collection of greyish corpses between the lines. After a day
or two their features became swollen, and there was no expression
in them. They lay in the dirt not in gallant positions, but stiffly,
like store-window mannequins. Their bodies were horribly
plump; they were in truth swelling out of their clothes. Nor did
the stretcher-bearers who collected them have an enviable task,
for there were many on both sides who took a malicious pleasure
in sniping at them.

Only the artillery never entirely ceased any day or night.
Every shell had a personality of its own and could be identified
with fair accuracy by old timers. Most cannon were light horse-
drawn field pieces which fired small shells, usually shrapnel,
about three miles. The British 18-pounder, the famed French 75,

3

and the German 'whiz-bang' 77 were all in this category. They
were not too difficult to detect en route and gave the men several
seconds to dive into cover. On the other hand, high-velocity
pieces were hated because their projectile was thrown at terrific
speed in a nearly straight line and gave almost no warning. And
except for the great railway guns the howitzers were the largest
of all: gaping monsters that tossed their fat shells almost straight
up and down. The men called them 'crumps'.

The German 5·9s were also polite and gave the recipient some
small time for acquiring shelter. The last part of its passage was a
deep roar; one was safe if the roar lasted, but if one were in its
path it descended fast and the best that could be hoped for was an
extreme case of shell-shock. These were called 'coal-boxes'.

The sounds of the projectiles created a bizarre symphony.
Field-gun shells buzzed in a crescendo and burst with a clattery
bang. The heavies flung their black bodies like great loaves of
bread (they could be seen in flight) across vast reaches of the infinite
sky and approached with the roar of an oncoming express train.
Over valleys they all echoed distractingly and defied prediction.
Those that fell in hollows burst with terrible suddenness and a
double crash. Fabulous indeed was the blast of the 30·5 Australian
trench-mortar. And there were shells that screamed, shells that
hissed, gas shells that exploded with a simpering pop, shells that
whistled, and shells that wobbled across heaven rattling like a
snare drum. Finally there was drum-fire, reserved for special
occasions, when all the instruments blended into one homo-
geneous mass of sound of such intensity as cannot be described, all
bursting into jagged fragments of hot metal that slammed into
the bodies of men and mules with familiar results.

The troops hated artillery more than machine-guns, more than
snipers, or bayonets, or even gas; for there was no fighting it, nor
could much really be done to elude it.

And above it all flew the airmen in their rickety little machines
—Albatross, Spad, Nieuport, Fokker and Sopwith fighters,
De Havilland bombers, RE-8 observers—fighting, bombing,
strafing and watching the motionless scene beneath them. Yet

the men in the trenches had no great hatred for the fliers who thus plagued them, but looked up to them with mingled fear and admiration. For the moles felt a certain inferiority, weighed down as they were by a score of impediments, wedded to the earth in shell-holes, mine galleries, trenches and underground pits where man was never intended to exist, except in death.

But for these feeble biplanes and triplanes that droned and flickered aloft, there was no longer any military motion of consequence along the Western Front. Sandbagged trenches, in themselves, were splendid for defence. Tanks were almost unheard of. A single machine-gun could stop 500 men. There was no real air power. Barbed wire often ten rows deep was staked out to trap and retard advancing foot soldiers. (A mordant comment when a man was missing from an informal roll-call was, 'Hanging on the barbed wire'.) Concrete pill-boxes peered sullenly through narrow slits of eyes from which protruded the swaying muzzles of machine-guns and semi-automatic rifles. And there were booby traps, sharpshooters cunningly hidden in devious nests, contact mines underfoot, and armoured short-range artillery ready to blast any small target that appeared— even a single sniper revealing his hideaway, or a guide chancing a short-cut to the latrine.

The use of gas also helped the defence, not only because it burned, blistered and asphyxiated, but because it forced attacking troops to advance through the yellowing swirling fumes in cumbersome equipment. The clouded mica of the masks made accurate rifle-aiming impossible. Soldiers tired quickly, and moved slowly and vulnerably across the nerve-racking strip toward the opposing trenches.

After the Somme débâcle two and a half million men had been killed on the Western Front out of nearly seven million total casualties there; and still the lines held. The titanic armies sat— squatted, as the arm-chair critics contemptuously put it—amid scenes of unique desolation. Everywhere near the battle zone where the trench system had finally congealed lay the debris of war—smashed, rusty rifles, empty haversacks, stricken and abandoned heavier equipment, here and there among the scrub a lonely grave adorned by a single wooden cross, as well as growingly formal cemeteries. Trees were nude stumps. Moon-craters studded the landscape. Peasants' houses gaped in the middle of their patch of ground. Inside one might still salvage scraps of clothing, broken crockery and sundry rubbish. Always the roof was half off. Potatoes rotted in the cellars, cupboards were torn open, pictures blew in the breeze, old French and Flemish prayer books invariably lay tattered in a leeward corner. The people had long since left the advance zones of battle. For over two years the Allies and the Central Powers had contemplated each other balefully out of the ruins of the countryside and the wreckage of their respective war plans.

2

The Home Front

IN London the tone of the New Year was set by Lord Curzon, Lord President of the Council, in a message to the Primrose League: 'It is impossible to say as yet that the end is in sight. . . . It seems likely that well into another year, perhaps longer, must we continue the dreadful tragedy that is turning the world into hell. . . .' This was hardly news to the people of the home island, who by 1917 had relapsed into an apathetic silence that concerned their leaders almost as much as the enemy. It was not that revolution was likely, but that a negotiated peace might become necessary some day unless matters took a turn for the better. The prospect, though as yet no larger than a cloud the size of a man's hand, definitely existed now and was ominous to contemplate. Nor were the Germans making matters easier. Their recent peace overtures, though scornfully rejected, had created much embarrassment. Even now, three weeks later, *The Times* was still rejecting them; on New Year's Day, a Monday, their leader writer wrote: 'To the illusory peace proposals of Germany the Allies with one accord have given a definite negative. . . . Germany's conduct demands penalties, reparations and guarantees. . . .'

And, as if to add emphasis, another peace meeting in Victoria Park was broken up—this one conducted by the notorious pacifist, Miss Sylvia Pankhurst, and four of her lady cohorts, all of whom had voiced the usual inflammatory sentiments concerning the nebulous Allied war aims, the motives of David Lloyd George in not exploring the German proposals, the logic of attempting to solve political problems by so-called organized murder, and so on. A sizeable crowd had listened in silence, but the surrounding police had made no move until an opportunity presented itself: 'During the speeches two little dogs rushed in and made an opening for active interference. Two old soldiers, waving the Union Jack and singing "The Red, White and Blue", made for the platform, and with the help of the crowd swept it away with all upon it', throwing the five ladies to the ground.

Nowhere in any newspaper that day was there a single item about New Year's Eve celebrations. No gay parties were reported, no drunken uproars out of the ordinary, none of the usual whimsies of the January-the-first press. Instead, the columns were full of firm resolves, grim warnings, and dour expressions of determination to carry on to ultimate victory regardless of cost. No more cheerless fare could have greeted the average Londoner at breakfast.

Certainly there was little enough to celebrate. By now nearly every family knew at first hand the meaning of death, capture, or injury at war. London was a city of women, children, old men, and walking wounded. The ingredients for merry-making were missing. The glories had long passed, along with most of the starry illusions of 1914. Those had been days when the men had volunteered in overwhelming numbers (now they were con-scripted), days of the exciting spy-mania, when one child had pleaded about her family's old German house-servant, 'Mummy, *must* we kill poor Fräulein?', when bands had played daily in the streets, when women had rushed by the millions into any kind of war work, when flags had everywhere fluttered. Then it was that excited girls thrust white feathers at young men who failed to join up quickly, and the newspapers had published that splendid recruiting song, 'Your King and Country Need You':

> Oh, we don't want to lose you,
> But we think you ought to go;
> For your King and your Country
> Both need you so.

We shall want you and miss you,
But with all our might and main
We will thank you, cheer you, kiss you,
When you come back again.

In sullen obstinacy people had by 1917 become resigned to the
necessity for winning the war, hating it, seeing no end to it, no
longer able to understand it by standards that had once seemed so
brilliantly clear. Now it was only necessary to get the thing over
with, to sweep it out of existence, and to try, somehow, to restore
life to normal. But beneath it all was a suspicion that it really
might never end. The people of Britain were like a person in a bad
dream—half awake, half knowing it to be a bad dream, but a very
long one which somehow did not end, as other bad dreams always
did.

Especially disillusioned were the Liberals. Before the war they
had been opposed to participation. When Britain did declare
war, they fell off the pacifist train and became the most ardent
warriors of all. Suddenly electrified, they looked forward to a
world cleansed and socially advanced, once this last war of history
was won and Prussian militarism smashed. But now they felt
tricked. The war, it turned out, was just another cynical and
sordid affair. There was nothing to hope for, nothing to do but
win it. Their misery was the greater, for they were ashamed of
having been trapped, and because they had flown so high before
falling so far.

Only among duller minds, by that January the first, was the
war still a splendid canvas without warts. One writer, after a
conversation with a worker of this mentality, reported, 'Like
much general talk in war-time, it was vague, jumpy and incoherent. The man's views reflected oft-repeated prejudices; he
showed total failure to grasp historic sequence of happenings. He
displayed a loose kind of ignorance. You felt that he was incapable
of acting on reasoned grounds or steering among the heap of
prejudices that jostled one another in his mind.'

People seldom exclaimed, 'How sad!' at news of others'

deaths or casualties but hurried on to tell of their own misfortunes. Rumours flew thick as locusts: Turkey was leaving the war, Austrian emissaries were discussing peace terms in Switzerland, the German Crown Prince was dead, the United States would declare war next week, a German regiment near Bullecourt had mutinied, and so on. But neither false reports nor optimistic speeches could lift the general depression for more than a moment. The French Minister of Munitions, M. Albert Thomas, had been dismayed during previous visits by the serene attitude of the British toward the war. But now when interviewed by the *Chronicle* he was struck by their proper grimness: 'The whole "tonality" is different,' he said, with satisfaction.

Food was scarce, especially meats and fats. On New Year's Day the Food Controller ordained only 'straight-run' flour for bread. 'White Loaf in Exceptional Cases Only' was *The Times* heading. But still there was no rationing (it might alarm the populace, the government thought), and there were queues for meats and margarine, and sometimes for sugar, potatoes and even tea. Housewives tramped from shop to shop in hopeless quests for certain supplies. All imported foods were desperately short because of the German submarine blockade, now reaching its peak; and servicemen had first call on whatever did get through. The people did not understand all the reasons for foreign shortages (much data and many facts having naval significance were withheld) and complained sourly that Britain was not fighting the United States and the Dominions. There were food meetings, food demonstrations of great size and organization, food complaints, and endless food conversation among the bedevilled citizenry. It was far and away the favourite routine vexation of the war, surpassing even that concerning the Zeppelin and airplane raids which by 1917 had killed or injured nearly 3,000 British in London and various coastal cities.

Rivalling all this was the coal shortage, and many were the comments with regard to the private profiteering and hoarding of that commodity. By 1 January, 1917, the coal queues were starting to rival the great food queues in size. There was much shivering and actual suffering that winter in Britain, and people who lived where gas or coke were burned enjoyed a great popularity.

Without petrol for owners of private cars, unless they were engaged in important war duties, the crush in trains, trams and buses had become astonishing that winter: 'Getting home during rush hours was a daily terror. . . . The crowds of office workers were vastly increased and the scramble to get into some of the longer distance trams and omnibuses constituted a bear fight out of which those of both sexes, who were worsted or driven off the overladen vehicles by the conductors, retreated to the pavement with hats bashed in, umbrellas broken, shins and ankles kicked and bruised, in a dazed and shaken condition. The darkened streets added to the confusion of people returning from work.' And that Monday *The Times* told of

'Dearer Travelling Today.
Fewer and Slower Trains.'

As for taxi-drivers, surely they were the most hated of all human beings. Their independence, rudeness and profiteering were positively infuriating. To travel alone in a taxi was unheard-of; and it was usually necessary to bribe the driver in order to change his dourly premeditated route.

Inflation, that disreputable cousin of war, had arrived on the scene from the beginning. Women's stockings had risen from 1s. 8d. in 1914 to about 3s. 8d. in 1917, and an average man's suit from 28s. 6d. to 60s. The food index stood now at 187 compared to the 1914 normal. And, of course, the official figures told only part of the story, for in the absence of rationing and price control everything sold for anything the seller could get. In the case of rabbits, cereals, most luxury items or whatever else was really scarce at the moment, such prices became scandalous. And the people complained bitterly over the exorbitant profits made by business out of the misery of war. Wages had increased, but longer working hours, ugly working conditions, speed-up routines and higher prices created much discontent. By 1917 strikes were commonplace, and these in the very depths of war.

John Bull, that frenetic scandal magazine of the day, had achieved an enormous circulation by pungently expressing the people's weariness and disillusionment. Its editor, Horatio Bottomley, roared out in stories headed by captions like these: 'Who are the Liars?'—'What a German Officer Told Me'—'Still Taking Odds'—'Why Haig is Silent'—'Murderers, not Ministers'—and after the German peace overture: 'No more Peace parleying with the enemy—no more damned nonsense about consulting the wishes of the niggers in the captured German colonies.' The people loved it, and clamoured for more.

That New Year's Day there were clearances everywhere, and the newspapers (pitiful, shrunken things due to governmental restrictions) were full of the advertisements. And elsewhere in *The Times* were other items heralding the glad new year. Sir Douglas Haig, that silent, humourless, grey-moustached, level-eyed Scot who had long considered himself the right-hand man of God in this holy struggle, commander on the Western Front, was named a Field-Marshal. The King and Queen, Princess Mary, Prince Henry, Prince George, and Princess Victoria all went to the intercession service that morning at Sandringham Church. An Amsterdam correspondent reported 'CRIMINALS FOR THE GERMAN ARMY' and enlarged glowingly on that vulnerable theme. *Samson and Delilah* was still hanging on at the Aldwych Theatre. Gilt-edged stocks had closed firm that morning, and bank shares rose in brisk trading. Madame Tussaud's Wax Exhibition advertised, among other delights, a 'Lifelike Portrait of the RIGHT HON. DAVID LLOYD GEORGE . . .'.

The military reports were unusually dull. Russia reported that scouts had captured nine men in a trench west of Koniuchy. The French told of a '*coup de main* against a small German post south of Chilly [which] gave us a number of prisoners. Everywhere else the night was calm'. British G.H.Q. in France spoke of artillery fire south-east of Le Transloy, but concluded that beyond this 'there is nothing further to report'.

The only war items of the slightest interest were a German communiqué to the effect that in Rumania the Russians had been thrown back as far as the Braila bridgehead (even *The Times* admitted that 'the enemy are making ground'), and another concerning the sinking of the French battleship *Gaulois* by a submarine in the Mediterranean.

And, despite the shortage of newsprint, a few items of a more pungent nature were included in the 16-page New Year's Day *Times*:

Under the heading 'GERMAN SAVAGERY AT SEA' it was told how the skipper of the U18 had deliberately murdered a Danish captain and sailor by striking their lifeboat broadside with his submarine.

And in a related vein:

THE MURDER OF A RACE

HOW ARMENIANS WERE EXTERMINATED

MOSLEM EVIDENCE

Among the abominable cruelties and extensive massacres perpetrated by Germany and her Allies . . .

Everywhere women had taken over the bulk of civilian duties. By the dawn of 1917 they were heavily engaged in munitions work; they were firemen, tram conductors, taxi-drivers, window cleaners, chimney sweeps, horse and mule trainers, farmers, ambulance drivers, even mechanics. And, of course, they had enlisted by the hundreds of thousands in the Army, the Navy, and the Red Cross. While all of this had at first been wonderfully new and thrilling, the bloom now had worn off and much cynicism had become rampant among the women as well as among male workers and soldiers. Nowhere was this more evident than in the squalor and hopelessness of the East End, where poverty traditionally reigned, especially now that the heads of the families were gone to war. There had been a great movement of women and girls from this district into heavy labour and surreptitious prostitution. Soldiers' wives moved in with other men, and the civil authorities were deluged with morals complaints.

Liquor was served in restaurants and night clubs in unprecedented quantities. To evade the 10 o'clock ban, Scotch whisky was customarily poured in coffee cups, and champagne in lemonade glasses. Soho, 'that square mile of vice', was in its heyday. Nearly 200 disreputable night clubs, countless ladies of unfortunate repute, thugs and confidence men thronged the area in wait for the soldiers and sailors who drifted there as though magnetized, almost begging to be set upon for their money in the age-old ways. Luridly, Sir Arthur Conan Doyle appealed for the protection of these young men (whether they wanted to be protected is debatable) 'preyed upon by harpies' in darkened London, and, along with many others, he asked for official State Regulation of Vice. By 1917 there were an average of 4,000 monthly convictions for drunkenness alone in England, Scotland and Wales.

In Germany everything was much the same that dismal New Year's Day. Prices had gone up even more. The sea blockade was total. The Crown Prince of Germany in his memoirs tells bitterly how

> . . . as early as the beginning of the year 1917 . . . weariness of the war was already very great. I also saw a great and menacing change in the streets of Berlin. Their characteristic feature had gone; the contented face of the middle-class man had vanished; the honest, hard-working bourgeoisie, the clerk and his wife and children, slunk through the streets, hollow-eyed, lantern-jawed, pale-faced and clad in threadbare clothing that had become much too wide for their shrunken limbs. Side by side with them jostled the puffed-up profiteer and all the other rogues. . . . Nevertheless, nothing was done to remove the evil . . . whoever wished to profiteer profiteered—profiteered in state contracts, in essential victuals, in raw materials. . . .

And as one German woman later wrote to an English friend:

> One of the most terrible of our sufferings was having to sit in the dark. It became dark at four in winter. It was not light until eight.

Even the children could not sleep all that time. One had to amuse them as best one could, fretful and pining as they were from under-feeding. And when they had gone to bed we were left shivering with the chill which comes from semi-starvation and which no additional clothing seems to alleviate, to sit thinking, thinking, thinking. . . .

By New Year's Day 1917 most British people of democratic views had become dismayed by the Defence of the Realm Acts, which had generally torpedoed civil liberties and had substituted courts martial for much civil law. Any 'reports likely to cause disaffection or alarm' had become an offence. The police and military were given the power to search and inspect any premises at any time, to seize documents or 'anything' else which the military had reason 'to suspect' was being used, or might be used, for subversive purposes. Anyone could be arrested without a warrant. Suspects could be detained by the military police almost indefinitely, until they could be dealt with in the normal course of civil jurisdiction. Military boards could force anyone to live or not to live in a specified area. These and other regrettable regulations had reduced most citizens to a paranoid furtiveness. They tended to avoid strangers, to utter nothing critical, and to refrain from reading or listening to anything defeatist or anti-patriotic. In stereotyped phrases they backed the war effort.

Only a few courageous possessors of dissident views spoke, wrote, or acted in such manner as almost deliberately to invite intervention by the authorities; and primary among these were the conscientious objectors, who even at this late stage were still being treated as this group is always treated in war.

One of these was the writer, Lytton Strachey, who, though he had been classified physically unfit, preferred to go through the mill as an objector. At the military tribunal he inflated an air cushion to sit on, in protest against the hard benches, an opening gambit which did not endear him to his inquisitors. When the chairman stated the usual preliminary: 'I understand, Mr. Strachey, that you have a conscientious objection to war,' he replied in his curious falsetto, 'Oh, no—not at all; only to this war.' And to the triumphant stock question: 'Tell me, Mr.

Strachey, what would you do if you saw a German soldier trying to violate your sister?' he had replied with pious virtue, 'I would try to get between them.'

But the great masses of tired and depressed ordinary people merely got on with the war: not for them the calculated protest, the sardonic analysis, the deliberate affront to entrenched power. The ignorant saw no reason to doubt. The religious prayed. The poor worked. The Liberals wrung their hands. Few surrendered to thought. The very rich called Sunday their 'munitions day', when they replaced regular war workers, and survived the war coldly and determinedly, drinking hard at the better places, flirting and love-making, dancing, dressing to the fashion, and living as usual, but more so.

And while life variously went on in the cities and farmlands of Britain, death held sway on the Continent, where, on the Western and Eastern and other fronts, after the near-truce of New Year's Day, the gigantic armies turned again to the business of war. General Smuts said: 'We cannot contemplate without feelings of profoundest emotion this spirit of self-destruction which has come over our civilization.' But when was it all to end, and in what fashion? By New Year's Day 1917, the answers to these questions were as obscure as the early morning fog that drifted over the Thames and locked in its grey arms the towers of the Houses of Parliament, the riverside wharves, and the labyrinth of Piccadilly.

'We are going to lose this war,' remarked David Lloyd George to a Cabinet official as 1916 drew to a close. It was, perhaps, an unduly pessimistic statement, especially for him, but after the cruel disappointments of 1916 few in command or authority expected any longer to win a clear-cut victory. It was a period of drift, uncertainty, irritability. Everybody pretended to have a pet solution, but at heart nobody knew just what to do. Hope was flagging in London and Berlin that dreary New Year's Day. Both sides were exhausted. People high and low had begun to forget what they were supposed to be fighting for. At the top there was much concern about protocol, personalities, politics and gossip—always a sure sign that a dead end has been reached—and a vulgar search for scapegoats, both military and civilian. There were lightning shifts in command. Always officials were resigning, or threatening to resign, or meticulously pointing out conditions under which they positively would resign. But upon one matter everyone was agreed (with the exception of a very few who thought the war was coming along splendidly)—and that was that the war was coming along miserably. The Rumanians were finished. Bulgaria had joined Germany. Russia was fading fast, and by the end of the year was heading for civil chaos and military ruin. The naval battle at Jutland had been a confused, indecisive disappointment. The German U-boat campaign was reaching its triumphant apogee. The Somme fiasco had just ended. The Americans were still maddeningly neutral. And the Northcliffe press fanned the flames of despair: *The Times* and the *Daily Mail* castigated the politicians, of whom there were twenty-three in the War Cabinet. Placards reading 'Wanted: Twenty-Three Ropes' were displayed on the streets to advertise a late edition.

Everybody blamed the leaders. Nobody blamed the Germans. The military blamed the politicians. The politicians blamed the military, or other party members in the Coalition government. The masochistic conviction that England herself was at fault had sputtered slowly for two years and had exploded after the Somme, causing the fall of mild Mr. Asquith and his replacement by David Lloyd George, the violent Welsh politician, a passionate, imaginative, scheming man who knew well that his one and only mandate was to conduct the war more effectively.

His first problem was not Ludendorff, but the War Office. For it was from this quarter, Mr. Lloyd George believed, that policies had emanated which had brought the empire so near exhaustion. It was the War Office, so intent on holding the reins of military power, which Mr. Asquith had said 'kept three sets of figures, one to mislead the public, another to mislead the Cabinet, and the third to mislead itself'. It was the soldiers' War Office and its specious statistics that Lloyd George himself had once compared to desert sands: when the wind changed, the humps turned to hollows and the hollows to humps. And why these deceptions? To Mr. Lloyd George they were plainly designed to ensure an enormous flow of drafts and munitions to France and Belgium, and nowhere else.

For after the military paralysis had set in, two schools of strategic thought had arisen. On one side were those (mostly soldiers) who thought the war had to be fought on the Western Front against the main concentration of German strength. On the other were the so-called Easterners (mostly civilians) who considered it hopeless to attack the enemy where he was strongest and who recommended various other ways of outflanking, or dismembering, or blockading, or otherwise demoralizing and defeating him. The position of Lloyd George was stated in his own words: 'I never believed in costly frontal attacks in war or politics, if there were a way round.' He considered General Haig a clumsy, murderous fool. His own plan was to turn the Western Front into a holding operation, and by means of certain peripheral operations to leave Germany isolated, heavily outnumbered, and set up for the final kill.

Amateurish nonsense of this sort was resisted doggedly by Sir William Robertson, Chief of the Imperial General Staff, as well as Douglas Haig and other high British officers who felt that the only sure way to ultimate victory was to exert pressure continuously in France and Belgium.

Winston Churchill, at the moment merely Member for Dundee, was in turn contemptuous of such strategy. All the agility and subtlety of his mind revolted against generals whose idea of warfare was to throw vast amounts of men and guns head-on against a prepared enemy and then, when it was all over, to 'count heads' and compute who had won the battle. His 1915 Dardanelles expedition designed to knock out Turkey, reinforce Russia, and slice through the soft underbelly of the Central Powers had been bungled by half-measures in London and by commanders on the spot, and Churchill had fallen into disfavour.

For a time he had even served as a battalion commander at the front. Now he was back in the Government with vivid plans for the Balkans, the Middle East, and the Baltic Sea. He had ideas regarding tanks and other revolutionary new weapons, and he envisioned diplomatic and naval manœuvres to stun the enemy. All this represented a philosophy designed to by-pass further failures on the Western Front.

But the commander on that front would not willingly release a single man or gun for service elsewhere. Though the Somme campaign had depressed most observers, it had fairly satisfied Sir Douglas Haig. Inflexible, impassive, he stated his unchanged intention of fighting a war of attrition on the Western Front. There was no substitute for killing Germans: that principle seemed so obvious to him that any other one smacked of imbecility, at best, if not outright treason. Momentarily Haig in 1916 had been induced to toy with the idea of an amphibious landing on the Belgian coast behind the German lines. After discussing it with Admiral Bacon he had learned of the need for special landing craft (which did not yet exist) and, in view of steel shortages, he had on sober second thought dropped the plan. Anyway, his heart was not in such shallow trickeries. War seemed simple to Haig. An ex-cavalry officer, he felt that battles were won by charging at the enemy and trouncing him in a straightforward fight. To do this, what else was really needed beyond superiority in men and material, an enemy that could not run away, a crucial sector, and sound planning? In November he had even suggested to Lloyd George that Italian troops and guns should be transferred to the Franco-Belgian front; and he recorded hopefully in his diary that the (then) Secretary of State for War 'said that he was much struck by my suggestion'.

After the Somme, Haig had written a paper for the Government summarizing his views. In keeping with his character and beliefs it was optimistic. 'There was reason to believe' (a phrase of which he never tired) that German casualties were far greater than those of the British and French. The morale of the enemy had shown 'marked signs' of deterioration, while the British army

4

was 'confident in its proved superiority'. Bad weather alone, he
continued, had prevented total victory. The effect of the campaign
on German civilians had been demoralizing. And, finally, if yet
another similar campaign were to be waged soon there would be
'full justification' for expecting decisive results. (A year later
Haig was to issue another such appraisal.) This memorandum
confirmed Lloyd George's suspicion that the man was quite
hopeless. The Somme was the nadir of the war, to date, and almost
everybody else knew it. From this moment on, his marginal
confidence in the European commander dwindled almost to
zero.

But, in a sense, the Somme had cleared the air. Opinions
solidified. The majority thought it had gained nothing but a few
devastated miles at enormous cost. The minority believed that
the German army had suffered a great blow, was tottering, and
would fall after one more of the same. In support of this view they
referred to the German peace feelers late in 1916, circulated
immediately after the German capture of Bucharest. (These
overtures had led President Woodrow Wilson to call upon the
various nations to state, once and for all, exactly what they were
fighting for. 'That ass President Wilson has barged in and asked
all belligerents for their terms', noted Sir Henry Wilson irascibly
in his diary, 22 December, although he was sure there would be
no negotiations; and in this he was correct.)

And of those who considered the Somme a failure there were
two subdivisions: one, as described above, which was now certain
that the war could never be won militarily on the Western
Front; and another which flatly recommended making peace.
This latter view was spectacularly summarized by Lord Lansdowne, who circulated to the War Cabinet a reasoned and
meticulous letter suggesting that a meaningful victory was no
longer possible. 'Can we afford to go on paying the same sort of
price for the same sort of gains?' he asked, and pointedly suggested,
'Let our naval, military and economic advisers tell us frankly
whether they are satisfied that the knock-out blow can and will
be delivered.' A large uproar followed. Lloyd George called it

'a terrible paper'. Winston Churchill and Lord Balfour felt that Lansdowne's argument could not be brushed aside. Haig replied coolly that the prospects were 'excellent' for 1917. And when also asked for an opinion, Robertson stated innocently to the Government: 'Quite frankly, and at the same time respectfully, I can only say I am surprised that the question should be asked. The idea had not before entered my head that any member of His Majesty's Government had a doubt on the matter.'

Lloyd George joined in rejecting Lansdowne's heretical views. As impending Prime Minister, the former knew that the Coalition Government in Parliament was not there to make peace but to contrive victory.

In this vein, by that New Year's Day, there was much talk by the Easterners of reinforcing the Bulgarian Front, where, at Salonika, the Germans had bottled up hundreds of thousands of Allied troops. The French were even more inclined to transfer supporting troops there than the British, fearing that the front might otherwise collapse, though as it happened the Germans had no intention of attacking what they had derisively labelled their 'largest internment camp'.

And there were operations in Turkey, Mesopotamia, and Palestine, having mainly to do with oil, where the Easterners saw further possibilities for outflanking the deadlock, or at least forcing the enemy to thin out his inventory of men and munitions. After all, the combined manpower of the Allies on all fronts was still far greater than that of the Central Powers.

To these schemes the Westerners objected. The interior lines of the enemy, they said, would make it easy for German reserves to be switched back to the Western Front in a pinch. Furthermore, the whole idea of knocking the props out from under Germany was a mistake. No success against Austria, for example, they said, could make the Germans give a single yard on the Western Front.

Not true, said the Easterners. Germany could not simply abandon her main ally, and thus expose herself to a gigantic enemy influx from the south-east.

But every Allied soldier transferred to 'side-show' operations, said the Westerners, increased the danger of a German break-through in France.

Demonstrably wrong, said the Easterners. The whole history of the war thus far has proved the impossibility of such a break-through on the Western Front.

But, insisted the Westerners, even if all the fringe campaigns in Italy, Turkey, Salonika and elsewhere were to succeed, the Boche would be strategically unaffected; for even then the Allies could not muster enough strength north of the Brenner Pass to menace the south German frontier.

Whereupon the Easterners proved to their own satisfaction that this argument, too, was a deception designed merely to salvage the fading reputations of dull-witted warlords seeking vindication and personal glory. And the war of words went on, in bitterness and frustration.

Meanwhile the military leaders were proceeding with strategy as they saw fit. On 15 November Joffre, Haig, Robertson and other Allied officers had assembled at Chantilly to decide what to do the following year, and obvious enough conclusions had been reached: The French and British (especially the British) would attack along the Western Front in February. Simultaneously the Russians, Rumanians and Serbians would attack on their respective fronts. And later in the spring the British alone would proceed to clear the Germans out of Belgium. This decision for the two major powers to continue, in effect, their Somme offensive did not meet with unanimous agreement. Most generals of every other country questioned the concept strongly and wanted basic operations to be switched to the Balkans for the coming year. However, the greater weight of Joffre and Haig had won out.

Meanwhile the despised politicians were also converging on Chantilly. They arrived the next day to find that the generals had outflanked them with a programme which, remarked Lloyd George, would reiterate 'the bloody stupidities of 1915 and 1916'. Everybody—Britain's Lloyd George and Asquith, Russia's Isvolsky, France's Briand, and other civilians, plus all the military officers—sat down and tried to argue it out. The generals explained that the Germans were in trouble and that 'wisdom demanded continuous hammering of the weakening vital spot'. On 16 November there was much confused bickering. The conference ended indecisively. None-the-less Haig and Joffre proceeded with their preparations.

Soon afterwards everything fell through. In December Joffre (patting his great head, no doubt, as he often did, and murmuring whimsically, '*Pauvre Joffre!*') was removed as Commander-in-Chief and replaced by General Robert Nivelle. The new French leader had a rather different concept, one which would change the complexion of the war in 1917, and which through a chain of unforeseen circumstances would soon bring in its wake a time of troubles for Field-Marshal Haig and several hundred thousand lesser men.

3

The Overture

HARD by the windswept curve of St. Andrews Bay lie the treacherous undulations of Scotland's Old Course, most famous of links, where Douglas Haig was so often to golf in later years. He was born some miles away at Cameron-bridge on 19 June, 1861, of a noted and wealthy family, and there spent his entire childhood. Later at Oxford he failed to distinguish himself scholastically, and was looked upon as 'headstrong, bad-tempered, and intractable'; and while he soon suppressed the second characteristic and became the most even-dispositioned of men, the other two he would find more difficult to master.

At university Haig had become, if nothing else, an outstanding polo player. It was a talent which was to have an effect on his life, for after Oxford he entered the Royal Military College at Sand-hurst, and from there gravitated naturally into a commission with the 7th Hussars. At once he became a member of the finest polo team in the army. Now in his middle twenties, aloof, hand-some, with hardly a thought in his head but for polo, hunting, the social pleasantries, and more polo, he appeared a typically shallow career officer. But with maturity came the stirrings of ambition. He began, somewhat indiscriminately, to read military history and to study cavalry tactics. This was extremely unusual among young cavalry officers, a group not known for intellectual pursuits, in a branch of service the lackadaisical members of which were seldom distinguished by talent or diligence. Haig's superiors were surprised to find that they had a military scholar on their hands. Under the auspices of the Prince of Wales he began to advance.

He became adjutant of his regiment in India, and attracted further attention by rewriting and finishing the *Cavalry Manual* started by Sir John French. In 1896 he was awarded a special nomination to the Staff College. And even here his individual ways persisted; he showed contempt for certain superior officers; he ignored studies in which he had no interest; he wrote letters of protest and criticism. Yet in two years as a captain he had become staff officer to the cavalry commander during the Sudan and South African campaigns.

He continued to correspond with extreme frankness—to his friend the Prince of Wales, to the Adjutant-General. He berated his own commander-in-chief, Kitchener, as a planless leader who had invited disaster and was 'truly fortunate' that the Dervish army was so inept as to rescue him from folly. His superiors, in short, were 'old fossils'. The future King Edward was amused but worried; such criticism, he suggested, 'may be correct, but it does not do'. To this Haig referred in another letter: 'What a stupid letter it would be if I did not express an opinion . . . but whether I am right or wrong . . . I consider our worthy authorities are old stupids, ignorant of the first principles of war.'

But while his own work as Chief Staff Officer to French was methodical, he had failed dismally to lay hands on the elusive Boer partisans while in command of a group of columns. Concerning this operation one Intelligence officer had in fact predicted:

Haig will do nothing! He's quite all right, but he's too —— cautious; he will be so fixed on not giving the Boers a chance he'll never give himself one. If I were to go to him one evening and offer to land him at daybreak next morning within galloping distance of 1,000 sleeping Boers, I know exactly what he'd do; he'd insist on sending out someone else to make sure the Boers were really there—to make sure no reinforcements were coming up to them, and to make so dead sure in fact, that when he did get there not a single d——d Boer would be within ten miles of him.

From a rather contemptuous, free-swinging youth Haig now veered toward orthodoxy, precision, and a hardening of the creative impulses. It was becoming increasingly difficult for anyone to change his mind. Silent in the past, he became more silent. The demands he made on his troops were exacting, his punishments severe. The appearance and precision of his command became famous. In 1903 he was named Inspector-General of Cavalry in India with the rank of Major-General. He began to be called 'Lucky Haig'.

His great favour with the King and with Lord Kitchener (whom he had criticized so severely in private correspondence) certainly had much to do with his appointment and future rise. By now he was spoken of by the King as 'my best and most capable general'. While a guest at Windsor Castle for the 1905 Ascot Races he was introduced to one of the Queen's ladies-in-waiting, Dorothy Vivian. Two days later he proposed and was accepted. The wedding took place in the chapel of Buckingham Palace; never before had it been used by anyone but members of the royal family.

His powerful connections, his dominating personality, the efficiency of his staff work, his fantastic rise, had made him an outstanding power among the military clique—if not with the politicians, whom he distrusted, and who generally disliked him in return. There was some talk about appointing him Chief of the Imperial General Staff; but this was going too fast, and an older officer received the assignment.

A disquieting event took place in 1912, when during war games Haig commanded a corps and was seriously outmanœuvred. The official report referred significantly to the way he had pursued fixed aims without regard to new information. A conference was held at Cambridge in which Haig tried to justify his actions. With the King himself presiding, Haig according to a biographer 'became totally unintelligible and unbearably dull. The University dignitaries soon fell fast asleep. Haig's friends became more and more uncomfortable; only he himself seemed totally unconscious of his failure.' Throughout his life Haig was to be plagued by this inability to convey his military thoughts in words.

What were his military thoughts? As a cavalry tactician he was devoted to broad concepts in the Napoleonic vein that were no longer appropriate. He wrote that the 'role of cavalry on the battlefield will always go on increasing'. His one great axiom—that 'mass tactics' were the basis of this arm—had been abandoned long ago by even the most ardent cavalry officers. He believed that bullets had 'little stopping power against a horse'. He conceived of cavalry as the basic instrument of war, to which infantry and artillery were secondary. He resisted innovations, and in later years was to deprecate the airplane, the tank, even the machine-gun. He had come to epitomize what a renowned French cavalry officer had once said—that 'the British cavalry officer seems to be impressed by the conviction that he can dash or ride over anything; as if the art of war were precisely the same as that of fox-hunting'. Sir John French wrote of Haig that he would 'show to greater advantage as a superior Staff Officer than as a Commander'.

When war came, all the qualities of Douglas Haig—his underlying intelligence, almost inhuman grasp of detail, coolness under stress, complete self-assurance—were matched by certain corresponding defects. In writing he advised His Majesty to sack Sir John French as commander on the Western Front, explaining that the field-marshal 'is quite unfit for his command at a time of crisis in our nation's history'. And throughout 1915 he continued to pour scorn on him in letters to the King and Kitchener, the impropriety of which never seems to have occurred to him.

But Haig himself had been strangely inactive as a corps commander during the 1914 retreat. His troops had retired (in an incorrect direction) while the adjacent corps under Smith-Dorrien stood and fought. Though Haig was only partially to blame, the fact remained that he had not met his first great test impressively. Later, at Ypres, he conducted defensive operations with skill. On the other hand, his attacks against the hardening German trench system were turned back with heavy losses.

When French was relieved of his command, largely through Haig's insistence, there was, at any rate, no one much better to

take over the British Expeditionary Force in France and Belgium
than Sir Douglas. He accepted—if his diary is any indicator—
with no more exhilaration or surprise than if he had been handed
a set of cuff-links for his birthday. The date, obscure but fateful,
was 10 December, 1915.

Yet his appointment was not received everywhere with
enthusiasm. Among his intimates he was respected for methodical
planning and firmness of will, but most of them considered him
something less than a brilliant general. Even the sympathetic
official historian writes that 'it appears true that Haig himself was
not swift of thought'. George Bernard Shaw visited the Western
Front soon after Haig took over, and appraised him similarly:
'. . . he was, I should say, a man of chivalrous and scrupulous
character. He made me feel that the war would last thirty years,
and that he would carry it on irreproachably until he was super-
annuated.'

Haig had expected the assignment and he had done his part
behind the scenes to stage it. He believed that God had chosen
him as a man of destiny. At spiritualistic seances had he not been
told 'to do much good and benefit my country', and that the
spirit of Napoleon was 'always near me'? And respectfully he
consulted the medium on matters of more specific import—
whether a battalion or company clerical system was more
efficient, how the Territorial Army problem should be solved, and
so on. But primarily he consulted God. 'I feel that every step in
my plan has been taken with the Divine help', he wrote in 1916,
just before the Somme offensive unrolled, where he lost sixty
thousand men the very first day for no appreciable gain in ground
—a portent of further such developments in this campaign.

Winston Churchill recalls how Haig once referred to a brigadier
as an officer who 'did not show a sincere desire to engage the
enemy'. This remark, says Churchill, was 'the key to his whole
military outlook', and he continues thus:

He presents to me in those red years the same mental picture as a
great surgeon before the days of anaesthetics, versed in every detail

of such science as was known to him: sure of himself, steady of poise, knife in hand, intent upon the operation; entirely removed in his professional capacity from the agony of the patient, the anguish of relations, or the doctrines of rival schools, the devices of quacks, or the first-fruits of new learning. He would operate without excitement, or he would depart without being affronted; and if the patient died, he would not reproach himself.

By 1917 Field-Marshal Haig had lost not a particle of his optimism and self-esteem, though all his offensives to date had miscarried, the war was a stalemate, British casualties exceeded a million, and his fitness to command had become a known matter of debate in Parliament and especially the War Cabinet. If he had doubts, he reinforced himself with prayer. No trace of a sense of humour could evoke in him wry reflections on his omniscience. Still in perfect health, an imposing figure of a man, gentle in outward manner, fanatically supported by his staff officers, totally confident of eventual victory by smashing open the front and releasing his beloved cavalry for the kill, convinced that the Germans fought for the Devil against him and God, he stood on the threshhold of his greatest crisis with the calm certainty of a genius or a fool. Time alone would deliver a verdict of one or the other or something in between.

While David Lloyd George and Douglas Haig had always disliked each other, this had not mattered much until the former became head of the government. Both wheels spinning in opposite directions then moved into contact, and the friction began to throw off sparks and heat. At Chantilly, where Lloyd George found himself faced by a *fait accompli* diametrically opposite to his views, he had argued to no avail his Eastern philosophy of war. Bitterly he refers to the generals' plan as 'mildewed . . . a legacy of inevitable disaster'. Not yet being in power he was unable to head it off. But as Prime Minister he *sotto voce* began expressing doubts concerning the decisions reached by Haig and Joffre, and to call for a new conference in January, at Rome, to decide once and for all how to fight the war in 1917.

It appeared that Sir Douglas did not consider these coming conversations much of a threat to his established plans, nor did he even plan to participate in them. On 3 January he met at Rollincourt with his Army Commanders—Rawlinson of the Fourth Army, Plumer of the Second, Gough of the Fifth—and laid down the theme for coming operations in terms more or less similar to those suggested at Chantilly. 'Rawly' was told that he would be sent up north to kick off the main offensive in the Ypres Salient, following a preliminary French attack. Thus Haig chose to ignore Lloyd George and to imply disapproval of any plans to the contrary developed at Rome. His main regret, which he stated freely, was that he was forced to deal at all with politicians of this stripe, and that in theory he might actually be bound by their inept military thinking.

Some degree of conflict between the two men would have been inevitable in any event, even aside from their strategic differences.

Haig was bound to suspect the glittering, dangerously clever Mr. Lloyd George, that 'mass man'—the new phenomenon of democracy—who differed from old-style aristocrats and warriors in his modes of thought as though he were an organism from another planet. But there were few indeed who truly fathomed David Lloyd George, and Haig was far from alone in despising and suspecting him. As a hard-bitten politician Lloyd George had never been reluctant to throw overboard anybody who rocked his boat. He had entered public life as an accomplished Liberal orator and writer at the age of seventeen. Avid for power, he campaigned in a harsh, radical fashion for Parliament only ten years later, and won. This was 1890; he was to represent Wales from the Caernarvon Boroughs for fifty-five more years. In Parliament he flung himself precociously into affairs, and almost at once was in conflict with the veteran Gladstone, who admonished him icily: 'I ask my honourable friend not to interpose unnecessarily, not to search with something of a feverish heat for arguments of all kinds. . . .' The appeal had no affect on the barrel-chested young man with the hard blue eyes.

As Prime Minister he had not mellowed, and was still capable of violent hatreds, especially for mental nonentities. To this day he had not a real friend in the world, though he was acquainted with thousands of people, had a thousand enemies, and sat on the shoulders of a thousand faceless lackeys. But—cohort, foe or slave—he would use any of them on Friday and cut them dead after the week-end. The only man with whom he had something resembling a true kinship was Winston Churchill—and even he, this forty-two-year-old upstart, could be (and sometimes was) shrivelled by the fiery tongue of the master.

Possibly Lloyd George was the most accomplished orator of modern times in the melodramatic mode. His repertoire included hoarse screams of fury, ingratiating smiles, ghastly whispers, ominous scowls and mutters. With all this were intermingled the gaunt finger of shame, silky sneers, irony that could slash like a razor, and pure wit of high or low sophistication. Or he could move audiences to tears with pathos, with the Welsh-accented poetry of his words. All these were the traditional marks of the charlatan. But his friends and enemies knew him better, and realized that behind this theatrical façade existed a complex brain and a fair amount of principle. He had been a Liberal almost from birth, and his hatred of war and championship of the under-dog were not entirely a pose designed to snare votes, though it was seldom that he allowed conscience to block his way to fame and power.

He was completely lacking in military training or sympathies. But like other semi-amateurs—such as Caesar, Cromwell and Napoleon—he seemed to possess an unorthodox low cunning in war. The generals hated him for his encroachments on their terrain, and the debate over his military talents will never end; for the approach he advocated was never tried. He was passionately, stubbornly wrong at times. Often he was devious. Culturally he was lopsided. Intellectually he ranged from the sublimely penetrating to the blindly prejudiced.

This is the man against whom that silent, simple Scot, Field-Marshal Sir Douglas Haig, fought the battle of wills which was to mean so much to so many.

Lloyd George had been Prime Minister of Great Britain for one month when the Rome Conference convened. His position then was far from secure. The empire's military and naval leaders opposed him almost to a man. The Conservative members of Parliament tolerated him apprehensively and only for the moment. Many of his own Liberals suspected his personality and past tactics. The very way in which he had acquired office (a rather disreputable imbroglio had taken place, not entirely behind the scenes, in which Prime Minister Asquith had been shunted to a siding) had not inspired confidence in the serenity and character of his forthcoming leadership. The Press had made these vulgar political manœuvres known to the people. So even in the most important sector—that of the general public—Lloyd George's reputation was weak. That January he was holding on by a thread, and it was touch and go whether he would last out the spring. To do so would require not only leadership far more resourceful than that of his predecessor, but a good deal of tact and compromise, at least in the beginning. As yet he did not feel strong enough to fight his powerful opponents to a finish at Rome.

At this sprawling conference of Allied military and civil leaders Lloyd George led off in a way that appears to have confirmed the suspicions of Robertson that the man really was a menace and a cad—a 'cur', in Haig's melodramatic word. It was not that Lloyd George circulated a long speculation ('an amazing document' Robertson coldly termed it) on what he believed to be the military situation. Nor was it that this civilian recommended again his stale plan for an Eastern operation. The unkindest cut was that the formula had been sprung on the assemblage without the knowledge of a single British general. Sir William ('Wully') Robertson, Chief of the Imperial General Staff, had crossed the Channel with Lloyd George and accompanied him on the train to Rome; and all this time not a word had been said about scuttling the Chantilly arrangements. The General was furious, and except for a few sullen expressions of dissent said little for two days. He left Rome in advance of the break-up of the conference, presumably confident that Lloyd George's suggestion would wither on the vine.

This turned out to be the case. The Italian general, Cadorna, had at first been delighted with the idea of shifting the centre of Allied gravity to his poor front, but had learned all too soon that neither Haig nor Robertson knew anything about their chief's surprise package, nor did they have any intention of buying it. In deference to these awesome personages he reluctantly backed off.

As for Briand, the French Prime Minister, he gives the impression of having entered the conference in a state of indecision. He knew all about the plans jelling around his new French commander, General Nivelle, to conduct an assault near the old Somme battleground. He could not very well undercut his own man. Yet he agreed with Lloyd George that it would be futile in 1917 'for each general to continue punching on his own front'. Though wedded as a matter of political principle to operations on the Western Front, emotionally he distrusted slaughter-house Somme-type offensives. He sympathized mildly with the plan to smash Austria, especially since large numbers of French (and British) troops would not be called into action there; Lloyd George asked only for an Italian offensive backed up by a terrific concentration of French and British artillery. He was aware of the deposed Joffre's warning that the French were so weak that their war effort was almost done, and that they were good for only one more grand offensive. If this assumption were true, and Briand accepted it, it seemed a pity to attack so soon after the last Somme débâcle, and in the same bloody locale. Yet Briand was afraid to join the isolated British Prime Minister and feared to weaken his own front by transferring any of his forces or material elsewhere. In the end, after soulful deliberation, he too opposed the Italian adventure.

And the British generals in attendance, headed by Sir Henry Wilson (he referred to politicians as Frock Coats and boasted in his diary on 6 January that 'we never touched on Lloyd George's paper all day') and the dour, heavily handsome Sir William

Robertson, openly blocked their own Prime Minister right down the line.

Lloyd George had plunged into all this with typical enthusiasm. He loved conferences. In front of large audiences all his talents of speech, personality and mental gymnastics came through in fine style. Yet by 7 January his first big entrée on the world's stage had turned out a humiliating failure. If Chantilly had been indecisive, Rome settled matters. For the moment at least the fluid military scheme for 1917 had frozen into solid and massive shape: the Westerners had won; the battle of the Somme would be fought all over again. Lloyd George was thrown a dry bone: his Italian scheme would be studied by the various Staffs, so it was soothingly said.

Baffled and in a murderous frame of mind, Lloyd George left Rome for Paris. Huddled in his overcoat while the train jolted along, he improvised moodily regarding the military policy of his commanders, who knew only the British sector of the Western Front and nothing of their allies. 'We must strike again against a soft front', he insisted to Robertson, Kiggell and the French representatives. 'The country would not stand much more of that sort of thing', he warned, speaking of Somme-type offensives. Scowling and in a rage he shouted that he would not drive thousands to slaughter like cattle. Men who are needed on the farms and in factories are not going to be used for cannon fodder, he said. For three years we have been promised certain victory in France and Belgium. What is there to show for this ceaseless battering? And now another of the same! General Kiggell, Haig's chief of staff, a Westerner and anti-French zealot, worsened matters by arguing with the Prime Minister. That evening he wrote Haig that Lloyd George had

poured out a lot of heretical, amateur strategy of the most dangerous and misleading kind and was far from complimentary to what had been done by our armies here. He ruffled me so thoroughly that I argued vehemently with him and I fear without displaying the respect due to his high office. . . . Robertson threw in a contribution now

Field-Marshal Sir Douglas Haig

General Sir William Robertson
and Field-Marshal Ferdinand Foch

Marshal Joseph Joffre, Raymond
Poincaré, King George V, Foch
and Haig

and then backing me up, but said little. Afterwards he told me
privately that he had to meet this sort of stuff all day and every day,
and was doing his best against it. . . . Robertson's line I gather is to
delay the commission of serious mistakes and try to fill us up with
all we want before the P.M. succeeds in sending things elsewhere.

Nobody's mind was changed in the course of this querulous
dialogue, the only result of which was that in the Prime Minister's
book Kiggell was henceforth labelled an insulting boor. And as
the day dragged on, the talking dwindled accordingly.

When the train jolted to a stop near Paris, General Robert
Nivelle was found to be awaiting them. He saluted Lloyd George
and introduced himself. Lloyd George had heard from him in
writing directly after his succession to Marshal Joffre. He knew
that the Frenchman had a scheme for resuming the Somme
offensive; in fact, he had received a memorandum about it on
Christmas Day. This he had surveyed with total lack of interest.
Its only redeeming feature was that it was to be mainly a French
effort. Nivelle had asked Haig to take over twenty-five extra
miles of front so that the French would be free to exert maximum
force in the chosen sector near Champagne. Lloyd George had
passed the request on to Haig passively and washed his hands of
it. It was suggested again by Briand at the Rome conference;
this time Lloyd George condescended to scorn it. Another Somme!
Would these ridiculous generals never learn?

But now in the crowded, smoke-filled railway car Lloyd
George began to size up the Frenchman and his scheme with more
respect. Certainly the man's reputation could not be laughed off.
A clever, suave tactician, he had been in field command at
Verdun, had stemmed the tide there and had been the hero of
the recapture of world-famous Fort Douaumont, in which
operation certain new artillery methods had been used with
surprising success. Lloyd George was surprised to find that this
general could speak English without an accent and with capti-
vating phraseology. Here was actually a French war leader he
could understand—a man of subtlety and fresh ideas. His mother
had been English. He was a Protestant. His way of thinking came

5

closer to Lloyd George's than any other Western Front commander. It turned out that Nivelle was not by any means advocating another Somme. His blow would be a two-handed affair on
both sides of the wrecked woodlands where the previous offensive
had failed. It would not be a campaign of attrition. It would be
a 'rupture of the front'. It would be an audacious plunge, 'a
single stroke'. It would involve new, fool-proof methods. For
better or for worse the issue would be resolved 'in 24 or 48
hours'. It would be a 'decisive battle' and its aim would be
nothing less than 'the destruction of the principal mass of the
enemy'.

The Prime Minister surveyed the trimly moustached, slit-eyed
little general, calm to the point of arrogance, yet hat in hand.
Perhaps his puzzling new formula would work. Anything was
better than nibbling on granite. Of course all generals were always
confident. Lloyd George decided, at any rate, to invite him to
London on 15 January to explain his plan before the British
War Cabinet.

Nivelle arrived on that date and charmed everybody. Lloyd
George began to entertain a positive enthusiasm for the proposed
offensive. It was settled that operations would commence no
later than 1 April. Haig would take over part of the French front-
line positions as far as St. Quentin with six new divisions from
England. The Frenchman described the offensive with his usual
lucidity: The British and French would attack in such fashion
as to attract and magnetize the enemy's reserves. Then the French
would strike on the Aisne River front, using special tactics made
famous at Fort Douaumont. If successful, and success was
'certain', the attack would be broadened and intensified to the
last ounce of men and material, and the drive would be pressed
all the way to the Belgian coastline. If not, theoretically speaking,
it would be instantly abandoned, and Haig's long-cherished
scheme of a third campaign in the Ypres Salient—toward the
same objectives—would go into effect as soon as possible, spearheaded by the British Expeditionary Force.

Haig agreed to all this resentfully. He himself had hoped to attack in February, but now he would have to wait on the French. Furthermore, he mistrusted Nivelle's plan. Referring to a French memorandum on troop dispositions, he called it 'a most misleading document. ... I felt it was disgraceful that the French Staff should have put forward such an untrue statement of facts at such a time as this.' And after the decision to back Nivelle was settled he confided in his diary 'I must say that these conclusions were hastily considered by the War Committee.' Robertson, who was deathly afraid of Haig and almost never knowingly disagreed with him, also thought the programme had 'many fallacies'. Even the French demi-gods, Foch and Joffre, felt that the attack would fail. None the less, it was now policy, and, like a derelict locomotive running downhill, could no longer be stopped by the hand of man.

At the moment, however, peace talk was overpowering the sound of the guns and the bickering of the warlords. It emanated from across the Atlantic where President Wilson was hoping to keep the United States out of war by ending it before the actions of Germany made his country's entry inevitable. He had tried (perhaps condescendingly) several times in the past, without success, to bring about negotiations among the belligerents, but this plea was by far his most dramatic. On 22 January, before the Senate, he made a last desperate attempt to bring the warring nations to the conference table. He introduced the idea of a post-war league of nations to enforce 'peace without victory'—one which would humiliate and deplete no nation, would guarantee freedom of the seas, and would see to it that all rulers would govern their nations with the consent of the governed. The reaction of most statesmen and soldiers to this proposal is perhaps typified by the entry in Sir Henry Wilson's diary: '... an amazing speech about peace without victory—all countries to have access to the sea, and much other dangerous nonsense. Doumergue and Castelnau, and all Frenchmen, are furious ...'

British newspapers cast scorn on the President. The various diplomats tried to phrase a tactful no-thank-you. Their embarrassment was relieved quickly. On 1 February, the Germans delivered one of several thunderbolts which were to make the first four months of 1917 among the most dynamic in modern history— they announced unrestricted submarine warfare. Neutrals were told that all waters around Great Britain, France and Italy would henceforth be barred, and that any merchantmen therein would be liable to sinking without notice. This policy nullified assurances given Wilson by the Germans nine months previously, and two days later the president broke off diplomatic relations with Germany. But to the dismay of the European Allies there was not a word in his congressional speech about declaring war. February dwindled, and still the two countries remained at peace with each other. The stunning thought began to be voiced that this weird state of affairs might continue indefinitely. The puzzle, the riddle, of America's continued neutrality might face them sphinx-like for the duration of hostilities. Was it really possible?

The hard-headed men of war paid little heed to these speculations. Neither Lloyd George nor Haig in their published memoirs refer to President Wilson's peace formula or Germany's reversal of naval policy. Wilson's proposal seems to have struck both men as beneath contempt. Naval matters were usually ignored by Haig as a matter of professional policy; to meddle in them unduly, he felt, would be most presumptuous. As for the Prime Minister, for once his spacious outlook failed him; he seems to have underestimated the reluctant decision of Ludendorff to give the admirals a free rein. That February intense Allied plans were under way for gigantic military blows which were intended to win the war. Nothing else mattered. Shortly there was to be another conference. It would be held in Calais on the 26th and, for a change, would not be another of those tumultuous, argumentative affairs, but would concern itself decorously with the chronic congestion of the Nord railway which for many months had impeded British operations in France and might even wreck the forthcoming spring offensive unless improvements were worked out.

On the Saturday before the Calais talks, the War Cabinet held a secret meeting. Robertson was telephoned by its Secretary and told that he need not attend this meeting unless he had special questions to bring up. That seemed strange, but the Chief of Staff drew the necessary conclusion and stayed away; and in the course of the long Monday trip to Calais an interminable conversation between him and the Prime Minister divulged nothing about the Cabinet meeting, nor did the civilian drop any hints about the forthcoming agenda.

In France Lloyd George quickly brushed the transport problem into the hands of a technical committee. Then the bomb burst: Haig and his armies were to be placed under the supreme command of Nivelle. 'The enemy has but a single army,' the Prime Minister explained. 'We should secure for ourselves the same advantage. If we do not we cannot hope for success.'

Robertson hit the ceiling. 'Get 'aig!' he roared.

The idea that all British units would be considered a group of armies in the French line of command, that Haig, as he notes helplessly in his diary, 'would apparently only administer the discipline and look after reinforcements', and that Nivelle's orders would be transmitted to the British Commander-in-Chief via an intermediary, struck the British military chiefs like a slap in the face. They 'agreed we would rather be tried by court martial than betray the Army by agreeing to its being placed under the French.' Robertson suggested that they all resign *en masse*. Haig that night confided to his diary: 'And so we went to bed, thoroughly disgusted with our Government and the Politicians.'

In the end it was compromised; Haig would be technically subordinated to Nivelle only for the duration of the latter's private offensive, but would have the right to appeal. Henry Wilson (whom Haig despised) would be the liaison officer. But the incident left Haig barren of any further respect for the Prime Minister, if, indeed, anything of the sort had remained. To his wife he writes:

Why I cannot think but I am told that L. G. finds himself slipping down the hill in popular favour, and is looking about to find something to increase his reputation as the 'man of the hour' and the saviour of England. However, I am doing my best and have a clear conscience. If they have someone else who can command this great Army better than I am doing, I shall be glad to hand over to him, and will be *so happy* to come back to my darling wife and play golf and bring up the children.

Feeling that the arch-devil Lloyd George was at the bottom of the scheme, Robertson wrote to Haig, 'I can't believe that a man such as he can remain for long head of any Government. Surely *some* honesty and truth are required.'

And Sir Douglas, who had secretly told all and offered his resignation to the King, entered in his diary, 'All would be so easy if I only had to deal with Germans.' And finally he wrote to Nivelle in a more friendly way, '... I feel confident that "unity of effort" will be assured with absolute certainty if you and I are allowed to settle our affairs together without interference from London or Paris.'

There has been a suspicion that the incident was engineered to bring about the resignation of Haig and Robertson. Certainly Haig was not oblivious to the possibility. It was at about this time that he was visited at G.H.Q. by General Gough, one of the rising young stars; Haig for once was worried, and remarked, 'Of course, if they don't approve of me, they had better appoint someone else.' Then he looked at Gough suspiciously and added, 'Is it going to be you?' Though Gough protested that such a thought could have crossed nobody's mind, much less his own, both men were quite aware of the crude affront delivered to Haig at Calais, that his status in the eyes of the Prime Minister was close to nil, and that his replacement was now a definite possibility.

To rub salt into the wound, Nivelle now began ordering Haig about in communications so peremptory that the latter quietly exploded and called upon his Government for a further clarification of the distribution of power. Referring to one of Nivelle's orders, he wrote to Robertson: 'Briefly it is a type of letter which no gentleman could have drafted. . . . I intend to send a copy of the letter with my reply to the War Committee with a request to be told whether it is their wishes that the Commander-in-Chief of this British Army should be subjected to such treatment by a junior *foreign* commander.' In later years this communication was to plague the Scottish Marshal. Nivelle *was* plainly a foreigner. And since France had a different grading system, technically he *did* hold a lesser rank, though he was Haig's senior in service. As one historian has suggested, the phrasing is none the less of interest 'if one is to understand the subconscious working of the military mind'. But these regrettable piques subsided in time, and Nivelle was left in peace with his own difficulties with his own politicians, who were, if possible, even more obstructive than Haig's.

So it went early in 1917. Two generations later these fitful quarrels and portentous conferences were to fade all but forgotten down the dim corridors of time. But at the moment nothing seemed more important to their participants. Even Lloyd George, head of the British Government, was far more alert to his own political fences, to impending French plans on the Western Front, to the immediate problems of troops, material, food, and submarines than he was to remote international developments. But now came events of overpowering magnitude.

The Russian Revolution detonated in March, with the Army and Navy in effect following George Bernard Shaw's bland advice: 'that if the soldiers had any sense they would go home and attend to their own affairs'. This exodus from the Eastern Front began upon the abdication of the Czar, who had made 'every possible mistake' and in autocratic blindness had denied his country even the rudimentary glimmerings of democracy. A moderate provisional government took over. Now the Russian soldier-peasantry, who had been butchered since 1914 in numbers far more (both relatively and absolutely) than even the French—ragged, underfed, half of them still without rifles—began to

clamour for release from a war which had even less meaning for
them than for the soldiers of the other Allies. The first provisional
government, like the one to follow, tried to walk a tight-rope
between war and peace. From the beginning it encountered fore-
seeable difficulties. Colonel A'Court Repington, military writer
for the Northcliffe press, began to refer to serious concern among
the warlords in France and England, and called attention to
allegations that the new government did not seem to be capable
of pressing the war effort. General Robertson stated glumly to
Repington in an interview 'that the Russian position is rotten',
and confided that Russia was about finished because the people
behind the Army were good for nothing 'except music and
dancing and tommy-rot love stories'. The Germans well knew
what a ripe plum had fallen into their lap; it was the greatest
stroke of luck they had enjoyed thus far in the war.

Strangely enough there were those in Britain who thought the
revolution would benefit their side. These were the Liberals, who
heretofore had been so bravely despondent. Suddenly they were
revitalized. The once naughty member of their coalition—
despotic Russia—had finally seen the light and was turning
towards democracy. At last the war had a shred of meaning and
voices were raised in hosannas. On 17 March the leading Liberal
paper, *Daily News*, contained an ecstatic article on 'The Twilight
of the Gods'. It was 'the greatest victory that had yet fallen to the
Allies'.

Until then there had been little enough to celebrate or even
hope for, except desperately to pray for the entry of the United
States into the conflict. Rumours to that effect had not ceased
in three years. After German-American diplomatic relations
ended, the speculations and yearnings swelled. The *Daily News*
Washington correspondent reported: 'It may be safely said that
the country [America] is nearer war.' But this was an old, tired
phrase. Was there really any truth in it? By now everybody was
in a state of exasperation over the dilatory tactics of the overseas
giant. It was always a 'puzzle' or a 'riddle' when any neutral,
especially America, failed to 'come in' quickly. And after Wilson's

'peace without victory' speech there were many who despaired, because it further seemed to imply non-intervention.

Until the Russian revolution it had been a dreary winter, mostly marked by soothing speeches and optimistic predictions. For example, Haig had limned 'The Coming Break-Through' ... 'We shall break the German front completely—we shall strike without respite and terribly. ...' The *Daily News* spoke cheerily of the 'Splendid Success of the War Loan'. And there was Lloyd George's 'Inspiring Message to France' in which he promised what would happen 'when John Bull gets his teeth in ...' and so on. But all these hypodermics could not for ever stimulate the idealists or the people at large.

Then at last on 3 April: 'AMERICA IN WITH ALL HER RESOURCES'. Near-hysteria followed. The Liberals professed to see wonders in Woodrow Wilson's war message to Congress even greater than guns and dollars and troops, and the *Daily News* intoned:

In this great utterance we seem to hear at last the authentic voice of humanity stating the issue and pronouncing the judgment, awakening the conscience of the world to the mighty things at stake. Never in history have there been such declarations as those made in the past few days in Russia and in Washington. Deep has answered to deep, and across the sundering ocean the democracy of America clasps the hand of the democracy of Russia, freed at last from the gyves of centuries. In the light of this prodigious union we see the issue of the war emerge with a grave simplicity of outline.

By Easter the paean had far from subsided. In the *Daily News* one journalist wrote a hymn for the occasion:

> I hear a noise of breaking chains,
> I hear a sound of opening doors;
> It comes from Transatlantic plains.
> Across the green Atlantic floors.
> She sings the old redeeming songs
> That Lincoln taught her lips to sing;
> The death songs of a thousand wrongs,
> The birth songs of a thousand springs.

And so on and on until the ghastly finale:

> And Britain with her sea-knit brood,
> Locked fast in world-wide conflict grim,
> Hears the high call of her own blood
> In Woodrow Wilson's Battle Hymn.

At a Savoy celebration one overwrought reporter wrote:

Gathered for lunch between the twined flags of America and Britain, we seemed to have recaught the glad, early spirit of the war. Youth was everywhere . . . an incubus of doubt was lifted. Even through the tobacco smoke, America's clear young eyes shone with that utter faith in a just cause which is the assurance of victory.

And Lloyd George, who was present, spoke more playfully about the 'bunkers' Britain had been in during the past three years; but now, he said, 'We have got a good niblick and have struck right on to the course.'

These glad tidings, one must conclude, failed to thrill Sir Douglas Haig to the fever pitch felt by other people. There is not a word in his published diary concerning the Russian revolution or America's entry. For a year he had been looking forward to his offensive at Ypres, one which he felt would be successful in breaking the German front, in reaching the Channel, thus dislocating the enemy communications and perhaps nearly ending the war. All this he intended to accomplish almost solely with British troops. He had little interest in the co-operation, then or eventually, of French or American forces. The Third Battle of Ypres was to be Britain's day of glory, and his plans for the conduct of this offensive were already complete.

Meanwhile he was forced to await the outcome of Nivelle's experiment. It was bound to fail, he knew; that was why the delay was so intolerable. As for Nivelle, he was an arrogant junior officer improperly promoted over the heads of other Frenchmen far more senior and experienced. Haig silently fumed. Worst of all, Nivelle was behind schedule. Why had his wretched battle not yet commenced? April 1st and 5th and 10th and 15th came and went, and still the French squatted. At this rate, the British offensive would not get under way till doomsday. Haig realized that the British should strike early in the summer, for later rains would make the Flanders plain difficult to operate on. The French would have to fight, fail, and retire quickly. But bad weather and supply difficulties continued to delay them. Two weeks after the deadline the French had still not moved, and now it was becoming really questionable whether Haig's Flanders offensive would get under way in time to force a decision before the rain, the snow and the paralysing cold stopped the British army dead in its tracks.

4

L'Affaire Nivelle

BUT surely nobody could have been more eager to attack on schedule than General Robert Nivelle. His appointment as Commander-in-Chief over the heads of such figures as Foch, Pétain and Castlenau, not to mention the exalted Joffre himself, had occurred, Nivelle knew, because it was hoped that he had something new to offer—a magical artillery formula, a scheme that would at last produce a breakthrough, an 'unlimited offensive' that aimed at total victory. Such, at least, were the anxious dreams of the French Ministers who had dumped 'Papa' Joffre because he had proved incapable of so delivering. And unlike his rival Pétain, the new commander knew how to deal with his politicians. Though secretly despising them (in a talk with Robertson he referred to all of them as 'foreigners') he was anxious to fulfil their desires and to vault from relative obscurity on to the centre of the world stage. His nomination to the supreme command went to his head; his normal good sense was unhinged by the premature position (his highest command heretofore had been a single army, which he had led for only five months) in which he now found himself. Drunk with the wine of history, he hoped to capitalize on his stroke of luck by attacking quickly and winning spectacularly. But many things had begun to go wrong almost at once.

First of all, his mentors, Briand and Lyautey, fell from power. Ribot, an octogenarian, became Premier and named M. Paul Painlevé as Minister of War. In the past Painlevé had been so bitterly opposed to Nivelle that he had refused to serve in the French Cabinet while that general continued in command. The

War Ministry, however, was too tempting a plum to refuse. Primarily a mathematician, an outstanding theoretical intellectual, a left-wing Socialist, Painlevé had often insisted that Nivelle's plan to seek a decision on the Western Front was the equivalent of mass manslaughter. There was no secret about his conviction that the proper general to command at this juncture was Pétain, who in turn had stated his opinion that the exhausted French armies must rest and go over to the defensive for at least a year. Instead Painlevé was now saddled with a man advocating, of all things, a grandiose scheme of attack. But instead of replacing him at once, as he had planned to do before the event, the War Minister stalled. Soon he was in so deep, Nivelle's preparations had advanced so far, the deadline was so near, that Painlevé submitted in despair and hoped only for the best.

He assumed office on 19 March. The following day he learned —'I might say by public voice', he wrote plaintively—that the offensive would begin on 8 April and that the British would attack near Arras on the 4th.

At this point it appears that conscience made him pause. Could he really sanction this madness? On the 22nd he summoned Nivelle to the first of a pedantic series of lectures designed to stop him. Nivelle remained adamant and a situation developed which Winston Churchill describes:

So Nivelle and Painlevé, these two men whose highest ambitions had been newly and almost simultaneously gratified, found themselves in the most unhappy positions which disillusioned mortals can occupy: the Commander having to dare the utmost risks with an utterly sceptical Chief behind him; the Minister having to become responsible for a frightful slaughter at the bidding of a General in whose capacity he did not believe, and upon a military policy the folly of which he was justly convinced. Such is the pomp of power!

But this was only the beginning of Nivelle's avalanche of problems. The weather turned wet, and day after day the already late attack was further postponed. The notoriously inept French hospital facilities resisted all last-minute attempts at improvement.

Under the load of gigantic preparations the efficiency of the railway system went from bad to worse. The Germans knew in a broad way what was coming, and as time passed French Intelligence in turn became alarmingly aware that the Germans knew. And the various means by which the enemy came to fathom Nivelle's intentions in detail are remarkable indeed.

First of all, the French newspapers proceeded to advertise the whole plan in its general outline. Nivelle himself was surprisingly careless. He had told all at a luncheon in London attended (in the icy phrase of Sir William Robertson) by 'several persons of both sexes'. Furthermore, the written plan sent by Nivelle to the British Foreign Office had been retyped and copies sent to at least ten individuals in England.

Next Nivelle had circulated innumerable copies of the detailed Order of Battle to front-line officers as low as company level. The sequel might have been predicted. On 3 March a French sergeant was captured by Germans in a trench raid and found to have one of these interesting documents on his person. The exultant reaction of Crown Prince Rupprecht is discernible in his words: 'This memorandum contained matter of extraordinary value . . . as to the particular nature of the surprise which the attacker had in view. . . . Graf von Schulenberg at once formulated the logical reply for the defence.'

All during March German officers intently watched the immense preparations proceeding under their noses. Aerial observation and other means of inference were also helpful. On 6 April another surprise raid captured another Frenchmen and another document—the order of attack of the French Fifth Army. The Crown Prince continues: 'In it the French attacking units were mentioned by name. . . . Fresh information upon the anticipated French method of attack was given. The last veil concealing the intentions of the French offensive was torn aside.'

By now the enemy knew Nivelle's plan with total accuracy and was preparing accordingly. A stream of reinforcements had already begun to flow toward the threatened sector. The nine divisions stationed there were increased to forty. Within a few weeks a vast new system of barbed wire, machine-guns, trenches, concrete strong-points, and mountains of ammunition appeared as if by magic. Hundreds of batteries were placed into additional positions, and special methods of tactical defence were established.

Meanwhile (and this was, or should have been, the last straw) the Boche simply proceeded to withdraw from the exposed salient upon which Nivelle's offensive was supposed to fall. Even before the birth of the Nivelle affair Ludendorff had long been wary of his potential weakness there and for months had been preparing a new defensive chord from Arras to Royon—the so-called Hindenburg line. As far back as February the British under General Gough had been astounded to discover that the Germans were bombarding their own front-line trenches. Cautious patrols were sent forward. They found the German positions deserted. In one dug-out only a black cat leaped out to greet Australian scouts. For several days local commanders continued to report the disappearance of the enemy. Eventually it dawned on everybody that the Germans were really conducting a mass disengagement from the front—in some zones as far back as fifty miles. The process posed an embarrassing question: Where was the Somme morsel now? What remained to bite off, when from Arras to Soissons the Germans had fallen back? For when they had finished the British Fifth Army was 'in the air' and three of Nivelle's five armies were also separated from the enemy.

As the Germans retreated from occupied France they laid waste the villages and the countryside. Key towns like Péronne were utterly devastated. Every house in the abandoned area was blown up. Wells were poisoned. Trees were cut down and laid across the roads. Orchards were devastated. At road intersections huge craters were exploded. Thousands of booby traps were laid everywhere, some of which were extremely ingenious. A new shovel lying among old ones would be wired to a bomb, a duckboard out of place awaited a neat-minded Englishman, an innocently open door, a closed door, fountain pens on a desk—these and other such devices inflicted many casualties on the Allies proceeding northward with glacier-like persistence. Delayed-action bombs were planted; the Town Hall of Bapaume was demolished by an explosion several days after the British moved in. The devastation was nearly total. Even the furniture in the houses was chopped apart, and the livestock carried away or slaughtered.

Of this operation, aptly designated by the German code word ALBERICH (the malicious dwarf of the Nibelung Saga), Ludendorff admitted, 'The decision to retreat was not reached without a painful struggle. It implied a confession of weakness. . . . But as it was necessary for military reasons we had no choice. . . . The retirement proved in a high degree remunerative.'

Yet it was not easy for the Germans to destroy the homes and orchards of the people with whom they had billeted for two and a half years. 'He wept when he told me that the village was to be destroyed,' one native said. And as the German tide receded it laid bare the hidden backwash of war. Seldom in history has an area been found so demolished, its inhabitants so impoverished. One correspondent who entered the area was first struck by the young French mothers with flaxen-haired babies of German fathers. Was this, too, the result of atrocities? And the answer was, 'They had no need to use violence in their way of love-making. There were many volunteers.' They rubbed their thumbs and fingers together as though touching money and said, 'You understand?'

But as to the matter of Nivelle's attack, even he had to admit that affairs had somewhat altered. 'The retirement of the enemy on the front of the Fifth British Army constitutes a new fact,' he announced in a directive to Haig rather less than brilliant in scope. But he was not alarmed. 'On the contrary, the so-called Hindenburg position is so disposed that the directions of our principal attacks . . . will outflank it and take it in reverse. In this respect the German retirement may be entirely to our advantage.' Therefore he decided 'not to modify in any fundamental way the general plan of operations already settled'. The more matters changed, it seems, the more they remained the same. Was it possible that in the face of these new facts Nivelle could still be right?

Albert Thomas, Haig, Joffre and David Lloyd George

General Sir Herbert Plumer, Major-General H. A. Lawrence and Haig

Yet the situation as it now stood was at least disconcerting. It would take two months even to bring up railways, roads, supplies and men through the ruined area. Even then, Nivelle would only be in a position to move against the strongest fortified defensive system on the Western Front. On the other hand, the only other sectors where an attack could be mounted without delay were on the flanks of the abandoned area. Thus it would have to be two disconnected assaults. This was not at all what Nivelle or anyone else had envisioned. On 12 March the massive German retirement began in earnest. Machine-gunners stayed behind to slow the gingerly advance of Allied troops. A handful of picked men with rifles, flares and mortars rushed up and down the deserted trenches to give the impression of substantial forces still in position. And, for better or for worse, the Allied follow-up was so slow that the methodical enemy retreat was consummated by the end of the month with the most trifling of losses.

Nivelle's reaction to this basic dislocation of his plan was an intensified show of bravado. He began by stating that 'if he had whispered orders to Hindenburg, the latter could not have better executed what he desired'. Though he was now faced with attacking a nearly impregnable line with a mere collection of three armies, he briskly predicted, 'Laon in twenty-four hours and then the pursuit.' When told about a third line of German trenches behind the other two in Champagne he retorted, 'Don't be anxious, you won't find a German in those trenches, they only want to be off!' He would break through with 'insignificant loss'. When his top general (Micheler) suggested caution, Nivelle refused even to discuss the point beyond commenting, 'You won't find any Germans in front of you.' Across the years these loom as the sentiments of a person divorced from reality.

The incredulity of Pétain, Haig, Robertson, Painlevé, and even his own generals only spurred Nivelle on to a greater frenzy of optimism and activity. On 1 April he told Micheler:

The character of violence, of brutality and of rapidity must be maintained. It is in the speed and surprise caused by the rapid and

6

sudden eruption of our infantry upon the third and fourth positions that the success of the rupture will be found. No consideration should intervene of a nature to weaken the *élan* of the attack.

Yet, as caustically suggested by Churchill, in war a commander though absorbed in his own plans must at times take the enemy into consideration. Painlevé tried to reason with his man. Let bygones be bygones, he begged, and pointed out, 'A new situation ought to be considered with a new eye.' Don't consider it a sign of weakness to reconsider; bear in mind, he said in effect, not only the German retreat but the imminent American entry, the Russian revolution, the threatening state of affairs on the Italian front.

The general would not yield. The German retirement played into his hands, he said. Concerning the Plateau of Craonne, 'he had it in his pocket' and only feared that the Germans would run away before being demolished. And if they tried to reinforce their troops they would only lose that many more. After three days and about eighteen miles of pursuit the French might pause for breath on the Serre River, but 'it would be difficult to hold the troops back once they got started.'

Meanwhile high French officers were secretly transmitting to the new Minister of War their professional opinions that the impending operation was no longer practical. The commanding generals of his three army groups—Pétain being one—openly stated that the concept of a breakthrough then and there was out of the question. Painlevé was now distraught. He decided to try once more to stop Nivelle and for this purpose summoned a conference at the War Ministry on 3 April which included himself, the Commander-in-Chief, and several Cabinet members. There, laboriously and meticulously, Painlevé spelled out all the objections to Nivelle's offensive.

The latter replied in character. He would not abandon the attack, though the politicians were invited to abandon him instead, if they preferred. 'Under no pretext will I recommend a Somme battle,' he insisted. Everything would be over successfully (or otherwise, theoretically speaking) within two days.

Was he not aware that to capture the third and fourth positions he first had to capture the first and second?

Naturally; and he smiled. Did they think him a child?

What about leaks of information to the enemy?

Exaggerated. The Germans knew nothing of importance regarding his intentions. Surprise would . be achieved. The front would be ruptured—brusquely, inevitably, and in great depth.

Confronted by such confidence, the politicians morosely surrendered. The meeting appears to have been sulphurous. General Wilson, gossip-monger and go-between, discusses it at length in his diary:

> I hear that the Government, aided by Pétain, wanted to force Nivelle to abandon his great offensive and have a small one instead. Nivelle stood firm and won. What time of day for such a proposal, and Haig not consulted. . . . Nivelle listened for some time and then weighed in by remarking that there were so many C.-in-C.s that he was confused, but as C.-in-C. he would not tolerate the present state of affairs, and would do as he pleased or resign . . . but I am quite clear that, if our coming offensive does not succeed or is only moderately successful, the politicians will unload Nivelle. What a scurvy crowd. I then discussed Foch having been sent to Italy on Thursday. . . . The whole thing is a mess.

As of 3 April, the Nivelle assault became a final certainty. Yet in truth the plan was far from unique. Substantially it was a reincarnation of Joffre and the Somme, conceived on the model of the local battle for Fort Douaumont in the naïve hope that what had worked on a small scale could be duplicated in a grand offensive. Furthermore, Nivelle planned to extend the front of the assault to include certain sectors so formidable that even Joffre had taken care to avoid them in his plans for 1917. Thus in the words of Winston Churchill, 'The effect of the Nivelle alterations upon the Joffre plan was to make it larger, more violent, more critical, and much later.' The Germans could not be touched at all for the ninety miles between the south of Arras and Soissons. This left only the marvellously fortified neighbourhood astride Arras itself and around Champagne. And, as we know, the element of surprise was even less than before the Somme offensive had been kicked off. This Nivelle must have known, for he had been told a dozen times exactly how his detailed plans had fallen into enemy hands.

The obstinacy with which he persisted was to some extent induced by two subordinate officers. Primarily there was a certain Colonel d'Alenson, his Chief of Staff, who had Nivelle's ear just as Brigadier-General Charteris had Haig's. Unfortunately d'Alenson was in the last stages of consumption, had very little time to live, and wished to be the architect of a supreme gamble for victory before he died. This tall, sullen sliver of a man had determined to risk his reputation and country on a last throw of the dice. Ceaselessly and autocratically he spurred on his chief and other French professionals.

To a divisional general he frigidly stated, pointing to a map, 'We shall advance there, there and there, and then there we are!'

'And if we fail, what then?'

'Well, if we fail, we will throw our hands in.'

Then there was General Mangin, Nivelle's sharpest sword and most dangerous fighting commander, swarthy and flamboyant —the Hero to some, the Butcher to others. Reckless, defiant, white teeth and eyes flashing, the true unsung hero of Verdun as a mere brigadier, the epitome of the offensive, he would command the vital Sixth French Army. Nivelle seems to have feared and revered this brutal, competent man who dragged him willingly into battle.

Thus the trio Nivelle–d'Alenson–Mangin, not one of whom was a balanced individual at the moment, drove forward to the fray against the warnings of every competent civil and military leader in the Allied camp. Now events began to unfold in a grim pattern.

The British moved first. In a gale of sleet on 9 April, Easter Monday, the Third Army under Allenby attacked at Arras with the aim of distracting the German reserves from Champagne.

Behind a curtain of artillery and gas shells which smothered the enemy batteries, Canadian and Highland troops quickly captured the entire Vimy Ridge. Then the advance began to slow down against hardening resistance; also a traffic jam developed in the British rear which snarled the movement of men, guns, and supplies, and furnished a vulnerable target for heavy German guns. Though Allenby kept the pressure on for weeks, nothing more could be gained, and the casualties kept mounting. Yet by the standards of the Western Front at that time, the battle of Arras was successful. The Germans had been kept busy for the moment. They had lost three to six miles in depth, 14,000 prisoners, and 180 guns; and the English Press was as enthusiastic as though a major triumph had been achieved.

Two days later the edge was blunted by the failure (also a success in the newspapers) of General Gough's Fifth Army at Bullecourt, an operation conducted by Australians and concerning which the Australian Official History says:

> ... everyone was aware that the 4th Australian Division had been employed in an experiment of extreme rashness, persisted in by the army commander after repeated warnings, and that the experiment had failed with shocking loss ... the gross blunders of the general plan ... have, indeed, never found a defender. ... It was indeed employed by British instructors afterwards as an example of how an attack should not be undertaken.

In this small enterprise the artillery failed, the tanks got lost, the division lost 3,000 men, gained no ground, and inflicted minimum losses upon the enemy. From this day on it became traditional among Australians to hate General Gough. It was not the first time the staff work of the Fifth Army had collapsed in a welter of airy inefficiency, nor would it be the last. When Haig was told by a friend 'of the opinions concerning Gough that were widespread in the army, he curtly intimated that he wished to hear nothing on that subject'. The course of this battle and the statement quoted have a bearing, as will be seen, on future events of greater significance.

On Monday, 16 April, General Nivelle finally had his day. It began to rain just before zero hour. Cold showers slashed against the crouched Frenchmen in their trenches and the coloured Senegalese, 'France's colonial children', who waited apathetically beside the whites for the signal to go over the top. If there had been the slightest question of surprise up to now, it existed no longer; a protracted artillery bombardment had alerted the Germans once and for all, so that again the French infantrymen were faced with the bleak prospect of walking forward almost helplessly against thousands of intact German field and machine-guns.

The first sour taste of things to come occurred soon: the Senegalese broke and ran, even boarding hospital trains to speed their departure. In general the offensive proved immediately to be a fiasco. By dusk, along the main front, 600 yards had been gained. Nivelle had predicted six miles. The essential advance of Mangin's Sixth Army was stopped cold. Other French armies, plus the British Third and Fifth, made small headway.

That evening French communiqués were studiously vague. They stressed enemy resistance and inexcusably bad terrain. Such phrasing was always a portent that things were going badly and would probably get worse. Sir Douglas Haig inferred as much, and before going to bed noted in his diary that 'the much talked of victory has not been gained by the French to date. It is a pity that Nivelle was so very optimistic as regards breaking the enemy's line.'

The Germans had been ready except in one flank sector where the decision to attack had been made at the last moment, and where a tangible gain had been achieved. German machine-guns had been the primary instrument in cutting the French attack to shreds. Several counter-attack divisions had been positioned through a fifteen-mile depth, and had gone into operation on a time-table basis. Light batteries—and this was the crucial manœuvre—had been temporarily drawn back out of the range of the French counter-batteries, and were rapidly wheeled into position when the perfect moment came. And, finally, the German troops, in superb morale and fighting trim, had proved that the assumption to the contrary had been a delusion.

Sir Henry Wilson, liaison officer between the French and British, wrote to Haig that the French

> will look about them for some excuse, one of them will be that the whole German Army is facing them, and that we have not succeeded in easing their load! This would be pure French, i.e., the woman's side of their nature, wounded vanity, jealousy and disappointment at their own failure and our success. I don't think luckily that the French losses are very heavy.

Wilson was wrong. By Tuesday Nivelle had lost just under 120,000 men. His maximum penetration was two miles. Over 20,000 German prisoners were taken, and the enemy had suffered only about twice that number in other casualties. Overnight Nivelle changed his tune and tried to convert the operation into one with more modest aims. But it was not humanly possible to forget his previous boasts. General Wilson wrote in his diary (in that war everybody seemed to keep a diary) that

> Nivelle will fall and that we will certainly have Pétain here. Painlevé will certainly aim toward that. At 4 o'clock I went to see Foch who had just come back from Italy. We had a long talk. Foch was clear that Nivelle was done, owing chiefly to the failure of the Sixth Army. Foch said that he knew that the positions which this army was told to attack were impossible—and after what I saw yesterday I agree. He thinks . . . Pétain [will be] put in his place, who will play a waiting game. . . .

For once a prediction of Wilson's came true, and sooner than even he might have expected. Lightning rumours flashed everywhere in France that Nivelle's casualties had been twice the real number. The troops felt that they had been betrayed by callous generals, that the preparations had been slipshod, that they had been sent forward on a gamble to almost certain doom. They learned that nearly everyone else in authority had known that Nivelle's scheme was hopeless, and yet had allowed him to proceed with it. Surely this was too much to swallow. The reaction was swift and was directed not only against the generals but against the government and the war itself.

Trouble began on 3 May when the 21st Division of Colonial Infantry refused duty. The ringleaders were arrested. Two days later the division went back into action (Nivelle was still attacking) and was almost wiped out. It was the first thunderclap in a stormy sky. The 120th Infantry Regiment rebelled next. Attempts to arrest the leaders of the insubordination failed this time. To the entreaty of their frantic colonel the reply was, 'We'll never enter the trenches again'. Within a week mutinies had spread to sixteen army corps. Regiments began to unfurl red flags and to present written lists of conditions which would have to be met before they would fight again, including amnesty clauses for the instigators. The government and the military command refused to negotiate. In general the mutinies took place only when the troops were ordered back into the front lines. Their views were expressed in such statements as: 'We'll defend the trenches, but we won't attack'; and 'We are not so stupid as to march against undamaged machine-guns!'

The fighting units elected councils to speak for them. Entire regiments left for Paris *en masse*, singing and firing off their weapons, to demand a negotiated peace and to voice other demands. Secret Service reports to French headquarters concerning the state of affairs at the front became panicky in tone.

One regiment being led to the front went docilely enough, but persisted in baa-ing like sheep to indicate that they were lambs being driven to slaughter. When reprimanded by their commanding officer, the mutineers simply returned to the rest billets from which they had come. An artillery regiment tried to blow up the Schneider-Creusot munitions works. One general was severely beaten; 21,174 Frenchmen deserted outright. Unit after unit refused duty. Officers who tried to use force on the recalcitrant men were killed or beaten. Trains were derailed. Strikes and riots broke out in the domestic interior. A total of fifty-four divisions—at least three-quarters of a million fighting men—were involved.

Meanwhile fact-finding committees of Deputies gathered like vultures at the front. The affair was converted by opposition spokesmen into a political football, and the scandal in most of its details began to filter back to Paris. Painlevé (he was at his wit's end) estimated that out of the sixteen divisions on the Champagne front only two remained loyal. Some trenches were hardly manned at all.

Of all this the Germans remained generally ignorant, so closely was the secret kept from them. They heard rumours, but discounted them, and when complete facts reached them later via Switzerland it was too late for them to act. In his memoirs Painlevé wrote:

> Resentment among the troops against the staff, and particularly against G.H.Q., became pronounced. . . . There were daily quarrels between the infantry, the artillery and the airmen, the former reproaching the latter for having massacred them or left them to be massacred. The French Army has never passed through so formidable a crisis.

A French official report claims that 60 per cent of the men engaged in revolutionary acts of 'indiscipline' were drunk. One is entitled to doubt this interpretation. Some of the finest units in the French regular army took part, and it is clear from the calculated, rational colour of the demonstrations that far more than wine had produced the débâcle.

Whatever the reasons, it was plain that France was finished for the moment as a fighting force and possibly even incapable of defending herself against a major attack. It was also obvious that General Robert Nivelle's brief candle of glory had flickered out. Within thirty-six hours after the attack had started, Haig had already received a worried note from Lloyd George. What should be done, he asked, if the French War Cabinet advised Nivelle to cease fighting? Haig replied that he himself would continue the pressure in so far as possible, provided that the French could co-operate at least to some extent. Painlevé himself even went so far as surreptitiously to ask the recommendations of Sir Douglas as to Nivelle's future and his possible successor. Haig refused to commit himself, though the French War Minister tried to coax him into suggesting Pétain.

Alexandre Ribot also visited Haig that hectic day—26 April—'a tall, old man of eighty years of age', Haig scribbled in his diary, 'a dear old thing, but I should think too old to deal with those tricky French politicians'. He too inquired casually about Pétain's merits, but again Haig hedged. The assets of Pétain were, of course, common knowledge, and the civilians were seeking moral support rather than confirmation of their views. Pétain, too, had made his reputation at Verdun as a methodical planner. He was a cold man, sardonic, logical, contemptuous of democratic devices, but genuinely sympathetic toward the sufferings of the French ground forces. As to offensive spirit, this he had only when he thought the occasion warranted it, which was seldom. It was a foregone conclusion that Pétain would take over. He was the perfect man for the job. Painlevé named him Chief of the General Staff on 28 April. Shortly Nivelle was asked to resign as Commander-in-Chief.

A disreputable and tragic scene followed at French G.H.Q. What had happened was all the fault of General Mangin and Micheler, protested Nivelle. Let *them* resign. In bitterness and fury they berated Nivelle in turn. The shouting could be heard by everyone through the closed doors; they accused him of moral cowardice; they poured scorn on him; they screamed at him. Nivelle nearly fainted. Without a further word in defence he tottered out. On 15 May Pétain succeeded him.

Next month Colonel d'Alenson died, arrogant gambler to the last—'a Napoleon devoid of genius'.

Meanwhile the new commander was taking prudent steps to end the French decay. Twenty-three mutineers were officially shot. Two hundred and fifty were marched to a quiet sector and annihilated by their artillery. Over a hundred ringleaders were banished to various French colonies. Especially mutinous units were sent to the most dangerous fronts. Pétain himself undertook laborious personal measures. For months on end he visited the front lines by automobile and talked to the men, promised better conditions of service, and especially of leave, and in the rest camps, and assured both officers and privates that there would be no more blood-letting of the type which had characterized French generalship in the past. When he was done he had visited a hundred divisions, and the French army was back on the road toward self-respect and fighting spirit. For the first time, the average *poilu* felt that in this stern patriarch he had a leader interested not only in victory but in the lives of his countrymen at the front. Incessantly Pétain said, 'We must wait for the Americans and the tanks.' The French troops took heart, went on leave in huge numbers (to the disgust of Haig and Robertson), rested, and were replenished by a flow of younger classes. But it would be many a month before the armies of France would again participate in a grand offensive in the grand old way—perhaps many a year, perhaps never.

Haig's reaction to all this was anything but poignant. He remarks in his diary that as to Nivelle 'some suitable post, probably Russia, will be found for him'. He advised Ribot (perhaps too gracefully) that he 'had no knowledge of what Nivelle was supposed to have failed in' and, he might doubtless have added, very little interest. His main concern, of which he writes Robertson, is that 'pressure on the German Army must not be relaxed in the meantime. This seems to me of first importance for the success of *our* plan'. Therefore, he wrote the War Cabinet 1 May, the French should take back those sections of the front which the British had manned during Nivelle's offensive.

The French had fought, failed, and fallen back, just as Haig had anticipated. Now it was the British turn—a little late, but was not late better than never? The question seemed to answer itself, but was it to prove quite that simple?

5

The Interlude

EARLY 1917 would have been a splendid time to stop the
war. Both sides were exhausted. A military stalemate
existed. The causes of the conflict were demonstrably trivial
and implausible; one is reminded of Orwell's *1984*, in which the
people no longer remembered why they were fighting but only
knew that they had to continue. Certainly the war which had
begun in 1914 had little enough to do with the welfare of the
ordinary people of Europe, who could scarcely hope to benefit
through victory in riches, security, culture, pleasure, social
advancement, or in any other way. Those called upon to fight
and die, to work, to be maimed, to be made homeless and
bereaved were instructed to do so (in effect) with no clear explana-
tion of the need for such sacrifices. From the purely nationalistic
interest of each belligerent nation, the war had to be won; but
since these interests turned on technical considerations of military
prestige, economic power, and governing ideology, other
arguments of a more melodramatic nature were mostly put
forward. Thus the British and French and Russians were instructed
concerning the mad Kaiser seeking world conquest, sadistic
robot-like Junkers, bloodthirsty Bavarians whose sport it was to
bayonet Belgian babies, and goose-stepping Huns ready to march
in and take over London, Moscow, Paris, and the inhabitants
thereof. Correspondingly, the common citizens of the Central
Powers were stimulated by fables concerning revenge-crazy
French politicians, blood-thirsty Sikhs, the demented monk
Rasputin, savage black Moroccans seeking blond Teutonic

fräuleins, the British king plotting to dismember Germany so that the Empire could continue to gorge itself on profits, and so on.

The propaganda was in the vein of the Old Testament. People were warned by their rulers with stories of sundry fates worse than death unless the enemy were crushed. There was remarkably little promise of happiness or even loot upon the achievement of victory; only its negative rewards were stressed. Yet all the people of Europe had embarked on the struggle three years previously more or less willingly, fairly convinced that they were victims of aggression, that their lives would be miserable if their country were defeated, and that the motives of their rulers were pure. Even the intellectuals and international Socialists, by and large, were convinced—often more fanatically so than ordinary patriots.

By mid-1917 all this had worn terribly thin. Fortunately for the sanity of the military commanders, a caste anything but schizoid in nature, their duty was one-sidedly clear. It was Haig's job, for example, simply to fight the war on the Western Front and if possible to win it there. To do this he needed an aggressive plan promising decisive results, and this he was certain that he had.

Long before Nivelle's failure, before the Chantilly conference, before the Somme campaign, and even before Verdun, Douglas Haig had determined to attack the Germans in the Belgian province of Flanders in an offensive mounted primarily by British arms and centring around the salient at Ypres, some thirty miles from the Channel coast. Since late 1914 the eyes of many other Allied planners had been fixed upon north-west Belgium as a focus of operations, primarily to clear the twenty-eight-mile strip of Belgian coastline held by the enemy. If this could be accomplished two large advantages would be gained: the ports of Ostend, Zeebrugge and Blankenberghe would be wrested from the German navy—its submarine facilities in particular. In addition, if an Allied army could be based on the coast in a position to move east, the main German mass would find itself between the two arms of a giant nutcracker, the other being the existing Western Front. As early as December 1914, Winston Churchill had suggested a combined naval-military operation along these lines; but at the time the French were too busy defending Paris, and the British could not handle it alone.

A year later a similar plan was again suggested by the Admiralty,

The Flanders Front: 6 June, 1917

and now it was that Haig seriously turned his attention to it for the first time. It struck him immediately that the potential there was far more interesting than in the ponderous Franco-British campaign on the Somme now being considered. Unfortunately there were drawbacks. The Belgians had flooded the lower Yser shortly after the war had begun, and this entire area was still under water. Between the flood and the Channel lay only two miles of sand-dunes. That was too narrow a frontage, Haig considered, for a blow of the magnitude that would be needed. Although Belgian experts replied that the Yser area could be drained off, they admitted that a month of dry weather would have to ensue before troops could operate on it. In turn this meant that the Germans would have a month of clear warning that an attack was coming at exactly that point.

The British field-marshal therefore decided to drop that approach. Why not, he suggested, first attack from the Ypres salient and capture the vital ridges that surrounded it? After that the British would turn west, the French and Belgians on the coast would advance, and the amphibious manœuvre would be launched.

This variation of the plan seemed an improvement, and it also possessed the bonus, if successful, of delivering the British from their death-trap in the Salient, where they were half surrounded and taking 7,000 casualties per week for not the slightest purpose or advantage. Haig set the wheels in motion in a directive dated 7 January, 1916, and throughout the balance of that year various army commanders and navy officers toiled dutifully at the detailed planning. Meanwhile the giant battles of Verdun and the Somme were fought, and throughout 1916 the Flanders offensive smouldered only in the brain of the British commander and his subordinates, awaiting the proper time to flare into action. Again it saw the light of day at the Chantilly conference in November, and again it was brushed aside while Nivelle tried his experiment. By the time Nivelle had failed, the Flanders scheme had developed into something of an obsession with the British commander. It was a year and a half since his tenacious mind had adopted it, and now there was to be no stopping its execution.

As time went on, the need for clearing the Germans out of Belgium had indeed become chronic. There was the afore-mentioned matter of the North Sea coastline. It was most embarrassing for the Germans to be holding even a small part of it. In doing so, despite the British navy, they were able to menace coastal shipping not only with destroyers but with aircraft based near there, with great land-based guns, and with their smaller submarines. (An all-time record of 800,000 tons of British shipping had been sunk by U-boats in April.) Psychologically, to deliver the Belgians from under the heel of their conqueror was natural and almost instinctive. And what if the Germans should manage to advance even further along the coast at some future time—perhaps as far as Calais, just opposite Dover? That prospect in particular was unpleasant to the British mind.

Thus, in proposing operations along the coast, Haig or any other Allied chief was certain to get a sympathetic hearing from the British War Cabinet Committee.

Haig had other motives. Alone among the British he knew of the nearly complete collapse of French morale, and feared a serious breakthrough if the Germans were to attack Pétain's line. He was determined not to give them that chance. His summary is best described in his diary 1 May:

> Success seems reasonably possible. It will give valuable results on land and sea. If full measure of success is not gained, we shall be attacking the enemy on a front where he cannot refuse to fight, and our purpose of wearing him down will be given effect to. We shall be directly covering our own most important communications, and even a partial success will considerably improve our defensive positions in the Ypres salient. This is necessary in order to reduce the heavy wastage which must occur there next winter as in the past, if our troops hold the same positions.

The idea of simply withdrawing from the Salient had been under discussion for two years; on political and psychological grounds it was repugnant to Haig and almost everyone else.

It is also beyond question that subjective factors existed. Since

Crown Prince Rupprecht of Bavaria

Field-Marshal Paul von Hindenburg, Kaiser Wilhelm II
and General Erich von Ludendorff

Général Robert Nivelle

General Sir Hubert Gough

1914 Haig had seen Foch, Joffre and Nivelle successively fail to win the war in grand offensives under their personal banners. Now it was his turn to try. Intensely religious, he felt that God would favour his design. It has been said, too, that with Haig optimism was not merely a state of mind but a matter of policy. Supernatural aid aside, he was confident of victory. And behind a grim façade, this silent Lowland Scot dreamed, as any man would, of the glory that would accrue to him if he could win where his predecessors had lost. Finally there was Haig's patriotism; for he hoped to break through with British troops for the glory of the empire before the Americans arrived.

In all these not unreasonable ambitions Haig had the backing of the Chief of the Imperial General Staff, Sir William Robertson. Together this powerful combination moved toward their objective, sometimes subtly with the moral support of the king (who disliked Lloyd George), sometimes blatantly with the propaganda of the Northcliffe press, sometimes directly by means of head-on verbal offensives against the politicians, and on occasion by less normal devices.

The trouble was that the plan had imperceptibly shifted. A coastal attack was one thing, but when it was abandoned, in effect, for yet another onslaught against the main German defences on the Western Front, that was something else. The new concept did look suspiciously like another Somme. True, there would be amphibious and coastal operations later, but these were conditional upon victory further south. And could success really be achieved at Ypres? Certain generals were already dubious. Primarily they feared the terrain. Years ago it had been a veritable swamp; through centuries of toil its inhabitants had converted it into farmland by a complex system of ditches, drains and canals. This delicate maze might be ruined by a prolonged artillery bombardment, nor was it conceivable that troops could advance without such an advance barrage. Matters could be worsened by the heavy, invariable summer rains. It was evident to Haig and Robertson that their politicians would require some convincing, for the offensive would require the sanction of the British War

Cabinet. Yet where else could Haig attack? Assuming that the Western Front would be the main theatre of operations in 1917, what alternative existed? The case for Haig was summarized methodically by Henry Wilson:

1. Somme—i.e. wearing down the Boches.
2. Verdun—i.e. whirlwind attack.
3. Pétain—i.e. do nothing.

We have tried 2 (Verdun), which has been a complete failure. There remains Somme and Pétain. To my mind the Pétain plan is one to be avoided, and a Somme, with intelligence, is our only chance.

But where? Certainly not on the Somme again, for a dozen sundry reasons, including the assumption of employing British troops in the main onslaught. On the Arras–Vimy front? That would not be worthwhile, because the French could not co-operate properly; furthermore (as of the moment) Allenby had just been stopped there. The Lens sector? Haig's staff ruled that out; the entire neighbourhood was so broken up by houses and little towns that the defence would have an unfair advantage. In the centre, along the Aubers Ridge? But British troops in that narrow position were too limited in scope to make the theatre attractive for a major operation. So Haig and his supporters decided, somewhat lamely, that it would have to be the Salient at Ypres 'by a process of exclusion'.

In truth, the theoretical possibilities there were exhilarating. If they could get to the Dutch coast, their communications would be shortened, and without any great prolongation of the British line the entire German position might easily be turned. Then the key would be the Liège gap, that narrow route between the Ardennes and south Holland through which ran a great railway; from this, in turn, fanned out all the smaller lines which supplied the German armies from the Aisne to the Channel. With these rails captured, a grand German retreat was inevitable. Primarily it all rested on the advance from the Salient to Ostend—'only' thirty miles, as per the adverb of Haig's planners. Was such a gain possible in 1917? To Robertson and Haig it seemed well worth the gamble.

Just before Lloyd George replaced Asquith as Prime Minister the latter had sent a memorandum to William Robertson which contained this sentence: 'The War Committee were absolutely unanimous on the very great desirability, if it is practicable, of some military action designed either to occupy Ostend and Zeebrugge, or at least to render those ports useless as bases for destroyers and submarines.'

Dated 21 November, 1916, the message was interpreted by the General as something resembling official approval. However, it must be observed that the draft was unfinished and unsigned, and intended only for the information of the Chief of Staff. It merely asked him to 'report' to Asquith 'at an early date what action you consider feasible'. Plainly these were not formal instructions. As it happened, no report followed, and Mr. Asquith left office two weeks later. And the reference, finally, was to a coastal manœuvre—not to an attack at Ypres.

Sensing that this document was not enough to commit Asquith's successor, Robertson made haste to nail down matters more firmly. On 1 December he wrote to Joffre that

> my Government desire that the occupation of Ostend and Zee-brugge should form one of the objectives of the campaign next year. I am accordingly instructing Sir Douglas Haig to place himself in communication with you with a view to this operation being given a place in the general plans of operations for next year, and the necessary preparations being made to carry it out.

General Plumer, commander of the British Second Army at Ypres, had always wanted to relieve his vulnerable position there by winning the Messines–Wytschaete ridge dominating the Salient to the south-east. This he envisioned as a purely limited operation, complete in itself. When he was told of the new grand plan, he balked. The ground was unsatisfactory, he pointed out, and the offensive might bog down with heavy losses. In reply, Lieutenant-General Kiggell, Haig's Chief of Staff, deprecated Plumer's thinking, insisted that surprise and mobile operations were possible, and ordered him to recast his scheme by 31 January along broader lines. Two weeks later these instructions to Plumer were repeated and elaborated upon. None of these documents was shown to Lloyd George or other members of the War Committee. Throughout that winter and early spring great military preparations went forward in Flanders; and while the politicians knew of them vaguely they were not aware of their exact significance. Thus events proceeded through the Nivelle affair; and now followed a spate of conferences and conversations. Let us consider the sequence. . . .

First the War Cabinet met 1 May in an air of gloom brought about by the failure of the French in Champagne, and by disquieting news that Russian soldiers were already fraternizing with the Germans. Some Cabinet members even talked of making peace, but Lloyd George squelched these views and insisted that the pressure would continue. For the moment he was willing to approve methodical operations on the Western Front in order to keep the enemy off balance.

On 4 May a meeting took place in Paris including Ribot, Painlevé, Nivelle (for momentary decorative purposes), and Pétain; Haig, Robertson, Admiral Lord Jellicoe, and Lloyd George. At the outset it was decided that defensive operations would not be considered but that attacks would be made 'relentlessly' and 'with all available forces'. Lloyd George accepted this. But, he said, the French must co-operate on a large scale—not with only a few divisions. Would they pledge to do so? They would, assured Painlevé. As for Lloyd George, he did not pretend to be a military strategist, he said piously, but he felt that the enemy must not be given a moment's rest. 'We must go on hitting and hitting with all our strength until the German ended as he always did, by cracking.' He would not try to dictate the military scheme, nor (for the sake of secrecy) did he even wish to know its details, but he whole-heartedly accepted the thesis that 'it is no longer a question of aiming at breaking through the enemy's front and aiming at distant objectives. It is now a question

of wearing down and exhausting the enemy's resistance. . . .'
Painlevé readily agreed. He too believed in a continuing offensive,
he remarked, provided that it would not be a bloody, futile
affair like those of the past.

The talks that day were friendly, and everybody agreed about
everything; yet there was an undercurrent of doubt about the
French. While only they and Haig knew the whole truth about
the state of the French army at the moment, Lloyd George
inferred that something was wrong. Why were they so reticent
about explaining the sudden end of their offensive? he wondered.
He found Pétain silent and mysterious. In the corridor later,
Pétain came to him and said playfully, 'I suppose you think I
can't fight.'

'No, General', the Prime Minister replied, 'with your record
I could not make this mistake, but I am certain that for some
reason or other you won't fight.' Pétain turned away with a smile
and said nothing.

Yet it seemed that the conference had cleared the air and that
the two Allies were in agreement. While the French never
intended to attack on a mass scale, they did agree to the idea of
limited offensives for small gains, at a minimum cost in lives,
provided that sufficient artillery could be collected at the points in
question practically to guarantee such gains. But Haig's private
Flanders plan was not that at all; it envisioned a break-through
on a grand scale—one in which great masses of cavalry would
pour through the gaps and reach the Channel coast. Privately
Robertson did not share in this expectation, nor was he as disinterested as Haig in the probability (known to both of them) that
the French would not co-operate in strength. Nevertheless Haig
assumed that the conference gave him sufficient authority to
attack in a big way at Ypres. Immediately he advised Pétain that
he would continue heavy pressure along the Arras–Vimy front,
and that he would move against the Messines ridge early next
month with sixteen divisions. And that same day he sent Sir
Henry Wilson a plan of operations to transmit to the French.
Here, for the first time, he stated to that officer that he would

begin his campaign to take Ostend and Zeebrugge in July.

Later in the week Haig held talks at Doullens with his army commanders and divulged the entire Flanders scheme. To the intense disappointment of General Rawlinson (Fourth Army), Haig announced that Gough (Fifth Army) would conduct the main attack, though he had originally told the former that the job was his. Plumer would run the Messines operation; meanwhile Rawlinson was to go into reserve near the coast and prepare to assist the amphibious operation. Also, Haig told them in strict confidence, the French were finished for quite some time to come.

On 11 May, Wilson wrote in his diary: 'Went to see Pétain. . . . He is opposed to Haig's plans of attacks . . . to big attacks, and favours small fronts and great depths.'

The following week Robertson advised Haig that the French, in a written resumé of the 4th of May conference, had omitted any reference to their own offensive. This, he warned, 'might signify that the French Government, on reflection, had decided not to bind themselves to that resolution'.

To clarify the point, Haig consented to arrange a private conference with Pétain for the 18th. The moment they met the Frenchman took issue with Haig on the scale of the Flanders operation. It was, he said, entirely too grandiose in its aims and went far beyond the previous area of agreement. However, he added, it was vital for the British to keep on attacking; and exactly how and where they did so was not his business. At any rate, he would try to co-operate, and promised to deliver four small attacks starting in June. Haig was satisfied. He found Pétain 'businesslike, knowledgeable, and brief of speech. The latter is, I find, a rare quality in Frenchmen!'

Wilson visited Pétain the very next day and was told that 'in his opinion, Haig's attack toward Ostend was certain to fail, and that his effort to disengage Ostend and Zeebrugge was a hopeless one'.

On 21 May Colonel Repington, the military writer, had an

informal talk with Robertson at York House. 'I gave him a warning', he writes, 'to keep out of Low Country fighting and said that I had warned Foch when he disclosed ideas to me in this sense. I said that you can fight in mountains and deserts, but no one can fight in mud and when the water is let out against you, and, at the best, you are restricted to the narrow fronts on the higher ground, which are very unfavourable with modern weapons.' Robertson does not seem to have argued the point, but Repington noted how closely he listened and began to suspect 'that some operation in this sense may be in the wind . . . .'.

On 23 May Henry Wilson wrote in his diary, concerning a letter from Pétain to Haig regarding their talk the previous week: 'I object strongly to this answer, both to its tone and to its substance . . . it absolutely ignores Haig's suggestions as to dates for French offensives. . . . Then he comes to a dead stop, never mentioning any further operations during the autumn. . . . Of course, all this is quite hopeless. There is no sign of combined operations at all.' This appears to have been especially annoying to Sir Henry, for as liaison officer between the two Allies such a non-meeting of minds might be traceable to his own lack of statesmanship. So again he interviewed Pétain and pressed him for more concrete assurances. Why, he asked, had Pétain's commitments seemed to end in July? Without elaborating, Pétain stated that he could promise nothing more.

'Very well, then say so', Wilson replied irritably. Fuming, he left for Paris. There he saw General Foch, and on 2 June records the following in his diary:

He wanted to know who it was who wanted Haig to go on 'a duck's march through the inundations to Ostend and Zeebrugge'. He thinks the whole thing futile, fantastic, and dangerous, and I confess I agree, and always have. Haig always seems to think that when he has got to Roulers and Thorout he has solved the question. So Foch is entirely opposed to this enterprise, Jellicoe notwithstanding.

And on 4 June this entry:

I saw this morning the notes made at the conference the day before yesterday. . . . They are disquieting. The French attack for June 10 is cancelled . . . the Marshal must understand that no infantry attacks would take place anywhere for at least a month. Gun and aeroplane attacks, yes; but infantry attacks, no. This endorses and underlines all that I have been saying for the last month or more, and I think, and hope, that it will finally dispose of Haig's idea of taking Ostend and Zeebrugge.

None of these objections to Haig's offensive was conveyed to the British War Cabinet Committee. The lack of French co-operation was concealed or minimized. And even Wilson, who had just been strongly prevailed upon by Haig, made light of the French mutinies in his report; they were 'not yet serious'. Thus Lloyd George and his colleagues at the moment had no reason for qualms over the impending military conduct of the war on the Western Front, nor had they yet been enlightened about the specific offensive Haig was preparing in the Salient. They only knew that Plumer was about to attack the Messines ridge that overlooked the British position from the south and south-east, and that this 'life-saving operation' was expected to begin at any moment.

And on the other side of the front the enemy also waited. Major-General Max Hoffman writes in his diary:

I am very curious to know what is going to happen in the West. I cannot suppose that the English are going to give up their great offensive without a word or an effort. I think they are going to collect their forces again somewhere else, perhaps in conjunction with a landing. The West is strong enough in reserves to face such an event with equanimity—thanks to the Russian Revolution.

As for Ludendorff and Crown Prince Rupprecht, they were fairly certain of what Hoffman seems only to have suspected— that the next big blow would be delivered by the British, and that it would be somewhere in Flanders. But even by the end of the first week in June, they were not fully aware that the exact locale would be the infamous Salient at Ypres.

The fields of Flanders are mostly flat, flatter than the plains of Kansas, flatter than the lowlands of Hungary. On such terrain a ten-foot rise is a military prize worth fighting for. This was once a land of grassy, tree-filled, primeval swamps. Even after three years of war its scrubby desolation still gave the impression of a forest clearing. The plain is part of the same one which runs from the Pyrenees to Russia, the only gateway into France which bypasses formidable mountains and plateaus.

Flanders at any time is a monotonous countryside. There are no landmarks except houses and the gentlest of ridges. Single hills are rare. One of the few is Mount Kemmel, the loftiest peak in all the land, 350 feet high. Rivers and canals wind their way at random, merge into each other, separate, flow toward the ocean, then away from it; for the slope of the ground is too slight to create a normal pattern.

During the rainy seasons the rivers cannot discharge their waters because of the slightness of the gradient. Most of them flood once or more yearly. When they do, they spread their waters far and wide. Many of them have been straightened and canalized. Dikes and drainage water-courses are everywhere, marshes have been generally reclaimed, but still the waters overflow to some extent yearly, especially in the late summer and autumn. And in the words of Sir Douglas Haig's Chief of Intelligence: 'Careful investigation of the records of more than eighty years showed that in Flanders the weather broke early each August with the regularity of the Indian monsoon.'

The one major exception to the flatness is the famous Ridge, an arc of feeble hills and highlands running from some miles north of Passchendaele southward to Messines and then west toward Hazebrouck. Its average elevation is about 150 feet. Yet the German holders of these modest heights enjoyed a great military advantage not only in observation but in the placement of guns and defensive fortifications.

Since earliest times military offensives have failed in this mildseeming land because of a physical obstacle not apparent to the glance. For in Flanders the ground is almost pure fine-grained

clay, sometimes with a crust of sand on top or a thin coating of
loam. In certain places there is no topsoil at all; these clay fields,
called clyttes, exist at their worst north of Ypres in the vicinity of
the Houthulst Forest. Because of the impervious clay, the rain
cannot escape and tends to stagnate over large areas. Unable to
soak through, it forms swamps and ponds and sluggishly spreads
towards one of the already swollen rivers or canals. The ground
remains perpetually saturated. Water is reached at an average
depth of eighteen inches and only the shallowest of puddly
trenches can be dug by the troops, reinforced by sandbag
parapets. When the top-soil dries during fair weather, it cracks
open. The next rain floods the fissures. Then the clay blocks slide
upon themselves, causing little landslides.

The problem of terrain has bedevilled military commanders in
Flanders throughout history. In the early 1700s Marlborough
told how 'our armies swore terribly in Flanders'. By a curious
transposition of numerals, in 1197 Philip Augustus was trapped
with his army in the morass south-west of Ypres, and similar
frustrations occurred during the days of the Roman conquest.
For clay plus water equals mud—not the chalky mud of the
Somme battlefield to the south, but gluey, intolerable mud. The
British War Office Archives are full of reports in this vein:

'Part of company bogged in communications trench south of
St. Eloi; two men smothered.'

'Three men suffocated in mud near Voormezeele.'

Men had to lie 'flat and distribute their weight evenly in order
to prevent sinking into the mire'.

'The trenches are very wet, and the water is up to the men's
knees in most places.'

'Trenches full of liquid mud 2 to 3 feet deep.'

Men 'in pitiable condition coming out of trenches; wet
through, caked with stinking mud from head to foot. . . .'

When one officer was instructed to consolidate his advance
position, he wrote back, 'It is impossible to consolidate porridge.'

'Trenches full of liquid mud. Smelt horribly. Full of dead
Frenchmen too bad to touch. Men quite nauseated.'

Everywhere by 1917 the water was contaminated, and the delivery of fresh water was a major operation. The filthy surface wash was locked in by the clay. Rivers and canals were polluted by refuse from the flooded land, and even the artesian wells had become poisoned. The decay and refuse of millions of men, alive and dead, sank into the soil and were carried by the blackened waters throughout the inland plain. These conditions were most severe on the maritime strip west of the Yser, where the land is lower than sea-level at high tide. Were it not for the drains and dikes some sections would be ten feet under water, and, in fact, this had become the precise situation after the Belgians inundated the area in 1914.

In October of that year the Salient was formed, following two great offensives hurled at each other simultaneously and ending in stalemate. Next year the Germans won the entire ridge, though not Ypres itself, which now lay in a protruding pocket held stubbornly by the British who did not realize that in time it would become a suicide trap half surrounded by Germans on the heights above them. For over two years the lines had remained stationary. But the fighting never ended, and innumerable were the tiny battles waged henceforth, mainly for meagre topographical advantages. By the spring of 1917 the salient that curved roughly from the Wytschaete–Messines portion of the ridge to Boisinghe was as rigid in its contours as a portrait in stone, feared and hated like death itself by soldiers of the Empire everywhere in the world. Already a quarter of all the British killed on land or sea since the beginning of the war had died here.

In this landscape nothing existed but a measureless bog of military rubble, shattered houses, and tree-stumps. It was pitted with shell-craters containing fetid water. Overhead hung low clouds of smoke and fog. The very ground was soured by poison gas. Not one building was intact. Only mounds overrun with scrub grass, interspersed with old brick and fragments of wood, showed where many houses had formerly stood.

In the centre of this incarnation of ruin lay the dead city of Ypres—'Wipers' it was always called—obliterated, crushed like a pile of discarded baby's toys left out in the rain. Yet this mournful corpse, like a skeleton in a nightmare, seemed to live; for though it no longer possessed a normal spirit it was a turmoil of military activity. The traffic on the roads and in the shattered market-place was enormous and without end, though the town was shelled day and night, and since 1914 had been bombed more than any other target on the Western Front. General Monash, commander of the 3rd Australian Division, in a war letter to his wife describes the scene thus:

> . . . streams of men, vehicles, motor lorries, horses, mules, and motors of every description, moving ponderously forward, at a snail's pace, in either direction hour after hour, all day and all night, day after day, week after week, in a never halting, never ending stream . . . ploughing its way slowly and painfully through the mud . . . a reek of petrol and smoke everywhere.
>
> Here comes a body of fighting troops, tin-hatted and fully equipped, marching in file into the battle area, to carry out a relief of some front-line division. There follows a string of perhaps one hundred motor lorries, all fully loaded with supplies; a limousine motor-car with some division staff-officer; a string of regimental horse- and mule-drawn vehicles going up to a forward transport park; some motor-ambulance wagons . . . a long string of remount horses, marching in twos . . . a great 12-inch howitzer, dragged by two steam-traction engines, returning from the workshops after repair of injuries received; more infantry, thousands of them, more ambulances, more motor lorries; a long stream of Chinese coolies, smart and of magnificent stature . . . dispatch riders on motor bikes threading their way skilfully between the gaps; a battery of artillery all fully horsed and clattering and jingling; motor lorries again, heavily loaded with artillery ammunition . . . wagons bringing forward broken stone and road-making materials . . . a mounted police detachment . . . an 'Archie' (anti-aircraft gun), steam-motor drawn, going to take up a more forward position . . . a Royal Flying Corps car carrying parts of aeroplanes to forward hangers; more ambulances; and so on and on and on in a never-ending stream.

In the centre of the town only two buildings could, with

difficulty, be recognized from out of the past: the enormous Cloth Hall, epitome of the power of the ancient merchant guilds of the fourteenth century, when Ypres was the centre of a hand-weaving industry; and the adjacent Gothic cathedral. Their interiors were open to the sun and the rain. Dense weeds and grasses waved, field-mice scurried, birds built hundreds of nests within the scribbly, bombed-out walls.

Ypres was completely surrounded by the remains of its medieval walls and moat. On the south were the infantry barracks, on the west the prison, the reservoir, and the water tower. In and under all these ancient structures lay a honeycomb of 900 dug-outs that housed troops and headquarters.

From the eastern ramparts there issued the Menin Road, past the wrecked Menin Gate and onward to the front lines. Full of water holes, weeds and mud, this was a nightmare path, swept by shrapnel, strafed by aircraft. By the spring of 1917 hundreds of thousands who still lived could recall it with a pang: its mess, its muddle, its ceaseless traffic of apathetic men, sleepy and stumbling, marching in the fine rain that always seemed to characterize the Salient. To the north the Dixmude Gate was used for traffic to and from the Poelcapelle and St. Julien areas. The primary artery for transport further back was the road from Poperinghe ('Pop') to Ypres through Vlamertinghe. Years ago it had passed through long lines of trim little houses and elm trees. Meadows and fields of flax, corn and hops blossomed on both sides. Now all this was gone. The houses mouldered under the clay, the trees were blackened stumps, the meadows were mud and reeking water. Only the road still existed, for the army had macadamized it and kept it in operation. Now it was lined by thousands of rotting vehicles, guns, equipment, and dead horses.

Other than that pertaining to war, all civilization had long ago left the Salient. The last inhabitants had departed early in 1915. Only some stray dogs and cats stayed behind, wild and terrified, still roaming the land where their masters had once lived and played with them in quiet farms and cottages.

Flanders lies at fifty degrees north latitude, roughly along the line which passes through Newfoundland, Southampton and Cologne. Its average mean temperature is about 49°. Rain falls on an average of every other day throughout the year. Fogs drift inland from the coast. Even during peace the climate is not inspiring. This was the countryside where the First and Second Battles of Ypres had been fought to a standstill, and where the Third Battle of Ypres would soon explode under the calm but relentless guidance of Sir Douglas Haig.

When German cartoonists drew the Salient during the war years they usually likened it to the mouth of a skull, the teeth of which were biting down on Ypres. For the British to push further into the open mouth would leave them in danger of being swallowed up altogether. Plainly it was necessary first to capture the Messine–Wytschaete lower jawbone, and then to proceed up the molars through Broodseinde, Passchendaele, and West-roosebeke. After that would occur the coastal operation under the navy and Rawlinson's Fourth Army. By June 1917 plans for the attack at Messines were completely and meticulously in readiness; and so was General Sir Herbert Plumer with his Second Army.

6

Triumph at Messines

SIR HERBERT PLUMER'S hair had turned white during his two thankless years as warden of the Salient. A heavy responsibility had been his, with no chance for glory, for there was hardly a point within the loop of ground held by his Second Army which German guns could not enfilade or fire into from behind, a state of affairs hardly calculated to improve the nerves of this commander or his troops. None the less he had made of the Salient a nut so hard to crack that the enemy had not tried to do so since 1915. An ideal officer to hold any position in bulldog fashion, Plumer was a prim little old man with a pink face, fierce white moustache, blue eyes, a little pot belly mounted on tiny legs. As he walked, he panted and puffed. Only the dour cast to his mouth hinted at the essential stubbornness of his nature. Yet he liked to give lifts to women and children in his staff car as he toured the Belgian roads behind the front; and he took childlike delight when troops of his own kind—Lancaster or London— accomplished anything useful in battle.

He was fortunate in possessing an extraordinary chief of staff, the cultured and wise Major-General Sir Charles ('Tim') Harington—also a cautious planner, but with, perhaps, an extra dash of imagination and verve. He was tall and thin, nervous, had a card-index mind and a sense of humour. The combination of the two men had proved outstanding in the war to date; and now they hoped to prove that they could storm an objective as well as hold one. Surely they had been allotted more than enough time to get ready. During the long, lean years while they had hung on, improving their defences, not looking for trouble, they had studied their terrain with microscopic thoroughness. Of Plumer it was said that 'he knew every puddle in the Salient'. Plans for capturing the Messines–Wytschaete ('White Sheet') flank of the ridge had been endlessly cast and recast in conference after conference, order after order. By spring 1917 the operation had been worked out with an intensity unmatched in the war thus far.

Plumer's trump card was a system of enormous land mines burrowed beneath the German front. This work had begun in 1915 with the construction of shallow galleries and small charges about fifteen feet underground. Next year the idea of concentrating on a deep-mining offensive, with tunnels and charges nearly 100 feet below the surface, was contemplated. But to penetrate secretly with galleries of substantial size the saturated, semi-liquid layer that made up the Flanders sub-soil was on the face of it quite impossible. Might there be another way?

The problem was studied by Lieutenant-Colonel T. Edgeword David, chief geologist of the B.E.F., and the Engineer-in-Chief, Brigadier-General G. H. Fowke, who analysed sand and clay layers and the variations of water in each. Perhaps, they thought, the layer of heavy blue clay lying even further down —between 80 and 120 feet—might be a practical medium for their purpose. At that depth the tunnels and charges could not be blown up, accidentally or otherwise, by mortar-fire or shallow countermines; and the sound of digging would be so muffled that secrecy might be possible. Under the harried conditions of war, with the time element so important, and specialized heavy equipment so scarce, was it possible to construct such shafts, to lay gigantic charges accurately under the key German front-line positions, within a reasonable time, and without being detected? Though the odds were not good, it was decided to try.

By January 1916 six tunnels had been started (the signs above them read 'Deep Wells'); and during the next year twenty of the largest mines in the annals of warfare were in place, or in process of being placed. Twenty underground communities

Stretcher bearers in action following the Battle of
Pilckem Ridge; August 1, 1917

Field gun bogged; Pilckem Ridge; August 2, 1917

Near Zillebeke; August 9, 1917

After the battle

came into being. From the sandbagged openings wooden stairs led down to sleeping quarters. Below these, planked passages slanted to headquarters posts and thence to the actual three-by-six galleries. In these bowels of the earth, the mole-like character of the war was fantastically intensified. The hum of pumping engines never ceased. The thousands of men who worked here with picks and shovels, coughing in the dampness, white of skin, shoved their tunnels a pitiful ten or fifteen feet forward each day under the glare of electric lamps; and as each gallery was completed a mine was laid in place (sometimes two) containing charges of ammonal up to 95,000 lb. Some tunnels were almost half a mile in length. By 7 June the total had come to a million pounds of explosive and almost five miles of gallery.

Meanwhile the Germans were also mining toward the British lines, but in a smaller way and much more shallowly, for they had neither the equipment nor the plan for deep works possessed by their enemy. Yet in places they did venture to considerable depths—sometimes nearly sixty feet down—and many were the times when the British, listening with microphones at the forward, boarded-up faces of their galleries, heard with dismay a German tunnel approaching their own. Early in 1917 the enemy had dug within eighteen inches of the British at the northern corner of the ridge.

A colonel came to Harington with the news and recommended that the mine be blown. Harington thought for a moment, walked to Plumer's door, knocked, and entered.

'"Mines" says we must blow the Hill 60 mines today.'

'I won't have them blown,' snapped the General. 'Good night.'

Work stopped, the British evacuated the tunnel, and by chance the Germans veered away.

The enemy knew that the ridge would soon be attacked. Preparations above ground were obvious, and they had captured many prisoners who had talked. One specifically told them on 29 May that the assault would begin on 7 June after eight days of bombardment. But what about the mines, the only element of

8

real surprise? The Boche had their suspicions. While they did not greatly fear the small, shallow charges they had become apprehensive concerning deep mining. They sent out many raiding parties primarily to bring back not prisoners but samples of the soil thrown up by diggings. On 9 April one of these parties returned with blue clay. While this was a sure sign that the British were constructing at least one mine at great depth, the Germans reacted inconsequentially, assuming evidently that the shaft was only an isolated one (if it existed at all), and that, since the attack was so imminent, little further mining could be accomplished by the British in the brief time remaining.

To the British it seemed doubtful that their opponents could not know of the twenty deep mines. Certainly, they worried, some prisoners had disclosed them by now. (Not one had done so.) Surely the Germans had been able to hear the work going on, despite many soundproofing measures. (They had not, due to the inferiority of their microphones.) For once even Sir Douglas Haig seems to have been troubled by nervousness. His greatest fear was that the enemy might abandon his front lines just before the attack, a suggestion in fact made by Lieutenant-General von Kuhl, Crown Prince Rupprecht's Chief of Staff, early in May. But this projected withdrawal, which would have dislocated Haig's plan even worse than the one which upset Nivelle, was rejected by Rupprecht. The blow to morale would be too great, he estimated, if such an outstanding defensive sector were to be discarded without a fight. It could and would be held. As for British mining, the Germans had rather decided by May that it had ended, except for small efforts of no importance. Only at Hill 60 was it definitely known that the British were still digging in earnest, and here, according to the German officer in charge, their work had been hopelessly damaged by countermining. Thus misled by faulty Intelligence, the Crown Prince could not see how the clear and above-board preparations of the enemy could possibly succeed.

Accordingly on 1 June he caused the XIX Army Corps to issue an order concerning Wytschaete and Messines: 'These strong-

points must not fall even temporarily into the enemy's hands. . . .
·They must be held to the last man even if the enemy has cut them
off on both sides, and threatens them from the rear.'

Furthermore, the German troops were told that they need have
no fear of a break-through. Reserves were already in place and
would move in swiftly to seal off any gaps that might occur. In
these orders and reassurances the opposing high command clearly
showed the value they placed on the east and south ridges of their
precious encirclement.

So Haig's one great worry was baseless; the Germans would
stay put and make their stand. Not knowing this, he recommended
in a conference 30 May that all mines be exploded before Zero
Day; next the troops would occupy the ground; and later they
would try to cross over the crest of the ridge. He also suggested
moving the target date forward a day or two. Plumer begged to
reject these last-minute changes, and Haig agreed to let matters
go forward on schedule.

The trepidation of the British is understandable. The greatest
series of simultaneous explosions in history was about to take
place (it would triple the former record set in New York during
subway construction late in the 1800s). Hundreds of thousands
of men had been working toward this one day for over two years.
The immensity, the importance of the operation was incalculable.
And it all hung on the feeblest of threads. One British private
soldier taken prisoner could have nullified it. German detection
devices could have been alert to the entire plan for months.
Aircraft observation might have detected any number of blue-
clay diggings, despite efforts to camouflage them as they were
hauled to the rear. How much did the Germans know? From
Haig on down, the British would have sold their souls for an
answer.

The very fact that German countermining continued was noteworthy, even though most of these efforts were at shallow levels.
In one place the Germans were known to be digging along a line
that was bound to intersect the British gallery. Again this was
near (or rather under) Hill 60, where the most spectacular mining,

countermining, and mine fighting took place. The state of affairs was later described:

> ... on May 9th the enemy was so near that work was stopped, and the branch gallery was loaded with 1,600 lb. of ammonal. The Germans had evidently completed their shaft and were driving a gallery past the end of the branch gallery. As, however, there was only a month to go, and the *camouflet* (a small defensive charge which ruins the enemy tunnel but does not open the surface of the ground) might detonate the great mine, or at least cause the Germans to probe vigorously, it was decided that the safest course was to accept the risk involved in letting the enemy work on, and not to fire the mine unless he touched the actual timbers of the branch gallery. . . . The Germans could now be heard putting in timber, working a truck, walking, and even talking. On May 25th in some other workings they fired a mine whose position was 'dangerously correct' directly above the Hill 60 gallery. It crushed in the junction of the galleries and entombed two listeners. One, Sapper Earl, in the Hill 60 gallery, coolly went on listening and heard a German walk down an enemy gallery apparently directly over the great mine. . . . The listeners had to be withdrawn, and from then onwards the staff could only trust that the enemy would not reach the British workings before the mine was fired.

At Petit Douve, near Messines, one mine, already laid and electrically charged, was discovered by the Germans. They blew a *camouflet*, wrecked the main British gallery, and the mine had to be abandoned. This left nineteen. It was a race against time at Spanbroekmolen, where the major in charge of the tunnelling company scribbled in pencil a note to division headquarters 6 June that it was 'almost' definite that his mine would explode the following morning of the attack.

It had indeed been a tense two years of underground digging and fighting, and the records of the period recall the strangeness of it all, and the peril:

> Captain Woodward and Lieutenant Clinton . . . heard the enemy 'hard at work' and earth falling within twenty feet of them. The gallery commander . . . ordered the nearest part of the gallery to

be at once silently loaded. While the charge—2,500 lb. of ammonal —was being put in, the Germans could easily be heard 'with the naked ear'. So close were they working that the vibration kept shaking down flakes of clay on to the tin containers of the ammonal, which had therefore to be covered with sandbags. Woodward reported the situation 'critical', and . . . when the Germans were probably ten feet away, the charge was fired.

Sapper Sneddon, having clearly heard the Germans boring and then charging the bore-hole, temporarily withdrew his men. As no 'blow' followed, Major Henry suggested that means might be devised of simulating work while the gallery was empty, so that the enemy might fire his charge uselessly. Before this was done, however, early on April 7th the Germans fired their mine, crushing the rickety gallery and killing Sapper Sneddon, who was listening there.

. . . he had been working underground for nearly two years in the dark saps pierced under the German lines, and running very close to German saps nosing their way, and sometimes breaking through, to ours, so that the men clawed at each other's throats in these tunnels and beat each other to death with picks and shovels.

So the digging went on, and the never-ending pumping out of water; and seldom it was that men could last in this work for even a few months without a breakdown of nerve and health. 'Listeners all a bit windy', one Captain Avery reported. Replacements flowed into the diggings, and as time went on the fighting infantry were relieved by labour battalions. Every tunnel had a name—the Newcastle shaft, the Snout, the Sydney, the Perth, the Hobart, the great Brisbane. One started from over 200 yards behind the British lines, descended to ninety feet, and, the men said solemnly, would in time lead to Berlin. It was called the Berlin Sap. By late evening, 6 June, these nineteen mines were in place and charged, their shafts were tamped down, and the only remaining question was how many of them—especially the old ones that had been laid down as long as six months ago—would actually explode next morning.

The mines were to be only a curtain raiser. Because to a large degree they were an unknown factor—nobody really knew how many would go off, whether each lay in exactly the right position, and how much damage they would do to men, trenches, and guns many yards above—the greatest artillery mass of the war had been arrayed against enemy lines between Ploegsteert ('Plug Street') Wood and Observatory Ridge, about a mile north-east of Hill 60. Over 2,400 guns and howitzers were to participate, fully a third of which were heavy pieces: one gun to every seven yards of front.

Other than the mines, as we have seen, there would be no surprise at all (except possibly for the precise moment of Zero Hour itself, and this was not officially told to the troops until the 5th); and the artillery preparations were unusually brazen. In single file the heavies were hauled directly to the frontal area from the rear towns and assembly points. Behind them jostled the little field guns, galloping up without the slightest caution, a wild noisy collection followed closely by their ammunition wagons. They were emplaced wheel to wheel, with no attempt to hide them. From 18 to 30 May the guns rumbled forward, and on the latter day they began shelling in earnest the enemy's wire entanglements, his roads, camp areas, supply dumps, and in particular the routes and points where it was known that water and food were being delivered to troops up front.

In the final days gas shells were thrown in vast numbers to force the enemy to don masks and lose sleep. And, further to confuse him, the bombardment was twice increased to pre-attack intensity, and twice the Germans reacted spasmodically to false alarms. By the morning of the 7th the British gunners were thoroughly rehearsed, every gun was registered on its target, and the Germans were weary and on edge. All that remained was the final performance, the efficiency of which was a near certainty from an artillery standpoint.

Tanks, too, were in readiness—seventy-two Mark IVs that assembled a few miles south-west of Ypres and waited under camouflaged shelters for the signal to proceed toward the front. On the night of the 6th they emerged, throbbing and clattering, and approached their starting-points under the cover of aircraft which flew back and forth to drown their noise. It was the first appearance in battle of these new models. While their best speed on battle terrain with a crew of eight was only about three miles per hour, their plating was impervious to German armour-piercing bullets, and it was hoped that they would be able to help the infantry overcome strongpoints.

Three hundred planes of the II Brigade Royal Flying Corps went into action late in May, mostly to assist the artillery by observation and photographs.

The attack itself was to be a straightforward operation along a ten-mile front toward a final objective two miles away at most, known as the Green Line, or Oosttaverne Line, running slightly to the east of that ex-village in a nearly straight line that formed a chord across the base of the German salient. Three Corps (IX, X, and II Anzac) would participate with three divisions each, and each corps would have one division in reserve, ready to leap-frog through upon signal. About 80,000 infantry would go over the top at dawn, at which moment the mines would be detonated and the artillery barrage would commence with every operable gun along the Second Army Front.

During the long months of working, waiting, and suffering almost helplessly under the guns of their tormentors ringed around them on the slopes, the British troops had practised their great freeing operation. Behind each of the three corps, training areas had been constructed. Roughly similar to the terrain that would be met on 7 June, they were marked with coloured flags and tapelines designating ravines, woods, strongpoints, and other objectives. In full battledress, infantrymen and artillerymen rehearsed their attack six times. A model of the entire Ridge was laid out in a field about the size of a tennis court, and here all officers studied the slopes up and down which they would soon lead their men. Various of the twelve divisions, too, made clay table-top replicas of their individual sectors.

As training progressed, and while the guns and supplies moved in opposite the German ridge-salient, commanders from Plumer down visited the front daily and saw to it that the movements of troops as small as corporals' sections were understood by the men and co-ordinated with the larger plan. Patrols increased their activity, seeking new information. Major-General Monash, leader of the 3rd Australian Division, distributed circulars among his men telling how Australian prisoners had been nearly starved by their captors in a dungeon after the battle of Bullecourt; whether this tactic fed the ferocity of his assault brigades is doubtful, though the tale was true.

The men waited, worked, and trained. For once, in the First World War, they approached Zero Hour with a sense of optimism, though they understood what they faced. 'The enemy will fight his hardest for the Messines Ridge', said one officer. 'He has stacks of guns against us.'

And another, who knew the Salient perhaps too well, peered at the German-held ridges, lofty and arrogant in the hazy distance, flaming with guns, webbed with row after row of sandbagged trenches, peppered with thousands of machine-gun emplacements, pill-boxes, and sharpshooters' nests. He turned to a newspaper man and murmured, 'It's a Gibraltar'. The mines would have to do their job.

Major-General Harington opened his advance Press conference with these words: 'Gentlemen, I don't know whether we are going to make history tomorrow, but at any rate we shall change geography.'

Let us examine now the German side of the coin.

The Messines–Wytschaete portion of the ridge had been in the past manned by a total of four divisions. When in January 1917 Ludendorff became aware of the growing danger there, he placed two more in reserve. In February it was noticed that new British batteries were moving into position. On 29 April a spy advised the German High Command that the British would attack the ridge two weeks after stopping their main effort on the Arras front—an estimate which was very nearly correct.

At about the same time, aerial observation disclosed that

British movement on the roads and railways behind the Salient was reaching alarming proportions, far greater than that which had preceded the assault further south under Allenby a few weeks previously. After weighing these and other Intelligence reports Crown Prince Rupprecht decided that the Arras attack was merely a large-scale feint and that the Messines ridge was Haig's true objective. From this moment on, and for the next five weeks, the Germans reinforced their positions substantially opposite Plumer's army.

But five German weeks were not equal to five British months. In those five weeks the German air arm covering the Salient was driven out of the sky, and the former's batteries were nearly crushed by counter-bombardment. A few figures tell the story, and in reading them one senses the intensity of this greatest of all counter-battery operations, and the despair of the defenders who helplessly watched the shattering of their artillery shield. By early June almost half the German howitzers, light and heavy, were out of action. Hardly one captured Russian gun remained operable. The Third Bavarian Division faced the coming attack with a total of only nineteen field guns; the 2nd Division up north had lost fifteen out of eighteen medium and heavy howitzers.

Under such conditions, German infantry could expect only trivial support during the coming fight. Ominously, they had already been driven from at least one strong-point even before 7 June and had been forced to take refuge out in open trenches. British gas shelling on an unprecedented scale had indeed accomplished its purpose of keeping the enemy awake for days, and the disruption of food supply had further demoralized him. The night before the attack a lucky British hit exploded a great ammunition dump near Menin, and gas quickly spread throughout the area. Many civilians who still inhabited the outskirts of this section of the rear zone were killed, as well as an undetermined number of corralled mules and horses. So shaken were the Germans by British shelling to which they could not effectively reply that five divisional replacements had to be consummated during the

Messines: 6 June, 1917

first week of June. One of these, as we shall see, was actually in progress during the morning of the 7th.

Too late it dawned on the Crown Prince that he was in trouble, and during the last few days he worked feverishly to save his position. More small bodies of infantry were hustled into action. Artillery was added, especially on the flanks of the threatened sector; more planes, pioneers, and machine-guns were thrown into the pre-attack fighting. On 3 June 13,000 gas shells were poured into the Australians around Ploegsteert Wood, and on 6 June, knowing that the attack was due next day or the day after, Rupprecht ordered an even heavier gas barrage, in an attempt to smother the enemy artillery and catch troops on their approach march to the jumping-off line.

These last-minute measures embarrassed the British but failed to hamper them to any large extent, except in the case of General Monash's 3rd Australians, 500 of whom were gassed en route. For once, the 48-year-old Bavarian Prince, field-marshal of the northern armies on the Western Front, descendant of the Stuart kings of Britain, brother-in-law of the Belgian queen, world traveller and gifted military commander, had been too late with too little, outwitted underground, outmanned and outgunned on the ground, and overpowered in the skies above. The battle of Messines was lost by the Germans before it began.

During the evening the men marched silently in columns of fours like groping tentacles toward the communication trenches, and thence to the front, where white jumping-off tapes lay on the soft wet ground of No-Man's-Land. They were troubled and wearied by the need for wearing their masks, for gas shells were plopping all about them, laying low the unwary and careless as well as many pack animals gasping and heaving in the poisoned air. It was warm that night. Fog lay on the Salient like a heavy caress, and in it not a breeze stirred. Overhead forked lightning played, accompanied by the mutter of thunder. At midnight a sharp thundershower broke. It lasted only a few minutes, and when it passed a three-quarter moon floated regally in a nearly

clear sky. Now brilliant flashes against the enemy slopes could be
seen, and the steady whamming of the big guns sounded per-
ceptibly louder as the blanket of fog melted away.

Half-an-hour before Zero Hour the British guns stopped firing,
and the night became so still that one could hear nightingales
singing in the nearby woods. The men fixed bayonets and
removed their gas masks. Some of them dozed. Officers changed
to other ranks' tunics and kept peering at their wristwatches.
Zero Hour would be 3.10.

At 2.52 the Germans threw up yellow and green flares, calling
for artillery fire—a disconcerting sign. How much did they
know? At 2.57 heavy bursts of shrapnel swept segments of the
British front; but quickly it ceased.

At 3.05 the first streaks of dawn filtered over the Messines
ridge. On Mount Kemmel the cocks began to crow. Two green
star-flashes burst directly in front of the New Zealand division at
3.06—then machine-guns and another flare. Had this unit been
discovered? (Some of their assembly trenches had been dug
dangerously forward in No-Man's-Land during the early
evening.) But at 3.09 the German guns stopped chattering. For
one minute absolute silence saturated the air, while at whispered
orders the troops crawled over their parapets and lay flat in front
of the tapes.

A few seconds before 3.10 some of the heavy guns rearward
began to fire. Then each of the nineteen land mines exploded
almost in unison. The earth quaked, tumbling and staggering the
British soldiers as they rose in awe to see the rim of the hated
ridge burst skyward in a dense black cloud, beneath which
gushed nineteen pillars of flame that lit the Salient with the red
glare of hell. The pillars fused into greater mushrooms of fire that
seemed to set flame to little clouds above. Then, a moment or
two later, the long roar of nineteen explosions blended and
reverberated into one long blast that stunned even the British
troops, awakened the countryside, rolled through Flanders and
northern France, hurtled the Channel, and was heard in London by
Lloyd George, awake in his study at Number 10 Downing Street.

From the German positions yellow flares soared imploringly high into the sky, the pathetic prayers of doomed men crying for help. As the villages of Messines and Wytschaete disappeared into oblivion, the heaviest of all artillery barrages struck the German front, and the British assault brigades scrambled over the top.

Plumer and his staff had breakfasted at 2.30, after which everybody went to the top of Cassel Hill to see the mines go up—all but Plumer, who returned to his room and knelt at his bed in prayer. When the first news of the infantry advance came, he burst into tears. It was quite clear that his Second Army was winning as planned, and with greater ease than had been expected. So swift and thorough was the British success that subsequent fighting came as an anticlimax.

The enemy was in a state of near shock when the British fell upon them. They surrendered *en masse*, weeping, waving handkerchiefs, grasping the ankles of their captors. Thousands lay beneath the ground, to be for ever entombed there. Some of the mine craters were 300 feet across and 70 feet deep. The wreckage of their front left many Germans cringing in derelict shelters 'like beaten animals' while the British walked along throwing Mills bombs at unresisting clusters of men too dazed to surrender. One Australian lieutenant reported how they 'made many fruitless attempts to embrace us. I have never seen men so demoralized.' Another distraught prisoner said that only two men in his section of the line had survived the blast. A captured officer reported that of his 200-man company only thirty were alive when the British foot soldiers arrived. The 3rd Bavarian Division was relieving the 24th Saxons precisely when the explosions and the attack burst; both relieved and relievers were decimated, and most of the balance were made prisoners.

While the British dug in near the crest of the ridge, German defences began to tighten. Machine-guns took a heavy toll of these furthermost troops and of those moving up in support. By eleven o'clock appreciable enemy infantry reinforcements were seen to be approaching the eastern slopes. Soon afterward, sporadic counter-attacks developed. Small bodies of Germans stubbornly

holding out at isolated points throughout the area redoubled
their fire. It was at this stage that hundreds of British were killed
and wounded by their own batteries and fellow infantrymen; for
as they descended the western slopes of the ridge after being
relieved they were mistaken again and again for German counter-
attackers. At other sectors along the front of advance errors in
direction were committed; some companies got temporarily lost;
others were held up by the great mine craters. Yet, all in all, the
general sweep forward proceeded on schedule.

During the middle of the afternoon, following the first long
pause, all three reserve divisions plunged forward with their
tanks and brushed aside secondary German defences. From a
previous line running some 600 yards west of the final goal the
new assault lapped toward the little village of Oosttaverne,
captured it within an hour, and reached the entire Green Line
by dusk.

For the next few days advance posts were established by the
victors, the new line was consolidated, the Germans continued
to counter-attack feebly; but in line with previous plans no
attempt was made by the British to exploit their success. The
battle of Messines Ridge was over, and would stand on its merits.
The south flank of the great Salient at Ypres no longer existed,
and now British troops stood astride that portion of the ridge
from which they had been murdered wholesale since early in the
war. The front had been pushed back two miles at the furthest
point; 7,300 prisoners were taken, and the Germans had suffered
almost 20,000 other casualties. These figures apply to the period
1 to 10 June. During the same time British casualties came to
something under 24,000. So, 'counting heads', the difference
between the losses in men on both sides was, after all, disturbingly
small, though the achievement as a whole was (or seemed to be
at the time) beyond question. Certainly the operation had been,
in the words of one writer, a 'siege-war masterpiece', one 'in
which the methods employed by the command completely fitted
the facts of the situation', a triumph of engineers in what was
essentially an engineers' war.

In his memoirs von Hindenburg admits:

The moral effect of the explosions was simply staggering. . . . The 7th of June cost us dear, and, owing to the success of the enemy attack, the price we paid was very heavy . . . it was many days before the front was again secure. The British army did not press its advantage; apparently it only intended to improve its position for the launching of the great Flanders offensive.

And in his dispatch dated 12 June Philip Gibbs wrote:

From Messines and Wytschaete [the Germans] had absolute observation of a wide tract of country in which our men lived and died —how complete an observation I did not realize until after this battle, when standing in Wytschaete Wood and on the mound by St.-Eloi, and on the ground rising up to Messines, I looked back, and saw every detail of our old territory laid out like a relief map brightly coloured. 'My God', said an officer by my side, 'it's a wonder they allowed us to live at all!'

Thus had Sir Douglas Haig cleared the first hurdle in his race against time and politicians.

7

The Signed Contract

IF Sir Douglas, jubilant over Plumer's triumph at Messines, had assumed that it would end once and for all the objections to his larger plan, he was to be unpleasantly surprised; for the more Lloyd George thought about what was next on the military agenda the more apprehensive he became. One by one he began privately sounding out various members of the War Cabinet for their support in blocking Haig, and he let it be known that he was still as strong as ever for a serious offensive on the Italian front. The Commander-in-Chief first learned of this in a letter dated 13 June from Sir William Robertson, which read in part:

> There is trouble in the land just now . . . the L.G. idea is to settle the war from Italy, and today the railway people have been asked for figures regarding the rapid transfer of 12 Divisions and 300 heavy guns to Italy! They will never go while I am C.I.G.S. but that will come later. What I do wish to impress on you is this:—Don't argue that you can finish the war this year, or that the German is already beaten. Argue that your plan is the best plan—as it is—that no other would be *safe* let alone decisive, and then leave them to reject your advice and mine. They dare not do that.

Haig was appalled. What hurt most was that even Robertson, despite his strong written support, was wavering too. In the course of subsequent conversation 'Wully' suggested that matters might become serious if Haig were to plunge into a long, bloody offensive without large-scale aid by the French. By autumn Britain might be 'without an army'! Was it not, after all, possible that Austria could be knocked out by one sharp blow?

Perhaps it might be wise to send at least heavy guns to the Italians and, if only for the moment, to stand on the defensive in the west.

Haig could scarcely believe his ears. Never before had a British officer dared to contradict him on this issue of almost religious faith. His own staff was packed with yea-sayers of the most dutiful and orthodox type—especially his Intelligence chief, Brigadier-General Charteris, he of the feverish optimism and Western zeal. Coming from his most trusted cohort, Robertson's words were heretical and incredible. Haig replied stiffly that the Germans were practically at the end of their rope, barely hanging on, and ready for the *coup de grâce*.

While this view had been emanating from Charteris for a year, few people other than Haig really believed it. Robertson brushed it aside. His own Central Intelligence chief at the War Office was saying exactly the opposite. Without the French, he feared, Haig would be walking into a political trap and perhaps a military dead-end.

But the French *would* co-operate satisfactorily, Haig replied. Had not Pétain promised him only yesterday that nearly 100,000 troops under General Anthoine were forthcoming, to be under Haig's orders? Pétain had said that he would be 'most anxious to help in every way', and that the situation in the French army was 'now more satisfactory'. As for the British assuming the defensive, Robertson could surely visualize its ineffable by-product—Lloyd George would, of course, seize the opportunity to snatch untold divisions from the west and squander them in Salonika or Palestine or Italy or heaven knows where else, or might even bring them back to England altogether, under some trumped-up excuse.

And Cadorna! Here both Haig and Robertson were in agreement. The Italian general plainly was incapable of handling a major offensive. Already his army had fought the Battle of the Isonzo River eleven times, and still it stood on the Isonzo.

Summing up, Haig felt that Robertson's opinion was, to say the least, unsound. He had, in fact, already formulated in his

9

diary a capsule of his attitude; the only thing to do immediately
was:

    1. Send to France every possible man.
    2. ,,   ,,   ,,   ,,   ,,   aeroplane.
    3. ,,   ,,   ,,   ,,   ,,   gun.

And on Sunday after church services attended by both men,
Robertson changed his mind. He was ready now to back Haig
to the hilt, and suddenly 'seemed to realize that the German
Army was in reduced circumstances'.

Yet it appears that the C.I.G.S. sensed, as others did, that
in spite of Messines things had not changed much. The Salient was
still a salient—perhaps not as bad as before, but the Germans still
had splendid positions and observation to the north-east; and as
to the rest of the ridge everything was quite the same. From the
Pilckem Ridge southward the enemy was as powerfully placed
defensively as ever, and a break-through was nearly as remote as
before 7 June. Perhaps it was even more remote, for many more
pill-boxes were being hastily constructed to meet the impending
assault, and an avalanche of reinforcements was moving in from
the Eastern Front. Luxuriously ensconced in their shell-proof
dug-outs that balmy June, the Germans fried their bacon, read
Goethe, peered through their telescopes, laid down more barbed
wire, trundled up more and more guns, played chess, oiled their
machine-guns, wrote letters, and with mingled apprehension and
confidence awaited the Third Battle of Ypres under conditions
that favoured the defence more than even before. And this time
there would be no British mines.

Furthermore there was still the time element. Was there really
enough time after the Nivelle and Plumer episodes to shift the
centre of gravity to Ypres and win a big victory before the rains
came? On this basis alone, many thought, the new plan was no
longer valid by mid-summer and should be cancelled.

And after Messines to achieve surprise was hopeless; visually
and on the basis of Intelligence reports the Germans knew what
was in store, just as throughout the war both sides always knew

when and where a big attack was due. German Fourth Army headquarters and Rupprecht individually agreed that it was 'certain' the next British offensive would be at Ypres. It was the same old story. To hide the immensity of the preparations was as impossible as ever, and, in fact, the enemy was aware of most of the exact details. The Crown Prince, ever shrewd and pessimistic, had begun to strengthen his front by early June, believing that the attack at the Salient would have the further aim of freeing the Belgian coast, along with an eventual landing from the Channel in co-operation with 'limited' (his word) assistance by the French. All these assumptions, as we know, were quite correct. Thereupon he brought to the crucial sector many additional divisions for front-line duty, reserve duty close behind the front, and for counter-attack after the British had been stopped. And, as we have seen, he hurried the construction of hundreds more of the most forbidding obstacle of all—concrete pill-boxes arranged checkerboard-fashion in depth all through his frontal area.

Later this month Canadian troops attacked at Lens. Still Rupprecht was not deceived. It was merely a feint, he announced; the British did not have the power to deliver two major blows at practically the same time, and the one that counted was coming soon enough at Ypres. On 6 July he reported that he was ready for an attack of any magnitude. By the 9th German artillery was stronger than the British, and leisurely engaged in blowing up ammunition dumps; and by now Rupprecht's staff wondered among themselves why the British guns did not open up in reply, to herald the hopeless advance of the foot soldiers.

Early in July, to add insult to arrogance, the Germans attacked Rawlinson's Fourth Army by surprise and drove most of it across the Yser river, where it had been sitting in anticipation of its future coastal operation.

Not even Nivelle's plan had been so apparent to the enemy, nor had it been awaited more placidly by the Germans; and precisely as in the Nivelle affair careless words had done their deadly work. Again prisoners had talked. Again the politicians had squabbled openly. On 7 July Painlevé himself had delivered a speech in which unfortunate reference was made to the small amount of aid French troops would be able to render Haig. One Australian on leave in England wrote in his diary: 'Everyone in England was talking of the coming British offensive. I heard more of it there than in France. . . . The first thing X— asked me was: "Well, Z—, when is the big offensive along the coast coming off?" I pretended to know nothing. It simply shocked me to hear the way people talked.'

In mid-June the *Frankfurter Zeitung* published a bland appraisal of British chances in the forthcoming attack at Ypres. Lloyd George read it next day. That settled matters, as far as he was concerned. Haig had to be stopped—and not by the Germans.

Much of the story of Flanders 1917 has to do with conferences —at Chantilly, Rome, Calais, Paris, and lesser ones elsewhere. Some reached sensible conclusions; most did not. Some only aggravated strained relationships between mutually exclusive soldiers and civilians. Many were dull and confused. A few were of importance, if only in settling some dispute for the worse, such as the final talk between Painlevé and Nivelle. The minutes of all of them lie fading and buried in the archives of the great states that fought the war, of interest now only to the scholar of minutiae and semantics. But the June deliberations in London are of a class apart. During three days a pitched battle was fought here between Haig and Lloyd George and their supporters from which three-quarters of a million men emerged dead or wounded five months later. It was the showdown between Easterners and Westerners. Haig had the advantage, largely because his opponents were divided among themselves, because neither he nor Robertson could be flatly removed without proving that the Allied cause was bankrupt, and because Lloyd George himself was not strong enough politically to sack them or override them unless they capitulated; and this they were not likely to do. The Prime Minister could only coax them to change their minds, and should this fail—as Painlevé failed versus Nivelle—he might be forced to let them have their way. The field-marshal and the general were in the driver's seat; they knew it, and refused to step down or hand over the reins.

To reinforce his position Lloyd George formed a new Committee on War Policy. Headed by himself, it included Lord Curzon, Lord Milner, and General Smuts of South Africa. The job of this select group of four was to direct and co-ordinate the entire British war effort on land and sea, and, the Prime Minister hoped, to offer a united front capable of bending the army high command to its wishes. We shall see whether the Policy Committee was indeed willing or able to accomplish this formidable task.

The Committee's first official act was to summon Haig and Robertson. Haig was at G.H.Q. in northern France. He drove from there to Calais, took a destroyer to Dover, and a train to Charing Cross. The Chief of the Imperial General Staff was already in London.

The deliberations that followed were grave and formal in tone. No direct recriminations were uttered. The name-calling by Lloyd George was so subtle, so polite, that the two generals were barely wounded at all. Superficially the talks proceeded on an unusually high level of objectiveness; though vast prejudices and preconceived notions lay submerged below, like an iceberg only a fraction of which shows above the surface of the icy, placid water in which it floats. Millions of words, spoken and written, made up the sum of the argument. Let us reduce them to simple terms.

The first meeting took place 19 June and was dominated by Douglas Haig. Here, for the first time officially, he revealed his Flanders campaign to the civilians in all its breathtaking splendour as based on a paper sent a week earlier to his army commanders.

He began by saying that the prospects for a successful attack were at the moment ideal. Russia was beginning a large offensive with 'excellent results', and so heartening was this to the Russian people that more such fine efforts could be expected.

Lloyd George commented that both these premises were incorrect.

Impassively Haig continued to the effect that the Germans were demoralized by a suspicion that their submarine campaign was a failure.

The Prime Minister thought that Haig was trying to play it both ways. If the submarines were failing, the Germans were demoralized and susceptible to attack. If the submarines were not failing, the Germans should be attacked so as to deprive them of submarine bases. Since Haig scored a point either way, again something must be wrong with his premise.

The moment was ripe, Haig went on. He described in detail how the campaign would unfold. The scene has been sketched by Lloyd George:

> When Sir Douglas Haig explained the projects to the civilians, he spread on a table or desk a large map and made a dramatic use of both his hands to demonstrate how he proposed to sweep up the enemy—first the right hand brushing along the surface irresistibly, and then came the left, his outer finger ultimately touching the German frontier with the nail across.

Curzon and Smuts were impressed to a degree, but Lloyd George, Bonar Law (who now and frequently in the future attended meetings of the Policy Committee) and Milner remained sceptical. They began to question Haig and Robertson in detail, 'tending to show', as Haig wrote in his diary that evening, 'that each of them was more pessimistic than the other'.

How could the French strike heavily, in view of their stunned military and psychological condition?

Haig replied that they could and would, and that Pétain had told him so.

Why had he said that the Germans were demoralized?

Because he had received unimpeachable reports to that effect. He quoted one emanating from an American committee: '. . . they realize that they are beaten . . . no longer present a smart appearance . . .' and so on. Furthermore, their despair was accentuated by the recent setback at Messines.

But was it not true that according to the War Office the Germans were superior in artillery, especially heavy calibres?

Haig doubted this, and went on to say that, at any rate, German guns were quite inaccurate.

Here Sir William Robertson first spoke up at length. Previously he had ventured only his usual grunts, harrumphs and muttered asides, for 'Wully' was, if possible, even a poorer extemporaneous speaker than Haig. Now he felt impelled to state in his husky soldier's voice that he considered his own War Office estimates exaggerated, and that German artillery superiority on the Western Front was a myth.

Since this left the matter of artillery hanging helplessly in mid-air, the politicians changed the subject to casualties. Certainly they were bound to be enormous, were they not? And were the two marshals not aware of the Government's manpower difficulties?

There was nothing to fear, replied Robertson. Observe what had happened at Messines in one day. If the new assault were equally successful Passchendaele Ridge would be seized in one day also, and with no greater losses.

Did he really expect to have enough guns, men, and ammunition to gain his objective?

More than enough; and he amplified this claim.

Speaking of objectives—in referring to the Passchendaele Ridge did the generals consider it a final or a preliminary target?

Haig answered shortly that the operation would end with the capture of the entire Flemish coast.

This statement was followed by a hush. Suddenly it occurred to the politicians that he really meant what he said. Heretofore nobody had inwardly felt that such an advance was possible or seriously contemplated by the generals. Even the official historian admits that 'the outline of the campaign may seem super-optimistic and too far-reaching, even fantastic. . . .' Yet here was Haig stating it as almost an accomplished fact. The self-assurance of the man was disquieting, and the civilians other than Smuts, disturbed as always by a sense of inferiority in discussing military matters with the leading military personages of one of the world's greatest military powers, fell silent and shuffled their notes and wondered uneasily who, after all, was right. Lloyd George, least impressed of all by 'the aerial tower built . . . by the industry and imagination of G.H.Q. to view this thrilling prospect', suggested calling in Admiral Jellicoe for his opinion. The melancholy and somewhat tarnished hero of Jutland appeared forthwith and intoned that unless the Channel ports held by the Germans could be recaptured Britain would have to end the war in 1918 through lack of shipping.

Like a leopard the Prime Minister leaped forward to denounce this bizarre opinion; but the First Sea Lord would not back down. The war was really lost unless Zeebrugge could be taken, he repeated. Haig and Robertson let the statement sink in. Yet, in the later words of Winston Churchill, Jellicoe's claim was 'wholly fallacious'. The Belgian ports housed only a few of the smaller U-boats and were by no means a worthy objective of a grand land offensive; and to deceive not only Haig and Robertson but the War Cabinet concerning their value to the German war effort made the Admiralty largely responsible for any decision that might follow.

It was now early afternoon. Soon Lloyd George would leave to attend the wedding of his daughter, and before doing so he delivered a few parting shots. To meet the voracious demands of the generals the Government was already 'scraping men up from munition works, mines, and agriculture, and from among those formerly rejected on medical grounds'. The population was growing resentful; and, while both he and the country wanted to back Haig, it would be regrettable if the army drained the nation dry 'on behalf of a failure'. The French were wounded and quiescent, the Americans were a year away, the Russians were a forlorn hope, and only Britain was carrying the main load. He appreciated hearing Haig's views, but under the circumstances the Committee could not possibly go along with them. And on this defiant chord the meeting of 19 June adjourned.

That afternoon Lloyd George sent Haig and Robertson a

written statement summarizing his outlook. Its key points ran as follows:

1. A failure might have 'disastrous effects on public opinion'.

2. The War Cabinet could not gamble with lives 'merely because those who are directing the War can think of nothing better to do with the men under their command'.

3. Before proceeding on an enterprise which might fail and result in 'premature peace' the responsible parties had to feel 'a reasonable chance of succeeding'.

4. Even counting the French, the Allies would enjoy only a 15 per cent superiority in men and mere equality in guns. In reserves the Germans had an advantage. To scrape the bottom of the barrel would lead to 'the same unrest, disaffection and labour troubles which have baffled all our other efforts to raise men'.

5. The French Army was in no condition to fight effectively, and 'it would be madness on our part to proceed on such an assumption'. Yet the British high command proposes 'that we should rush into the greatest battle of the War, against an enemy almost equal in number, quite equal in equipment, still the greatest army in Europe . . . with larger reserves than our own . . . holding formidable defensive positions which he has taken three years to strengthen and to perfect; and we are to launch this attack with doubtful support from our most powerful and important ally . . . if it pulls less than its full weight we shall be attacking the strongest army in the world with an actual inferiority of numbers . . . curious indeed must be the military conscience which could justify an attack under such conditions'.

6. Could Robertson promise anything better than Vimy Ridge and Messines . . . 'brilliant preliminary successes, followed by weeks of desperate and sanguinary struggles, leading to nothing except perhaps the driving of the enemy back a few barren miles —beyond that nothing to show except a ghastly casualty list'?

He turned to his alternative. Allied strategy had never recognized that 'the European battlefield is one and indivisible'. Why pit strength against strength and weakness against weakness? Such a policy could only protract the stalemate. But Austria could be knocked out by a strong blow. The country was half beaten and had already made peace overtures. Transfer heavy guns secretly to the Italian Front and let Cadorna attack. The latter was enthusiastic over the idea, and so was General Foch. Like a house of cards the Central Powers would topple. First Trieste would be captured; then would follow the collapse of Austria, the fall of Bulgaria, the defeat of Turkey. Now millions of Russians, French, British and Italian troops could be switched to the Western Front, and break-through and victory would follow in 1918.

The argument came to 5,000 impressive words, and had it been sprung on Haig and Robertson the following morning their defence might have been ragged, for they were notoriously unskilled in verbal counterplay. As it was, they had several hours that evening in which to draft a heavy counter-offensive.

This they delivered starting at noon of the following day.

After admitting that the German army was now ten divisions stronger than a year ago, Robertson rejected the notion that Austria could be easily knocked out. He doubted that heavy guns could be switched to the Italian Front unknown to the enemy. In any event, it would take six weeks to get them there. If pressure were taken off the Germans in the west, they might attack there with success or even beat the Allies to the punch in Italy. Therefore, he reasoned, transferring weight to Italy might bring about results exactly the opposite of those predicted by the Prime Minister.

Amidst death-like silence the C.I.G.S. continued. Without being hard-pressed in the west the Germans might even proceed further down the coast and take Dunkirk; and he said, 'I think we should follow the principle of the gambler who has the heaviest purse and force our adversary's hand and make him go on spending until he is a pauper'. Conceding that Russia might be about finished, he warned against the dangers on the Western Front should it be weakened by the Allies and strengthened by Germany.

'I deprecate as strongly as anyone our incurring heavy casualties without a corresponding return,' he went on, 'but the plan as outlined by the Field-Marshal should secure us against this mistake . . . while at the same time it permits of our easing off if the situation so demands.'

Here was the most telling stroke, the insurance policy, the protective clause which would be repeated many times in the future to the many prospects. For if the campaign truly would be stopped if it showed signs of approaching a dead end, nothing much would be lost by giving the generals their 'good try'. The question was whether they would really stop. Past history was not encouraging in this respect. Previous heavy offensives, such as at the Somme and Champagne, had ended only in utter exhaustion—not because Haig or Joffre or Nivelle had shut them down judiciously before tragedy set in. Could Haig and Robertson be trusted to use better judgment in Flanders? There could be no pat answer to this question.

While these thoughts flashed through the minds of the civilians Robertson was concluding: 'Germany', he thought, 'may yet take a great deal of beating'. On the other hand, she 'may be much nearer exhaustion . . . than we imagine'. Then followed an equally arguable sentiment—that 'great mistakes have been made by endeavouring to find a fresh way around. . . .'

Sir Douglas Haig now arose. He began with a complex book-keeping formula ('joyous arithmetic' Lloyd George later contemptuously termed it) which led to the conclusion 'that the Allies will have a considerable superiority in infantry at the point of attack—probably not less than two to one'. The assertion was received doubtfully. It contradicted estimates previously made, and evaded the likelihood of many German divisions being moved down from Hoffmann's Eastern Front.

He too deprecated the hope of defeating Austria, and feared 'very dangerous disappointment in France . . . a possibility of reverses on the Western Front' if the Flanders scheme were abandoned. Then he advanced Robertson's curious argument that if the Allies reinforced the Italians by weakening the west there would be 'a possibility of still more serious reverses on the Italian Front', whereas sustained maximum pressure in France and Belgium might very well win the war before the end of the year.

When Haig sat down it was clear that nothing at all had changed. Imperceptibly a sense of hoplessness invaded the quiet brown-panelled room off Downing Street where seven men meditated around the large rectangular desk strewn with papers, ash-trays and Haig's great coloured map—Haig cool and erect, Robertson burly and sullen, Lloyd George staring pugnaciously at the Commander-in-Chief, the pompous round-faced Curzon, saintly-seeming Smuts with his little white pointed beard, Milner narrow-eyed and balding, slim, handsome and tired Bonar Law. The two generals had not backed down, nor had their opponents. How was it to end? The war had to go on—there was no dispute about that; armistice overtures were out of the question. They could attack in Italy or Flanders. They could 'squat' and 'pull faces at the Boches', as Sir Henry Wilson put it, and wait for the Americans and the tanks. Each general could keep punching away at his own little section of the various fronts, in a limited and hopeless fashion. But regardless of what it was to be, the decision that had to be made was as far away as ever.

After a pause, Lord Curzon asked Haig whether in referring to 'a reasonable chance of success' he meant only the capturing of his first objectives. Haig replied that he meant the entire operation, from the Salient to the North Sea.

Lloyd George remarked dismally that of course he was all for Haig's plan if it was really practical and likely to succeed.

General Smuts, the only member of the Policy Committee who strongly backed the army chiefs, reported that Admiral Jellicoe had repeated his bombshell of the previous day to him in a private talk. It was decided to quiz the First Sea Lord again.

When he entered the council chamber Lord Curzon asked him to restate his views. This he did in even more pessimistic detail, ending with, 'There is no good discussing plans for next spring— we cannot go on.' The Prime Minister sardonically inquired whether he was basing his opinion on facts or whether, by implication, it followed merely from personal intuition. To ease the admiral's obvious discomfort it was decided to call for a proper investigation of the figures (nobody took this seriously), and morosely Jellicoe departed.

The meeting ended at about 1 p.m. After lunch the Committee members gathered to 'count heads'. General Smuts thought Haig and Robertson had presented a good case. Lord Curzon was not so sure. Lord Milner, Bonar Law and Lloyd George were completely opposed; however, Law watered down his opinion by adding that he did not think they 'were entitled to overrule the military and naval authorities on a question of strategy', a view which if carried to its bitter end should have dissolved the Policy Committee altogether, along with the very conferences now being conducted.

Milner and Lloyd George conceded that if they should ride roughshod over the military commanders they would probably receive no support from the War Cabinet as a whole. 'It was therefore decided', in the Prime Minister's words, 'that I should once more sum up the misgivings which most of us felt and leave the responsibility for decision to Sir William Robertson and Sir Douglas Haig, on the understanding that if the progress they made with the operation did not realize the expectations they had formed, it should be called off and effective help be rendered to the Italians to press their offensive.'

The generals had conquered.

The deliberations next day took place more for the purpose of absolving Lloyd George and his followers from future blame than to kill the now inevitable campaign in Flanders. In later years he was to state his opinion in language such as the following through more than a hundred pages of his memoirs:

... inexhaustible vanity that will never admit a mistake ... individuals who would rather the million perish than that they as leaders should own—even to themselves—that they were blunderers ... the notoriety attained by a narrow and stubborn egotism, unsurpassed among the records of disaster wrought by human complacency . . . a bad scheme badly handled . . . impossible orders issued by Generals who had no idea what the execution of their commands really meant . . . this insane enterprise . . . this muddy and muddle-headed venture. . . .

We were not informed that, so far from urging us on, the leading French Generals had done their best to dissuade us . . . thought it a foolish venture, which must fail.

We were not told that the French plan was to wait for the Americans. . . . Headquarters . . . felt it would be undesirable to confuse and distract our innocent minds. . . .

We were not informed that the new Commander-in-Chief of the French Army, and some of his leading generals, favoured a combined attack on the Italian Front. . . .

. . . we were told by the Commander-in-Chief that we should have a superiority of two to one in infantry—it was untrue; that the enemy had no effective reserves—that was not in accordance with the facts; that the German morale was so broken that they would not put up anything like the resistance which they had hitherto offered—that was misleading; that they had inaccurate guns and inadequate ammunition we found otherwise. . . .

. . . not a word was said about the meteorological drawbacks and the peculiar conditions which rendered the terrain of the struggle specially disadvantageous for a sustained attack.

But the most reprehensible . . . was the withholding from the Government of the fact that all the generals called into consultation by Sir Douglas Haig had serious misgivings about the whole project and had expressed their doubts to him. . . .

We were invited to discuss Sir Douglas Haig's plan not merely without full knowledge of the essential elements, but with a definite suggestion that the decisive facts . . . were quite contrary. . . .

A prospectus issued with a view to inducing the public to invest their capital in an enterprise must reveal all material facts. The Government were the trustees of the public and were asked to invest in this wild military speculation not only hundreds of millions of public money, but the lives of hundreds of thousands of brave men . . . they were invited to risk the fate of Britain on what Sir William Robertson later on called 'a gamble', where the truth that mattered was wilfully and skilfully kept from their cognisance.

In truth, Lloyd George was not nearly so uninformed as he later pretended to be. The record shows, and this narrative has in part confirmed, that he was more or less aware of French objections and counter intentions, of the doubts of at least some British officers, of the unsuitability of the terrain, of the contradictory estimates concerning manpower and German capabilities. But at the conference of 21 June his language and inferences were properly restrained. He began by pointing out that the ultimate responsibility for what might come lay strictly with the generals. Their military decision would not be thwarted by the Policy Committee; but he laid down one condition—that they would break off the attack if it bogged down. Then doggedly he proceeded to enumerate his objections, new and old.

First he referred to Robertson's sudden change of mind. On 4 and 5 May Sir William had told him that he was averse to heavy fighting unless the French could co-operate seriously, and now Pétain was admitting his inability to do so.

He turned to the prospects of success, and pointed out that the Germans already knew Haig's intentions. What reason, he asked, 'was there to believe that we could first drive the enemy back fifteen miles and then capture a place ten miles away?'—referring to objectives on the Channel coast.

The manpower superiority of the Allies on the Western Front was, he insisted, only 15 per cent, even counting the exhausted French. Surely this was insufficient for a modern-day offensive. Perhaps there might be initial successes 'but assaults on the German lines were like hitting India-rubber'.

He pointed out that in three years he had never seen an offensive begun without positive predictions of victory. This time he was even more dubious. The Germans had plenty of ammunition for defensive purposes, especially since experience had shown that a 5 to 1 superiority was needed for the attackers.

He referred to German reinforcements available easily and in great numbers from the Russian Front.

And what, after all, was so different between this proposed offensive and the Somme imbroglio, where the advance had been

only an indentation of a few miles at enormous cost? Certainly
there would be no greater factor of surprise.

Nobody on the Policy Committee, he said cruelly, whether
they were willing to go along with Haig's plan or not, really
expected it to work. Abandon it, he urged. Mark time with
limited punches here and there, or augment an attack against
Austria. For was it not futile continually to 'aim our spear at the
thickest part of the enemy's armour'?

He turned to Douglas Haig and asked him directly whether
he thought victory could be achieved this year.

The chance was 'very good', Haig replied. That very day he
had been advised by the diligent Charteris that 250-man German
companies were down to about sixty men, that only last week the
163rd German regiment had refused to attack, that some men of
the 1919 draft class were already at Rupprecht's front, and so on.

Lloyd George replied caustically that he welcomed such
'sanguine views, but did not personally attach great importance
to this sort of argument'.

Lord Curzon interposed that the Italians had done no good at
all thus far in the war despite their large superiority in numbers
over the Austrians.

Of course not, Lloyd George retorted heatedly; they had never
owned enough heavy guns and ammunition to support their
infantry. He turned again to the two silent generals, and in
measured tones stated that he and they 'were at the parting of the
ways'.

Speaking for himself and Haig, Robertson replied that he
knew this was 'the greatest decision of the war', that neither of
them resented the Prime Minister's opposition, and that their
written replies would follow. These were presented to the War
Cabinet a few days later, and in them the well-known views of
both generals were elaborated upon. The civilians decided to let
Haig's military preparations in Flanders continue. But still they
refused to render an official verdict, though by now it was
informally understood that the gamble was on, and that the die
would be cast across the soft Flemish plains as soon as the British

and French assault forces were ready. When would that be? By late June 1917, occasional delightful showers were already dancing across the budding fields of Flanders, hinting at more menacing weather soon to come.

Napoleon had once told his generals: 'Gentlemen, ask me for anything but time', a sentiment with which Sir Douglas Haig must have agreed that Belgian summer. He knew that his long-cherished offensive was dangerously behind schedule and that he could expect only a few more weeks of ideal weather. At the very latest he hoped to send his infantry forward by 25 July. This would give them perhaps two or three weeks of dry ground to fight on, which was still cutting things rather fine. He had once hoped to attack in the spring, but that was ancient history now; Nivelle had blunderingly intervened. Meanwhile Sir Douglas reflected that he was doing the best he could. Men, guns, ammunition, tanks, aircraft, food, petrol, road equipment, horses and mules, hospital equipment, and a thousand other impedimenta of war were being funnelled toward the Salient in quantities that made the Somme preparations look almost primitive by comparison and reduced the Messines episode to a mere sideshow. The days scurried by at alarming speed; still the War Cabinet hesitated; and Haig began to wonder just when his Ypres contract would be signed, sealed and delivered.

While Haig waited and the British Expeditionary Force in Belgium swelled in size and muscle, other events proceeded apace during the fateful interval between the end of the talking in London and the start of the shooting at Ypres. . . .

27 June. The Germans began shelling Dunkirk with a 15-inch naval gun at Leugenboom, and people with compasses excitedly computed that Haig's General Headquarters lay within its range. Whenever the gun was fired, someone at the front phoned the city, whose inhabitants received ten or twenty seconds warning in which to find shelter.

1 July. Kerenski finally got a Russian offensive going, with much Allied fanfare, until it quickly collapsed.

2 July. General Anthoine advised Haig that his six French

10

divisions, which were to participate in Flanders, would not be ready on time.

6 July. Robertson wrote Haig that the Prime Minister 'is more keen than ever on the Italian plan. . . . Smuts wants to land 150,000 men at Alexandretta (I do not know where he proposes to get them or the ships from), Milner is rather inclined to think that the Balkans would be a good place, while Curzon sticks to our plan. It is pretty difficult doing business under these conditions.'

7 July. General Gough, floundering with supply problems and worried about Anthoine, asked Haig for a five-day postponement. It was refused.

13 July. After a long talk with Gough the field-marshal reluctantly authorized a delay to the 28th.

17 July. Bad visibility and maddening difficulties on the part of the French in getting their heavy guns into position obliged Haig to move Zero Day back still three more precious days, to 31 July.

19 July. The German Reichstag passed a resolution, 214 to 116, expressing a desire for 'a peace of conciliation'. It was denounced violently by almost every military and civil leader in both camps.

19 July. Robertson wrote to Haig that though the War Policy Committee had been talking incessantly among themselves for days 'up to the present no official approval of your plans has been given. . . . I have twice reminded [Lloyd George] that time is running short.' Haig boiled over and sent a strong letter in return. It was 'somewhat startling to learn that the War Cabinet have not yet determined whether the attack is to be permitted to proceed'.

But unknown to Sir Douglas this message crossed another heading his way from the civilians—a poor, half-hearted thing, breathing in doubts and exhaling reservations. Yes, he might proceed with his Flanders attack, but it would have to be stopped if the losses were too heavy for the gains achieved, in which case the Italian scheme would take its place. Furthermore, Haig was to prepare at once for this alternate plan, should it become necessary to execute it. And finally they would like to know (for perhaps the fifth time) what his first Flanders objective really was, 'so that', in the words of an official historian, 'they might be able to judge whether the operation had, up to that stage, succeeded or not'. Haig replied bitingly. He resented the insinuation of the War Cabinet that he was not to be trusted, and asked whether the members did or did not wish to render confidence and support to his plan of operations.

Four days passed, and one can well picture the earnest deliberations of the politicians during this astonishing delay. Here was their last chance to get off the hook. They decided, instead, to swallow it even if it choked them. On 25 July the War Cabinet wired the Commander-in-Chief their 'whole-hearted support'. To say that it came in the nick of time would be an understatement, for three days earlier 3,091 British guns around Ypres had already begun the greatest artillery bombardment in the history of land warfare.

8

On the Brink

WHILE the great men pondered and argued in London and finally reached their uneasy agreement, events in far-off Galicia, of all places, were sharply raising the odds against Sir Douglas Haig's gamble in Flanders.

The Eastern Front had been generally silent all spring. Leon Trotsky in his history of the Russian revolution points out that a *de facto* armistice existed and that 'the Germans availed themselves of it for a wholesale transfer of troops to the Western Front'. This in itself was an extremely serious turn of events from the British point of view. Of course everyone knew that Russian troops had been deserting and fraternizing with the enemy in considerable numbers since March, and while defensively their front continued to be of value to the Allied cause Pétain had remarked with his usual insight into the ways of defeat and decay, 'The Russian army is nothing but a façade; it will fall to pieces if it makes a move.'

As we have seen, Kerenski forced it to make that move. In June with typical grandiloquence he told his commanding general, Brusilov, 'I command you—forward!' and in desperation the Russian commander tried to get some kind of an offensive going. With no staff preparations, no time-table, no co-ordination, no hope, local officers were simply told to start attacking whenever they could persuade or browbeat their more docile men into advancing. The absurd operation took place in piecemeal fashion, therefore, starting late in June—the major effort is said to have begun about 1 July—at various disconnected sectors along the

General Plan: July 1917

front. The main attack was against the Austrians in Galicia, and here, at first, some easy advances were made. Then came the counter-attack, and on 8 July the Russian 11th Army reported 'an overwhelming catastrophe'. From this date on it might be said that the Eastern Front passed into virtual oblivion, and about thirty divisions of the Central Powers were now free to turn their attentions to France and Flanders.

The British high command, only anxious to plunge out of the Salient at Ypres, paid surprisingly little attention to this ominous development. For in no other country—not even, any longer, in France—were the generals so indoctrinated with a spirit of the offensive, and by 1917 they were indeed a frustrated and embittered lot. In truth, they had not really won a victory of any consequence in Europe since the beginning of the war; and three years of deadlock had corroded their souls and driven them to an inchoate determination to smash through, to charge like a bull at the gate, to break out into open country, and there to continue attacking and attacking and attacking with infantry and cavalry, sweeping the enemy before them in the grand old way of traditional warfare.

And of all British generals with zest for the assault, the name of Sir Hubert Gough headed the list. In his hands Haig placed the spearhead of the campaign, though he and his army had never set foot in the Salient before. Because he was only forty-seven, impetuous, and an ex-cavalryman like his chief, Haig considered him more likely to crash through than Plumer and Rawlinson, both of whom were older and (in the past) more sympathetic toward limited attacks for partial gains—precisely what Haig did not have in mind at the moment. But the field-marshal could not possess the best of all possible worlds, and in appointing Gough for the main stroke he had also to accept a pair of attendant liabilities, like the man who in marrying the beauteous and rich widow also has to live with her two repellent children.

First, Sir Hubert knew almost nothing of the country in which he was asked to operate.

Second, he was saddled with a fairly incompetent staff, a bit too supercilious in its ways; and to these people Gough clung with an easy loyalty that did him no credit, though they had already compromised several operations conducted by the Fifth Army since its baptism in battle. Many combat officers resented the staff members. Some were barely on speaking terms with them. Gough himself was a balding but boyish chap of high military quality, always half smiling, invariably courteous, witty and personable. As an individual he was liked; yet the responsibility was indeed his for the occasional blunders of omission and commission emanating from his subordinates. All too often, in the past, Fifth Army supplies had arrived late or in the wrong place. Planning was far below the level for which Harington's group was famous. Tiresome, meticulous paper work to insure co-ordination between battalions and divisions was hardly a speciality of Fifth Army headquarters. Under such conditions Sir Hubert's reputation had been gravely damaged in the past—at Bullecourt, for example, to name an especially egregious instance. It would soon be ascertained whether affairs would be managed better starting 31 July.

Nor was Gough's Fifth Army the keenest blade in Douglas Haig's arsenal. It had formerly been the Reserve Army, had received its new name only nine months ago, and possessed a rather bad reputation for always being pushed and pulled here and there and everywhere, thrown into the most dangerous fighting, suffering far and away the heaviest casualties of any British army in the war. It was, in fact, a vast sprawling collection of shock troops. Men hated and feared to be assigned to it. Furthermore, its components were always being internally shifted about. By the summer of 1917 it was an amazing hodgepodge of regulars, reservists, conscripts, territorials, volunteers, and assorted units dropped into the cauldron for lack of any better idea of what to do with them at the moment. Officers were assigned, then re-assigned; and the shifts in personnel were so frequent and seemingly capricious that few troops knew the names of their battalion commanders. All this was most disquieting, but by late July there was no use discussing it, much less trying to do anything about it.

It is a cardinal principle of so-called military science that an attack from within a salient must be directed against at least one of the sides and not against the apex of the angle, where any advance would only thrust the troops still deeper into their deadly noose. Thus Gough's main blow, upon which everything else depended—even Rawlinson's bound along the coast—would be

The Attack: 31 July, 1917

almost due east toward the Gheluvelt plateau, rather than north or north-east toward St. Julien and Passchendaele. Simultaneously the Second Army under Plumer was to stand almost stationary and merely capture strong-points in the vicinity of Warneton. Next the Fifth Army would take Menin and the Pilckem Ridge. Sir Douglas Haig computed that within eight days the entire loop of the Ypres–Roulers–Thourot railway should be in Gough's hands—an advance of fifteen miles. Now, at last, Rawlinson's Fourth Army would move, the amphibious landing would take place, Plumer would turn north and north-west and take over the defence of the entire captured ridge, Gough and Rawlinson would join hands, the grand sweep up the coast would begin, and the German western flank would be turned in and pressed toward Berlin. Meanwhile the cavalry would be released for the charge and the kill.

How much of all this Haig really believed is not certain, though there is evidence that he had been temporarily sobered by Lloyd George's gloomy lectures the previous month. While in theory the field-marshal clung to his larger dream, he had evidently in practice come around to some degree, at least, of 'step-by-step' thinking, until an episode took place which proved that he still had his eyes mainly fixed on a super-victory. Originally it had been planned to advance only a mile the first day to the German second defence line which included the Gheluvelt plateau and the Pilckem Ridge, at which time and place there would be a two-day pause for establishing observation posts and bringing up artillery. Later Gough decided in a sudden, typical burst of enthusiasm to include the third German line in his first day's capture. And, he added, if his divisional commanders thought they could do so they might proceed without pause to the German Fourth Line running through Broodseinde—about three miles from the jumping-off positions. Three days later the entire Passchendaele ridge would be occupied. It would, he suggested, 'be wasteful not to reap all the advantages possible resulting from the first attack'. To this Sir Douglas surprisingly agreed.

But immediately Gough was challenged by Haig's own Operations Branch headed by Brigadier General J. H. Davidson. What on earth had happened to G.H.Q.'s original, laboriously conceived step-by-step plan? Gough's expectations were not practical, he predicted, and would not bring sustained results. For one thing, the fourth enemy line was even beyond the range of British field pieces. He urged the army commander to reconsider.

Gough responded that he still felt that his army should advance as far and as fast as it could. Now Haig was called in. He discussed the problem with Plumer. They decided to back Gough, provided that he would restrain his brigades further north at least until his right flank was firmly secured around Gheluvelt. Strangely enough, the once-cautious Sir Herbert Plumer had been the most vehement of all. As he pattered along with Davidson to the conference room, belly and moustache quivering, he burst out, 'Do you think that after making the vast preparations for attack on this position . . . after sitting in the Salient all this time, I am going to agree to limiting the progress and advance of my troops? I say definitely *no*, I would certainly not agree to any such limitation.' So here the matter rested; and thus the step-by-step technique which Haig had promised in London was scrapped.

Although the politicians were not told of this interesting development, some of them, as we have seen, had long been wary. On 22 July Winston Churchill, for one, wrote to Lloyd George confiding his regrets that Haig had been given a green light, and went on to say:

> It is clear however that no human power exists which can stop the attempt being made. The essential thing now is to arrive at a definition of success and 'great results' which will enable a new decision to be taken after the first or second phases of this offensive have been fought. Such a definition must, it seems to me, involve three conditions, viz. objectives taken; casualties sustained; and thirdly (very important) the time taken or required between any one thrust and the next. Thus it should be possible, by reference to these forecasts, to settle definitely after (say) six weeks of fighting whether there really is any prospect of obtaining 'great results' before winter sets in. . . .

The point was not one of verbal phrasing or psychological attitudes. Either Haig anticipated a fast break-through, and prepared for it accordingly, or he planned to wear down the enemy step by step, and prepared for *that* accordingly. In his 'mixture of motives lay grave disadvantages', an official historian later commented. In one case, surprise was vital. In the other, lack of surprise might be almost beneficial, so as to lure more enemy troops into the mincing machine. In either event, vastly different staff preparations would be needed. Which did Haig really aim at? Forty years later we can answer this hazy question with some assurance: He was hoping for a break-through but was willing to settle for more dead Germans than British—a victory of attrition.

Ignoring for the moment how the battle might end, let us first consider how it was to start.

It might first be noted that some officers mistrusted it on general principles. Among them was Gough's artillery adviser, Major-General Uniacke, who feared that enemy guns on the ridge to the right would be able to dominate the Fifth Army the moment it jumped off. His argument worried Gough, who passed it on to Haig with the radical request that Plumer's Second Army be given as heavy a share in the attack as his own. This Haig refused to do.

As to cavalry, two divisions were brought up on the Fifth Army flanks, ready to charge toward the Passchendaele–Staden ridge. There was much talk and preparation for 'putting the cavalry through the gap' and maps were issued to officers showing the terrain as far back as twenty miles behind the German lines.

About 180 aircraft were placed under Gough's immediate command. Intense observation work began during the middle of July. On the 29th, when air reports were most needed, the weather turned dreary and visibility from aloft became almost nil. On the 30th it was even worse; not one aerial combat was reported in Flanders that day and only a handful of planes got into the air at all. Buzzing along too fast and too low in the haze beneath a sullen ceiling of dense low clouds, they were unable to see much of anything.

Meanwhile Rawlinson, Fourth Army Commander, had been instructed by Sir Douglas Haig '. . . as and when the main attack to the east of Ypres made progress, to land with the assistance of Admiral Bacon's naval forces on the coast east of Nieuport, and eventually to advance, in conjunction with the main attack, upon Bruges. . . .' Although the Germans had embarrassed this army on 10 July by a lightning sortie and won commanding positions on the right bank of the Yser, thus complicating Rawlinson's problem greatly, his preparations continued in an aura of high enthusiasm. While Bacon and his marines trained in the Thames estuary for their amphibious operation, Rawlinson withdrew his 1st Division to the dunes south-west of Dunkirk. Here a secret training camp was built and surrounded by a wire fence. All leave was suspended. Mail was censored. The landing force began practising the scaling of the sea wall; tanks were constructed with special ramps to negotiate the steep slope and the artificial barrier behind the beach, and excited conferences without end took place between the army and navy officers involved.

The general line-up may be recapitulated briefly. Gough's main attack in the centre would take place along a seven-mile front and would initially employ ten divisions grouped into the XIV, XVIII, XIX and II Corps, running from north to south. Above them General Anthoine's First French Army would attack (primarily to guard Gough's left flank against German counterstrokes) with two divisions. Below to the south, acting somewhat as a holding operation in order to divert the enemy artillery, stood Plumer and his Second Army composed of three home divisions plus the New Zealand Division and the 3rd Australian Division. This totalled about 100,000 troops actually assigned to the assault; and behind these seventeen divisions were seventeen more, ready to move upon signal. The entire offensive front—Anthoine, Gough, Plumer—measured fifteen miles.

Directly opposite lay the German Fourth Army under General Sixt von Armin, whose chief-of-staff was Colonel von Lossberg, Germany's top defensive expert, who had been given a free hand to develop defences that would smother Haig's drive. Von Lossberg was in his element and had plenty of time. He increased the German trench and pill-box system to six lines—five and a half, to be exact, since the second one stopped short of Plumer's front. In general, his dispositions emphasised strong-points rather than rigid, densely packed frontal masses. Forward areas were held lightly. Several hundred new machine-gun posts were sprinkled throughout the forward slopes of the Ridge, and the riflemen were mostly withdrawn to prepared defences on the reverse slopes.

The crux of von Lossberg's formula, notwithstanding all the above, was counter-attack. Bodies of troops for this purpose were staggered in depth throughout the rear, with the strongest ones furthest back. In this way, he hoped, his retaliatory blows would get successively more powerful, should the need arise.

In artillery, opposite Gough's crucial front, the Germans emplaced 1,556 light and heavy guns, compared to the Englishman's 2,299. As for infantry, the Germans had arrayed three corps (groups) from Warneton to a point slightly south of Bixschoote. From south to north they were Group Wytschaete with five divisions, Group Ypres with three divisions, and Group Dixmude with one division. Close behind these front-line units were six reserve divisions. Behind these six were two more particularly mobile divisions. Behind these two were three more.

During the latter half of July it became depressingly clear to Allied officers near the front that the enemy was preparing for them in an unprecedented way. Shelling from the Ridge increased every day until no point along the entire front of the Salient could be considered safe. As at Messines the British field guns sat almost hub-cap to hub-cap directly out in the flat Flemish plain, with the heavies so close behind that the respective battery men could call back and forth to each other. Prior to Messines it had been the Germans who were in a salient, shelled and decimated from both sides; now the tables were precisely turned and the losses among British guns and gunners became tragically severe.

The enemy shelled selected areas without let-up, using everything from 8-inchers to 'pip-squeaks', and at night he drenched the area with mustard gas. The incessant uproar, the aggravating donning and doffing of gas masks, the lack of sleep, the heavy casualties—all this had reduced Allied artillery personnel to edginess and exhaustion by the 31st. And the ordinarily pessimistic Crown Prince Rupprecht noted in his diary: 'My mind is quite at rest about the attack, as we have never disposed of such strong reserves, so well trained for their part, as on the front attacked.'

Four of these divisions, by the way, had come from Max Hoffmann's Eastern Front in May. Many more were now available and, in fact, were streaming toward the Salient and other sectors of the Western Front. If Sir Douglas Haig was looking for Germans in vast numbers to kill, to exhaust, to bleed, and to capture in Flanders, he was about to find them.

The British Tank Corps in particular—all volunteers—was wild with excitement over its first test in battle on a large scale, but at the same time apprehensive about the ground and the weather. In the words of Colonel C. D. Baker-Carr, one of the brigade commanders: 'To anyone familiar with the terrain in Flanders it was almost inconceivable that this part of the line should have been selected. If a careful search had been made from the English Channel to Switzerland, no more unsuitable spot could have been discovered.'

He went on to remark that Ypres had once been a seaport, was now an inland city only because of the man-made drainage system, that every farmer had been responsible at the risk of heavy fines for the state of repair of the ditches and dikes on his property, and that 'To put it mildly, we were absolutely astounded at the decision to attack at this point.'

The possibility of flooding worried the tank people more than the thousands of shell-holes. Headquarters expected 216 Mark IVs to operate on the Fifth Army front regardless of circumstances and without excuses; nevertheless the Tank Corps staff began discreetly to acquire information from local inhabitants and the Belgian 'Ponts et Chaussées'. Their worst suspicions were confirmed: rain, plus a heavy bombardment which would wreck what remained of the watercourse system, was bound to revert the battlefield into a swamp. Since this would leave no suitable ground for tanks to move on (not to mention men, guns and vehicles) a warning memorandum was sent to the Fifth Army general staff. To this there was no reply.

Next the Tank Corps people forwarded charts which assumed the worst and indicated where the larger pools of water would collect. Now Gough's staff languidly bestirred itself and dispatched a curt note containing the following phrase: 'Send us no more of these ridiculous maps.'

If Fifth Army headquarters had few qualms, other persons including Sir Douglas were not so unconcerned. The field-marshal dreaded the thought of rain and especially what it would do to the area to the north-east, 'a tract of ground [in the words of one writer] which was difficult when dry but which became grotesque in its difficulties when it rained and the low-lying streams or "beeks" which meandered through it spread out into broad marshy bottoms'.

Colonel Repington sadly discussed the prospect with the commander-in-chief and said, 'I hate the idea of thrusting an Army into such a daedalus of mud and water'.

Haig replied that if he only advanced 'a bit, it was all to the good'.

So the confused, nagging guessing game went on, and the forebodings of private soldiers at the front were echoed down the corridors of command through battalion headquarters, brigade, division, corps, army, general headquarters, and at 10 Downing Street where Lloyd George sullenly awaited developments.

In those sunny days before the attack, while only the cannoneers duelled, a million British foot soldiers in and near the Salient rested and killed time and tried not to think of the future.

Day and night the dusty roads from Ypres ('Mecca of all good soldiers') to Vlamertinghe and Poperinghe were thronged with troops seeking sundry pleasures in towns, farms and rest areas far behind the front. Soccer and cricket were played on improvised fields. Red Cross canteens were crowded uproariously and good-naturedly as never before, and there was no end to the talk and well-worn phrases ... '*Hullo, I thought you were dead!*'—'*Are you enjoying the war?*'—'*Got a spare fag?*'—'*Remember me to Blighty!*' ...

In Y.M.C.A. tents kindly old gentlemen in vaguely military uniforms served cake, cocoa and packets of real British Wood-bines. The men swam in the canals and in little lakes like the Zillebeke and the Dickebusch, bargained with the farmers' daughters, got drunk, haggled over souvenirs. Far behind the restless front, where the big guns were only a rumble, it was a carnival time for troops who would soon be back at the business of war. In wonder and joy and with aching hearts they absorbed those common sights and sounds so long forgotten—leafy trees, splashes of sunlight on outdoor cafés, green fields, people at work at home and in their orchards. They polished their boots, scraped dirt from their uniforms, and filed into washing sheds singing that immortal ballad:

> Whiter than the whitewash on the wall,
> Whiter than the whitewash on the wall,
> Wash me in your water
> That you wash your dirty daughter
> And I shall be whiter than the whitewash on the wall.

And scarcely were they dressed again than a warning itch proved that they would be as lousy as ever next morning.

In backwater towns like Calais the streets were flooded with soldiers of all Allied nations—Portuguese, Belgians, a scattering of American engineers, blue-clad French poilus, brawny New Zealanders, French colonials of darker mien, Canadians, reserved Indians, Londoners, Irish, tall bronzed Australian farm boys not noted for classic discipline, always with soft hats and rolled-up brims. The beer was weak, the food was over-priced, but life was good. By the last week in July most leaves had ended, the carnival was over, and a great influx of returning men had restored front-line battalions to full assault strength. Back at the front nothing seemed to have changed, except that new tensions lay like a shroud over the battle zone and the guns boomed with a greater, grimmer intensity than ever before.

In London, too, everyone awaited the start of Haig's offensive and the good news it was sure to bring. The nation carried on as usual that relatively placid, pregnant summer.

On 7 July the most daring air attack of the war hit the metropolis from twenty 4-engine Gothas, killing and wounding 250 people, most of them in the East End. There was much recrimination in the Commons over the poor defences and the lack of proper warning.

After a naval action the Admiralty reported that destroyers *Swift* and *Broke* '. . . were fortunate in being able to save the lives of ten German officers and 108 men from the vessels which were sunk', a communiqué which caused intense disgust. The *National News* wrote of the 'crassly idiotic words and messages penned by a responsible government official. . . . Nothing could be calculated to throw contempt on the nation so much as official folly of this description . . . sentimentality . . . weak-kneed . . .'

On 28 July Colonel A'Court Repington, that haughty analyst of military affairs, wrote: 'We played tennis on Sunday, but were driven in later by the rain, and then played bridge . . . the guns in Flanders were heard very distinctly on the terrace at Glynde. It was a continuous throbbing, the noise of the heaviest guns occasionally rising above the distant din.'

In Parliament Mr. Pringle complained of the lack of discretion in calling-up notices, which had been sent to 'the maimed, the halt, the blind, the mute, the mad, and even the dead'. A large uproar ensued. Bonar Law insisted that the War Office was making 'an honest effort' to carry out the Review of Exemptions Act.

Early in July the *Daily News* published an editorial about the Russian offensive: 'The remarkable success attending the Russian army is due primarily, no doubt, to the spirit of freedom abroad in it. There is no spur in war like an ideal.' Scarcely was this edition on the street when the Russian armies melted away. Now came a sadder and wiser headline: 'THE TRAGEDY OF RUSSIA' and the writer stated dully, 'The Russian army would seem to have ceased to exist as a military instrument.'

As the month drew to a close, showery cloudy days spread

over most of England—a typical summer-weather front that moved slowly from west to east across the Channel and headed for northern France and Belgium.

Here on 30 July Sir Douglas visited General Gough in Fifth Army headquarters at Château Loewe and found him 'in the best of spirits, and full of confidence as to the results of tomorrow's fight'.

The British and French artillery bombardment might be said to have begun in earnest on 15 July. By the 22nd it had become ultra-heavy and continuous along the entire Flanders front. There had never before been such shelling—one gun to every six yards of line—and what with the German batteries replying and the flaming streaks of variously coloured signal flares, it was perhaps the greatest show of fireworks in history. On the 28th counter-battery fire began, but, as we have seen, on the 29th and 30th intermittent fog cloaked the battleground and made it impossible to carry out this final and most important task with much efficiency. It seemed, in truth, from the look of things, all too likely that rain was coming, and soon.

For three evenings prior to the morning of Zero Hour the assault brigades plodded toward their advanced assembly areas and then, more stealthily, into the front lines. The tanks rumbled towards their stations. Regiments of mounted cavalry cantered to their assigned flank positions. The early night of the 30th was warm and calm beneath leaden skies. As the infantry walked forward a signaller or runner occasionally flashed his lamp; then there would follow angry yells: 'Put that blasted light out!' Enemy shelling grew heavier by the hour.

Just before the attack a German machine gun facing 13th Sussex spoke: 'Taaa-t-t-t-taaa'. A British gunner replied: 'Ta-ta'. The men chuckled. They kept up the game till it got on everyone's nerves. Then a shell dropped into the lines. There was a suppressed commotion.

'Stretcher-bearers!'

'Coming up.'

'Someone hit.'

'Ay.'

'Lucky sod. He's saved a lot of trouble.'

The stricken man called out wildly for his mother, and a nerve-racked voice grated, 'Oh, put a sock in his blasted mouth.'

Trembling and with hearts pounding, the men fixed bayonets and touched hands. The youngest man in one platoon insisted on shaking hands with everyone. He was dead drunk. This time the troops had been given not the usual tea with rum before an attack but tea that was more than half rum.

Sir Douglas Haig, at his advanced G.H.Q. in a railway coach beneath a row of trees nineteen miles west of Ypres, recorded nervously in his diary: 'Glass steady. Morning dull and coldish. The bright weather reported as coming is slower in its progress than expected by our weather prophet.'

He dozed. At 4.15 he was awakened by the stupendous drum-fire of the barrage many miles away and by the ground shaking beneath his railway car. The Fifth Army had, in fact, gone over the top almost half an hour previously.

9

The Opening Phase

ESSENTIALLY the fate of the assault which unrolled that morning—one so monstrous that it appeared beyond the creation or control of the human will—depended on II Corps, commanded by the astute Lieutenant-General Claud Jacob, 53 years old, born and raised in India and in the Indian Army. He had been handed a most formidable task. That dark-grey morning his three divisions lay poised, armed to the teeth, aimed like a pistol at the scowling undulations of Gheluvelt Plateau. On both sides of this key objective some sixty feet high —a sizeable eminence in Flanders—the ground fell away into little valleys. From it the entire Flemish plain could be seen on a clear day as far west as the French border, occasionally as far north as the sea.

Within II Corps, one might say, everything depended on the 30th Division, composed mainly of Manchester and Liverpool battalions—a slender reed, for it had been hurt especially severely at the Somme last year and at Arras during the spring. Its personnel were not pleased at having been assigned to the deadly direct attack against the Ridge. Of this the Fifth Army staff seemed unaware. However, Haig's headquarters, somewhat more alert to military realities, had suggested interchanging the 30th with one of its two flank divisions. Perhaps the advice came too late; in any event the switch was not made.

Facing Jacob's young men along a three-mile front was the most domineering sector of the German reception zone—three major defence lines jammed together within less than a mile, dense with pill-boxes and lesser machine-gun posts. In the past British infantrymen had learned how to deal with isolated strong-points, but here each post defended another, so that men trying to knock one out would be exposed to fire from one or more close by. This entire system of brownish fortifications had been well camouflaged and was practically intact. Also, the bad weather of recent days had virtually grounded the attacker's air force and blinded his artillery. Thus the prior bombardment had been firing more or less at random rather than at specific targets such as these. German light artillery looking down on No-Man's-Land was massed heavily on the slopes east and south.

Everywhere along the Fifth Army front the ground was exasperatingly soft. Nobody had worried much about the showers of preceding weeks, but they had done their part to gum up the plain through which the infantry would have to pass before reaching the gentle upslopes.

Even Fifth Army planners had been anxiously aware of the problems in their path, and for weeks had bombarded divisional commanders with warnings and data concerning soil conditions and the abnormal intensity of enemy defence preparations. This is not to say that General Gough and his immediate officers anticipated a reverse. On the contrary, past failures had dissolved into nothingness in dark, forgotten recesses of their minds. As usual, they expected to win out after a brisk fight. In Churchill's words 'the hopes of decisive victory . . . grew with every step away from the front line and reached absolute conviction in the Intelligence Department'.

The confidence of British brass was matched by that of von Hindenburg:

I had a certain feeling of satisfaction when this new battle began . . . It was with a feeling of absolute longing that we waited for the beginning of the wet season. As previous experience had taught us, great stretches of the Flemish flats would then become impassable, and even in firmer places the new shell holes would fill so quickly with ground water that men seeking shelter in them would find themselves faced with the alternative, 'Shall we drown or get out of this hole?' This battle, too, must finally stick in the mud, even though English stubbornness kept it up longer than otherwise.

Somebody had to be wrong. Either way, the fate of the Third Battle of Ypres would very likely be indicated after the first few days of fighting.

As II Corps advanced due east toward the shrouded highland the men found themselves variously impeded throughout the outpost system by Chateau Wood (8th Division), Sanctuary Wood (30th Division), and Shrewsbury Forest (24th Division). In this pathetic jumble of débris, fallen trees, rusty barbed wire, and shell-craters, the heavy-laden troops laboriously picked their way to the accompaniment of a tornado of shrapnel. As for tanks, the first messages brought back by carrier pigeons were disquieting: 'Direct hit on tank by field gun. One killed, two wounded.' 'Ditched in German front line. Being heavily shelled.' Along Jacob's front the ponderous, clanking machines tried to advance through three narrow defiles; here they immediately came under heavy artillery fire. Not one reached its final objective. In the heavy going they could barely achieve a speed of one mile an hour, and soon they were left behind by the infantry. In No-Man's-Land dozens became trapped in soft spots. Their crews got out and tried to pull them free—a sight both pitiful and incongruous, for while the men shoved and hauled at their steel monsters in the midst of this most ferocious battle scene, they became the target of everything that could fire at them from land and air. Five tanks reached the 18th Division jump-off tapes and tried to push forward. Every one bogged down, and in a flash four were knocked out by unpleasantly accurate shell-fire.

The general attack had scarcely begun when part of the 30th Division ground to a halt a few hundred yards up the Menin Road, blocked by one enormous pill-box which could be neither captured nor destroyed by heavy guns. One by one the tanks that approached were knocked out by its anti-tank gun. Soon seventeen broken, abandoned tanks littered the ground, some smouldering; and as the men tried to get out they were machine-gunned by Germans within the intact pill-box. Thus was created the famous 'Tank Graveyard'.

Very soon the 30th Division lost all touch with its barrage, which was proceeding as stolidly as Frankenstein's monster at the rate of twenty-five yards per minute—a complete waste of ammunition—and while the first (Blue) line a few hundred yards ahead was reached early in the morning it began to appear doubtful if the men could fight their way forward any further without artillery support.

By ten o'clock a sorry situation had developed. The British artillery, still ignorant of the true state of affairs, had commenced its forward creep from the second to the third objective, though the infantry had not even left the first one. At 10.40 the commanding general of the division forwarded a message to II Corps headquarters near Poperinghe that 'apparently we are not on the Black (second) Line anywhere. . . .' The admission was a serious one, for if after seven hours the 30th Division had only been able to move some 500 hundred yards through Sanctuary Wood, it might be said that II Corps as a whole was stymied, that the Fifth Army had failed, and that Haig's entire plan had already blown sky-high.

What of the other two divisions in II Corps? Perhaps they had been able to salvage matters. But by late morning the 24th had advanced through Shrewsbury Forest only 300 or 400 yards, and the 8th was embedded in the nightmarish wastes of Chateau Wood. Everywhere the story was the same: the pill-boxes were far more numerous than Fifth Army Headquarters had anticipated, German artillery dominated the field from both flanks, the tanks were valueless except in a few isolated instances, British light guns were firing blindly at nothing that mattered, losses were high, the ground gained was far short of expectations. One brigade got lost altogether and reported that it had captured Glencorse Wood (it was, in fact, occupying Chateau Wood), and such confusion developed along the Menin Road that after a few hours eight separate battalions were milling around in the same splatter of shell holes just east of Sanctuary Wood.

II Corps was now really stalled, and to make matters worse communications were such that headquarters was unable to straighten out the jumble or even to visualize the tactical situation. Practically every telephone wire had been cut by enemy gun-fire, wireless instruments were dead, visual signalling was ineffective in the hazy light, and only pigeons and men were able to relay scraps of information back and forth. By noon every effort to push on had been fruitless and a long, sinister pause took place all along the front from the Ypres–Roulers line to Klein Zillebeke.

Elsewhere the news was far better. The French had fought spiritedly—this was strange, for according to Sir Douglas there was little or no spark left in the French Army—and by noon Anthoine's troops had proceeded nearly a mile toward Bixschoote.

XIV Corps up north had captured Pilckem by 1 p.m. and had advanced another mile to the Steenbeke. On its right, XVIII Corps also reached that stream and had even managed to cross it just north of St. Julien.

XIX Corps worked its way forward through the first German defence zone a distance of about a mile, and here again one of its divisions (the 55th) crossed the Steenbeke and pushed on a bit further.

Below General Jacob's unfortunate brigades the Second Army captured all its modest objectives by noon and then stopped to await further developments, if any, by II Corps on its left.

But all these peripheral profits did not constitute an unmixed blessing, for the deeper the three northern corps of the Fifth Army shoved forward into the German positions the more they constituted a salient (due to the failure of II Corps) into which enfilade fire increasingly poured. Thus as the day crept on and the British clung to their gains deep in No-Man's-Land they suffered steady losses of the most exasperating kind from machine-guns, mortars and 77s to their right, emanating from ground which Jacob's men had been unable to occupy. By one o'clock a sizeable but dangerous bulge about 2,000 yards deep had been created north-west of Zonnebeke. Since this area could not be held at reasonable cost, it was decided to evacuate it.

At one o'clock it began to drizzle. The fighting went on in a desultory way—quite heavily here and there—though by now there was no momentum left along the Menin Road and no real hope that II Corps could get forward any further that day. A west wind swept coldly across the plain. The scudding grey clouds imperceptibly thickened and became a solid mass beneath which a few rickety aeroplanes still sputtered, trying to glean some information from the colours of the men's uniforms and from occasional signal flares thrown up to identify units stranded far forward, awaiting the inevitable counter-attacks. Thirty British planes were shot down by rifle and machine-gun fire, some by their own men.

At four o'clock the drizzle turned to rain: a heavy, relentless downpour of the kind which gives one the feeling that it will never end. The water in the shell-holes, in the blasted canals and shallow streams, slowly and microscopically rose. Very little rain water sank in; it merely lay on the top-soil and began saturating the thin crust that hid the clay. By dusk the battleground was in the preliminary stages of flooding, and already all movements were becoming laborious.

That afternoon Sir Douglas visited General Gough, who was seemingly in excellent spirits, agreed with his superior that the first day was proving a 'great success', and reported that over 5,000 prisoners had been taken and that the ground was thick with dead Germans. A communiqué along these lines was issued to the world by British G.H.Q. One may only observe that it bore little resemblance to the realities faced by the fighting men in the battle zone.

The first of many counter-attacks had begun at 9.30 a.m. and increased in boldness throughout the afternoon and evening. The faces of officers in the concrete dug-outs of battalion headquarters were by now glum and—what is perhaps worse—indecisive. Further up the front the writing on the wall could be read even more clearly. Most company headquarters were established in shell-holes covered by waterproof sheets which kept out the rain but allowed the surface wash to seep in. Slowly the craters filled with scummy water. Here the junior officers, runners and platoon sergeants crouched with flash-lights over maps and messages. Tempers were short. One officer tells how 'I found myself suddenly threatening a sergeant-major with arrest for some unfriendly view. . . .' There had long been a legend in the British Expeditionary Force in France and Belgium that the Germans could make it rain whenever they wanted to. By this standard, the rain had begun precisely on Boche schedule. It kept pouring. An utterly black evening crept on, lit only by lurid flashes of the guns and reddish-white explosions as the shells whammed into the soft ground.

Most fortunate were headquarters personnel who had set up house in captured German pill-boxes. But the Germans turned their guns on these as well as No-Man's Land. When there occurred a direct hit against a concrete shelter or an occupied shell-hole, hell broke loose in the darkness; the wounded screamed and cursed; the dead were hastily shoved aside; groping, shouting figures milled around in terror and called for stretcher-bearers and stared hard into the gloom for signs of approaching Germans. All too often they came, and from St. Julien down the line to Warneton enemy troops kept sliding in and enfilading the Allied positions. Innumerable little brawls developed, with bombs and bayonets. The fighting was dogged and disjointed. As the shell-holes, concrete emplacements and mounds were battled over, attackers and attacked constantly changed places. Casualties among junior officers were heavy, as in all pitched battles of all wars. Sergeants, then corporals, sometimes privates became platoon commanders.

It was the classic picture, painted perhaps more sombrely than most, of a military *impasse* along most of the front, particularly on the right. While fortunes changed minutely throughout the day and evening, the new French and British line was little different by midnight than it had been at noon, except that it had been drawn back or forced back at several places.

As the fighting simmered down, the waste products of the battle, like the precipitate in a cloudy glass, moved rearward—the walking wounded and the stretcher-borne wounded ('very cheery indeed' according to Haig's diary), soaked, bloody, haggard with pain; the shrouded dead; the vague and stumbling shell-shocked. One artillery lieutenant had been struck in the throat by a bit of shrapnel. As the blood gushed, he walked 100 yards to a dressing station near Zillebeke, gasped to a doctor, 'My God, I'm going to die!' and immediately did so. The stretcher-bearers worked all day and night, helped by German prisoners, who also had begun to filter back early in the day—surprisingly young boys and older, grimmer veterans—all with sunken eyes, sodden clothing, boots full of water that squished at every step.

As the rain continued, traffic was forced to leave the open fields. On the roads sluggishly moving masses of men and machines, mules and wagons congregated—choice targets against which the German gunners now concentrated effectively. But as yet, because there was no need to do so, serious counter-attacks did not develop. Rupprecht's divisions on and behind the reverse slopes of the Ridge sat tight and awaited instructions, while smaller units along the Passchendaele sector, astride the St. Julien-Poelcappelle road, and atop the crest of Zonnebeke spur drove forward through the day and early evening. Preceded by brief, brisk barrages, they attacked strong-points here and there along the new line. After actions like these, the silence of the tomb settled for ever over many British advance posts, and certain localities such as at Kansas Cross and Schuler Farm had to be abandoned. But Germans, too, had to wade through mud and water up to their ankles, found the going hard, and often were thrown back with ease by the defenders.

On both sides the losses were already considerable, with the Allies deeper in the red than their opponents. By 10 p.m. the three assault brigades of the 55th (1st West Lancashire) Division had suffered casualties of 70 per cent. This was unusually high, though by the end of the day Gough's army had lost more than a third of its attacking complement in killed, wounded and missing. The first sobering shreds of this information began to reach Sir Douglas Haig late in the morning. When later he visited Gough he had seemed cool and confident, but that he was shaken is plain from what he said: The attack was to proceed, by all means, but only after heavy bombardment had stunned the defences and dominated the enemy artillery. For an hour the two men spoke quietly in the huge, ugly La Lovie Château which housed Fifth Army Headquarters, while rain slashed against the windows and the air trembled with the incessant roar of guns miles away; and as they talked they awaited further word—perhaps more encouraging—from II Corps. None came, and Haig took his leave.

Shortly before six o'clock Gough received a final situation report: General Jacob's infantry had still not moved and XIX Corps had retreated a mile to the Steenbeke. That settled it. At 8.45 Sir Hubert ordered both corps not to renew the attack for two days, after 'several adjustments' had been made.

Concerning the first day's operations, Sir Douglas stated in a note to the War Cabinet that the results were 'highly satisfactory and the losses slight for so great a battle'.

On the other hand, the fighting of 31 July (known henceforth by the British as the Battle of Pilckem Ridge, due to their comparative success there) was considered by the Germans to have gone clearly in their own favour. The Crown Prince's diary entry that evening was a jubilant one. He was especially pleased because his Group Wytschaete counter-attack divisions to the rear of Gheluvelt Plateau had hardly been employed at all.

Thus the following day, 1 August, in a phenomenon not rare for war-time, newspapers in London, Berlin, Paris and Vienna were all claiming the same victory. *The Times* proclaimed:

GREAT ALLIED ATTACK

YPRES SALIENT WIDENED

TWO MILES' ADVANCE

Everywhere our objectives were attained . . . the beginning is splendid. . . . Thus we have wrested from the enemy the last of the four great ridges which he held opposite our front up to a year ago.

And in another column:

We have broken the German line on the whole front attacked . . , our casualties seem . . . remarkably light.

It would be hard to cram more inaccuracies into a shorter compass. The Salient was not widened; in fact, salient-wise it was a worse one than before. At the point that mattered most the advance was not two miles but a third of a mile, nor was the average gain anywhere near two miles. The objectives were attained only at subsidiary points. The beginning of the battle was not splendid but a cruel disappointment, especially in view of the break in the weather. No ridges were captured. The main German line had not been reached, much less broken; only his outpost area had been penetrated. British casualties were not light; they were sufficiently severe to cause Sir Douglas to caution Gough against further headlong attacks.

Yet with slight embellishments the newspapers published only the news received by their correspondents from Haig's headquarters. Here it was that Brigadier-General Charteris handed out soothing opiates to the newspapermen. From 31 July to the end of the Flanders campaign it can safely be said that Charteris lied steadily to the Press, to the War Cabinet, and to his own chief, Field-Marshal Haig; and his almost psychopathic distortions during that time must be kept in mind in order to understand how and why the operation progressed as it did. That Haig implicitly trusted the man cannot be doubted. Charteris was to Haig what d'Alenson had been to Nivelle. In the words of General Gough:

Unfortunately Haig placed complete confidence in General Charteris, head of his Intelligence Service. Charteris was a good psychologist —if not a very strong character—and always told Haig something he especially wanted to hear. Thus Charteris would report that there were no Germans on our front, or that they were too exhausted to be capable of serious resistance. These misconceptions of the real situation cost the British Army dearly on more than one occasion.

Lloyd George particularly despised this forty-year-old Regular Army Glaswegian, to whom the news was always good. 'He could only be caught by a bright fly,' the Prime Minister writes. 'That he swallowed up to the gut'; and he refers cuttingly to how the Intelligence officer selected only those figures and facts which suited his fancy, and then issued hopeful reports accordingly. We shall hear much too much more of General Charteris as the campaign progresses.

Four days and nights it poured, and even Charteris, with a humility and despair uncommon for him, writes in his diary: 'Every brook is swollen and the ground is a quagmire. If it were not that all the records in previous years had given us fair warning, it would seem as if Providence had declared against us.'

The scene that existed has been well described by Sir Douglas Haig himself in a dispatch to the Government:

> The low-lying, clayey soil, torn by shells and sodden with rain, turned to a succession of vast, muddy pools. The valleys of the choked and overflowing streams were speedily transformed into long stretches of bog, impassable except by a few well-defined tracks, which became marks for the enemy's artillery. To leave these tracks was to risk death by drowning, and in the course of the subsequent fighting on several occasions both men and pack animals were lost in this way. In these conditions operations of any magnitude became impossible. . . .

On the morning of 1 August Haig instructed a French representative to urge Pétain to attack as soon as possible on his front so as to draw away Ludendorff's reserves from the Salient. Haig had claimed to be attacking largely to take pressure off the French; now it was the other way around. There is a whiff of sour grapes in his diary notation that evening, and a *non-sequitur* in the final phrase: 'A terrible day of rain. The ground is like a bog in this low-lying country . . . we are fortunate not to have advanced to the extreme "Red Line" because it would not have been possible to supply our guns with ammunition. Our troops would thus have been at the mercy of a hostile counter-attack; and a check might have resulted.'

Small attacks and German counter-strokes continued for three days without changing matters. Gough cancelled the big push scheduled for Thursday, 2 August. Pétain promised to deliver his diversion the following week. A lull set in; even the big guns quieted down. Haig was in despair as the Germans collected themselves. Air reconnaissance dropped to zero. The officers at Tank Headquarters, those spirited young men, issued a typically sharp memorandum: 'From a tank point of view the Third Battle of Ypres may be considered dead. . . . From an infantry point of view the Third Battle of Ypres may be considered comatose. It can only be continued at colossal loss and little gain. . . .' Fogs blanketed the Salient sporadically for the rest of the week, and the rain varied between drizzles and near cloud-bursts. On Saturday *The Times* soared to new heights of euphoria and spoke of important new gains, 6,122 captured Germans, and enormous enemy casualties. The French communiqué that day was in stark contrast :

AFTERNOON. The bad weather continues on the whole front in Belgium.
EVENING. In Belgium the situation is unchanged, and the bad weather continues.

Both sides settled down to bury their dead and minister to the wounded. Sixty-nine former members of the German 237th Reserve Infantry Regiment were buried in a mass grave while a Protestant chaplain, one officer complained, 'uttered offensive platitudes'. A Bavarian corporal with one leg torn off and an arm shattered kept crying over and over, 'Haven't you got a bullet for me, comrades?' His friends and fellow-wounded smoked their pipes and stared at him in silence. Here and there fallen horses screamed until they died or were shot. The card-players resumed their games. Behind the German front long lines of stretcher-bearers waited with their burdens to get into the dressing stations.

Near Zonnebeke, Father William Doyle of the 16th (Irish) Division dashed off another of his famous battle notes to the *Dublin Review*: 'All day I have been hearing the men's confessions, and giving batch after batch Holy Communion. My poor, brave boys—they are lying on the battlefield, some in a little grave dug and blessed by their chaplain. Do you wonder that, in spite of the joy that fills my heart, many a time tears gather in my eyes . . .?'

The diary of an English nurse assigned to a field hospital dangerously near the front also tells of the sequel to battle:

Soaking hopeless rain, holding up the advance; the worst luck that could happen. Poor Sir Douglas Haig. . . .

I got to bed between 2 and 7 and slept like blazes. This morning they really don't look so bad—for abdominals. Only 23 deaths.

. . . The abdominals coming in are very bad today—both Boche and British. The work thickens as the wards fill up and new wards have to be opened. We are to take Chests and Femurs too. . . . It is getting very ghastly; the men all look so appalling when they are brought in, and so many die.

. . . Can God be on our side, everyone is asking—when His (alleged!) Department always intervenes in favour of the enemy at all our best moments?

And another dispatch from the tireless Father Doyle was scribbled out and rushed to Ireland:

A moment's pause to absolve a couple of dying men, and then I reached the group of smashed and bleeding bodies, most of them still breathing. The first thing I saw almost unnerved me—a young soldier lying on his back, his hands and face a mass of blue phosphorus flame. He was the first victim I had seen of the new gas the Germans are using. . . . Good God, how can any human being live in this! As I hurry back I hear that two men have been hit twenty yards away. I am with them in a moment, splashing through mud and water—a quick absolution, the last Rites of the Church. . . .

And that same day, after many visits from officer friends to whom she served tea, Nurse Luard returned to her duties at the Advanced Abdominal Centre where a boy named Reggie in the Moribund Ward continued to wail, 'I do feel bad and no one takes no notice of me.' Fortunately that night (his last) he slept like a baby.

The rain stopped. An inventory shows that the British and French had lost about 35,000 men up to this point. The average Fifth Army advance was less than half-way toward the objectives planned for 31 July. Half the tanks were destroyed. The situation was, in the restrained words of the Official British Historian, 'only relatively satisfactory'.

General Gough decided to give II Corps another try on the 9th, with the rest of his army joining in on the 13th, and after a day's delay (due to atrocious weather which had broken in the meantime) General Jacob's brigades jumped off (crept off would be a better description) toward Gheluvelt. The attack this time was spearheaded by the 18th (Eastern) Division, a fresh outfit that had been in reserve. Fit or not, it did no better than the unfit 30th. The operation was a failure; and the grand offensive which followed three days later also accomplished nothing in the way of capturing ridge positions on the vital II Corps southern flank.

So desolate, so meaningless were these August struggles that the record of them in histories and memoirs fills one with a certain weariness. Listlessly the men assemble at the jump-off tapes. Behind the same familiar barrage they advance through the same narrow porridge-like strip of ground. The same hidden machine-guns greet them; the same whiz-bangs open up at them. Here and there a strong-point is captured, a new outpost is reached, to which a few riflemen forlornly cling. Some of these are held, and occasionally the line is advanced a few hundred yards. Brownish masses of German troops slog forward and everywhere nasty hand-to-hand encounters take place. The men on

12

both sides are lacerated and punctured, bleed and die, in numbers that baffle the imagination. Nameless new beings take their place, but nothing else changes.

Gaunt, blackened remnants of trees drip in the one-time forests. The shells of countless batteries burst deafeningly and without ceasing; the dank smell of gunpowder, wet clay, poison gas and polluted water spreads over the battleground and drifts eastward. The men hardly know what they are doing or how affairs in general are progressing. By mid-August they were told even less than soldiers are usually told: Move up there. Start walking that way. Occupy those shell holes. Wait near the barn. Surround that pill-box. Relieve those chaps (you can't see them from here) behind the canal and wait for further word. After two weeks such was the status of Haig's grand offensive which was to have burst out of the Salient, bounded across the Ridge, released the prancing cavalry steeds, and with flying banners captured the Channel ports.

And so far as the people across that Channel knew, all this did seem to be happening—not as quickly as had been hoped, perhaps, but none the less inexorably. Maps in the newspapers showed huge shaded areas captured from the Germans; but a closer inspection of the scale revealed that the gains were measured in hundreds of yards rather than dozens of miles.

The illusions of the times were not all the fault of Charteris and the G.H.Q. Press releases, nor were the correspondents entirely to blame. The newspaper moguls, the politicians, the industrialists, the people at large desperately wanted a victory. Almost unconsciously the editorials reflected that inner need, and created wish-dreams out of the copy at hand. The columns of *The Times* sound like a prayer meeting to bolster the faith of backsliding parishioners. On 17 August, under the heading 'Ypres Battle Resumed', splendid advances around Langemarck are described despite 'stubborn resistance'; and while it is conceded that most German counter-attacks were successful, these were 'at great cost'.

The *Spectator's* accounts were exceptionally slavish and inane:

Certainly we have reason to congratulate the General Staff. The strong and promising new blows which have been struck in the new battle are, we imagine, only the first in a long series.

The fourth year of the war is opening with all the lessons of the past three years being applied not only with science but with resolution. Our Staff work in the field seems to be irreproachable . . . the infantry, whose losses are said to be comparatively light, march behind the moving curtain of shells and bless the gunners as they go.

And *The Times* righteously told on 18 August of 'Enemy Lies Exposed: What the Germans are Told.—Falsification of Battle News.—The Lie as a Buttress of Morale.'

In another column the disappointing action of 16 August was outlined by a war correspondent in this vein: 'Our successes . . . were even more satisfactory than I dared to assume when tele-graphing yesterday afternoon . . . slaughter of the Fourth Division of the Prussian Guard. . . . Our progress . . . appears to have been swift and admirably executed.'

And contemptuously this writer pointed out that the opposing troops were young Prussians of 'poor fighting material . . . undernourished for the last two years before enlistment'.

The arithmetic of German casualties was in British numbers so enormous that, looking back after forty years, one wonders how any but the most gullible could have been deceived by them. Haig reported an even 100,000 on 21 August and flatly stated that the end of Germany's resources was at hand—this on the basis of a paper written by Charteris, who, however, protested in his diary (he does not seem to have protested elsewhere): 'D.H. has not only accepted *in toto* my report . . . but he has gone much further.'

Constantly throughout August the German armies were 'visibly cracking'. There was 'proof that they were preparing for emergencies'. They were alleged to be burning some villages; 'this might be preliminary to a withdrawal'. Lloyd George remarks that even the War Cabinet and other politicians believed the campaign was going well, and again he attributes this to the evil genius of General Charteris, to Haig, and to Kiggell:

It naturally pleased Haig to have carefully chosen and nicely cooked little tidbits of 'intelligence' about broken German divisions, heavy German casualties, and diminishing German morale served up to him. . . . He beamed satisfaction and confidence. His great plan was prospering. The whole atmosphere of this secluded little community reeked of that sycophantic optimism which is the curse of autocratic power. . . .

As for General Kiggell, the Chief of Staff, he had the air of a silent craftsman, whose plans, designed and worked out by his art in the seclusion of his workshop, were turning out well and proceeding inexorably without a hitch to the destined end.

To the disgust of Sir William Robertson the Prime Minister, sensing the débâcle in Flanders, revived on 23 August before French and Italian dignitaries his old scheme of attacking the Austrians. Furthermore, he vowed, the Belgian operation was positively to be stopped in ten days. (Foch agreed that matters were hopeless on the Western Front.) 'Wully' wrote to Haig saying that Lloyd George 'is a real bad 'un. The other members of the War Cabinet seem afraid of him. Milner is a tired, dyspeptic old man. Curzon a gas-bag. Bonar Law equals Bonar Law. Smuts has good instincts but lacks knowledge. . . . The rain is cruel luck but it will get fine in time.'

And when Haig heard that the Prime Minister had been questioning Foch about British strategy he commented heavily: 'I could not have believed that a British minister could have been so ungentlemanly.'

Meanwhile *Punch* continued to divert its readers with cartoons showing groups of cringing Germans throwing up their hands quavering '*Kamerad!*' to nonchalant individual British privates. The public was happy. At last the war was going properly; all records were being broken in the manufacture of British munitions; the Yanks were coming; and if there were any among the masses of the people who doubted the gladness of it all they were not to be quoted in the periodicals of the day.

Yet as early as 7 August General Headquarters had questioned whether the original objectives were any longer obtainable.

Suddenly it was suggested that the plan was not, after all, to reach the Channel coast but mainly to wear down the Germans. Should not, therefore, the break-through idea be abandoned in favour of the original May step-by-step plan? To this, Rawlinson, for one, still twiddling his thumbs near Nieuport, agreed enthusiastically. In a written summary of his views he remarked that the British army in the west had never really tried to carry out a campaign of attrition, had never issued orders to the effect that limited objectives reached after a series of hard, fast blows were not to be exceeded. Furthermore, he continued pointedly, if the enemy morale were to be broken by such methods it would become common knowledge—'not a matter of conjecture built up on the reports of prisoners and deserters'—plain to every Britisher as well as to the Germans themselves. He urged that the high command stop assuming airily that the German army was breaking down. Further efforts should never again be undertaken without full artillery cover. Never again, he insisted, should the infantry be assigned targets beyond their physical capacity.

Gough went even further. In a sudden fit of revulsion and pessimism he advised Haig to close down the campaign altogether. Success was no longer possible, he said, except at the price of disproportionate losses.

But Plumer wanted to continue, and the fighting went on; though now Haig tacitly sanctioned step-by-step methods. He instructed Gough to attack again. On 22 August Sir Hubert did so, but in an extremely limited fashion—just enough to comply technically with orders but not enough to bring about another blood bath. So all August every day there was fighting, intense and otherwise, and the rains continued in unprecedented quantities—it turned out one of the wettest Augusts in thirty years—and by late that month the line had been pushed forward another few hundred yards on the northern flank, though II Corps lying at the base of Gheluvelt Plateau was still as stationary as ever.

Sir Douglas, perturbed over Gough's failure on the 22nd, made a radical decision that afternoon when it became clear that Jacob's corps was getting nowhere at the usual high cost in men. He drove to Second Army headquarters near Cassel to visit General Herbert Plumer. A delicate conversation followed. The commander-in-chief spoke of the regrettable delays in capturing the high ground to the east and the importance of doing so before the larger plan could be realized. Would General Plumer, who knew the Salient so intimately, consider extending his frontage northward to include the II Corps sector? The rotund little officer had suspected what was coming, had discussed the matter previously with Gough, and was not thrilled. He had been in the Salient for two miserable years, he grumbled, and had no desire to push himself into another. Taking over the main advance along the Menin Road seemed like a fine way to ruin one's reputation. To throw good money after bad is a thankless and hopeless business in war or peace. He suggested that they talk it over with Gough. Later that day the three men met at G.H.Q. and the decision was consummated: Plumer would take over, and in three weeks would begin a new drive founded upon a series of meticulous, strictly limited operations.

That Gough was relieved, in both senses of the word, there can be no doubt. He was glad to be rid of his wretched chore even at the risk of his professional standing. And there were others who were happy to see the Fifth Army leave. As usual, criticisms had mounted concerning Sir Hubert's headquarters. Philip Gibbs, the war correspondent, stopped to talk to a group of officers leaving the Salient. 'You must be glad to leave Flanders,' he said, and bitterly one man replied, 'God be thanked we are leaving the Fifth Army area!'

But under the conditions that now existed to the east of Ypres, could General Plumer do any better?

On the 24th there was another attack, this time toward Inverness Copse. It failed. (The *Spectator* reported next day, 'This has been for the Allies the greatest week of the war'.) On the 27th another try was made. It also failed. Between these efforts, and after them until the end of the month, and before them incessantly on dates not mentioned in this narrative, there were more attacks all down the line by Frenchmen, Irish, English, Welsh, Scots, Australians, New Zealanders, Canadians—all for nothing, under hateful conditions, persisted in for no reason that anyone (outside G.H.Q.) could any longer discern. Over and over the Germans counter-attacked. Inverness Copse changed hands eighteen times. The senselessness of it all grew like a cancer into the minds of the Allied troops. One historian writes that 'these strokes, aimed at the morale of the German army, were wearing down the morale of the British'. In the past Crown Prince Rupprecht had been impressed by the coolness of British captives, but on 16 August he was surprised to hear one say that he and his comrades would have been happy to shoot down the officers who made them attack. The following week Rupprecht noted in his war diary that British captives were still bitter against their officers, and that officer prisoners were now blaming the staffs. On 25 August he was advised that the once-tenacious British were now surrendering easily. All these reports were passed on to Ludendorff. He knew how badly his own troops were suffering; but the Germans, at least, were winning most of the August battles.

It was during this month, therefore, that Ludendorff felt free to transfer some nine divisions away from Flanders to help the Austrians. Though General Gough was discouraged he tried to put up a good front at Fifth Army conferences. Baker-Carr, one of the tank specialists, has told of the many times that Gough opened proceedings with a statement such as this: 'Gentlemen, I have just come from an interview with the Commander-in-Chief and he tells me that everything points to a complete break-down of the enemy morale and that one more hard thrust will crumple up his defences'; but the younger officer comments that: 'There was not another single member of the Conference who did not know how grotesquely inaccurate this statement was in fact.'

One trouble was that most generals were too distracted by the pressures of staff work to find time to visit the battle zone. During August Baker-Carr delivered a tank lecture at the Staff College Course at G.H.Q., and after lunch he candidly amplified his views. The fighting, especially as it concerned tanks, he said, was

'as dead as mutton', and had been precisely that ever since
1 August. His words were met by stony silence. After lunch
Brigadier-General John Davidson, Haig's Director of Operations,
asked to see him in his office. When Baker–Carr arrived he found
the general seated at his desk with his head in his hands.

'Sit down', he said. 'I want to talk to you.' Baker–Carr
complied.

'I am very upset by what you said at lunch, Baker. If it had been
some junior officer, it wouldn't have mattered so much, but a
man of your knowledge and experience has no right to speak as
you did.'

'You asked me how things really were and I told you frankly.'

'But what you say is impossible.'

'It isn't. Nobody has any idea of the conditions up there.'

'But they can't be as bad as you make out.'

'Have you been there yourself?'

'No.'

'Has anyone in O.A. been there?'

'No.'

'Well, then, if you don't believe me, it would be as well to
send someone up to find out.'

Yet there was, perhaps, more behind it all than met the eye.
The Germans too were being hurt—not as badly as their attackers,
but enough to worry Crown Prince Rupprecht. As for Ludendorff, here we find a discrepancy. In August 1917 his words and
actions were those of a man who had no qualms, whereas in his
later memoirs he writes:

The costly August battles imposed a heavy strain on the Western
troops. In spite of all the concrete protection they seemed more or
less powerless under the enormous weight of the enemy's artillery.
At some points they no longer displayed that firmness which I in
common with the local commanders had hoped for. . . . I myself
was being put to a terrible strain. The state of affairs in the West
appeared to prevent the execution of our plans elsewhere. Our
wastage had been so high as to cause grave misgivings and exceeded
all expectation.

But the British and French had lost some 74,000 men between 31 July and the end of August; while German casualties were about 50,000.

In the *Daily News* H. G. Wells asked 'Why . . . does the waste and killing go on? . . . the declarations of public policy (on both sides) remain childish, vague and disingenuous . . . they chaffer like happy imbeciles while civilization bleeds to death.'

For one blinding moment the evil sorcery, the taboo, about discussing peace was broken. On 16 August Pope Benedict XVI sent from the Vatican a note to all belligerent governments crying out against the war: 'Shall, then, the civilized world be naught but a field of death? And shall Europe, so glorious and flourishing, rush, as though driven by universal madness, toward the abyss, and lend her hand to her own suicide?' He suggested broad means of ending the conflict and settling the issues. *The Times* denounced the Note as 'pro-German and anti-Ally . . . permeated with German ideas'. Every major power on both sides rejected it. The fighting would go on till somebody won. At Birkenhead Lloyd George estimated in an impromptu speech that 'we shall just win', to which the *Nation*, that irreverent organ of the Left, innocently asked, 'Win What?'

August ended as it had begun—with new torrents of rain. Battalions in reserve, such as at St. Omer, waited apprehensively for orders to return to the front. Rumours drifting back from the Salient were indeed chilling. They told of subhuman grappling in swamps, of tanks shattered by the hundreds, of careless plans and alarming casualties, of furious generals, of stubborn attacks doomed before they began. The *B.E.F. Times* tried to keep spirits up—how successfully we shall never know—with humour, verse, and satire such as the following 'want-ads' of 15 August:

WANTED.—To rent for the winter season, DRY WARM DUG OUT. Must be commodious and in healthy locality; untroubled by hawkers and Huns . . . Apply: Reggie, c/o of this paper.

FOR SALE.—TWO TANKS. Slightly soiled. Price moderate. Or would exchange for a pair of rabbits. Apply: 41, Dammstrasse.

FOR SALE.—PLEASANT COUNTRY ESTATE, situated in one of the nicest parts of Belgium. Heavily wooded. Has been shot over. Owner desirous of leaving. Apply: Feddup, Glencorse Wood.

Late in the month Father Doyle was killed. Nursing Sister Luard reported in her diary 27 August that three of her men would die that night and that one boy 'who's had a leg off . . . is to lose an arm and an eye tomorrow'. As the month closed Sir Douglas inscribed a familiar entry in his own diary: 'Glass falling slightly. Weather unsettled. Heavy showers of rain fell throughout the day.'

Philip Gibbs wrote of new enemy counter-attacks and reported that although Inverness Copse had changed hands for the nineteenth time, and was now held by the Boches, fighting continued at the usual pitch of sublime British courage. The *B.E.F. Times* advertised a great 'Special Attraction: Haig's Company in a Stirring Drama, Entitled: *Pilckem's Progress*.'

Gradually the great guns became silent. On the chessboard of Flanders the opening phase had ended. The pawns lay still, filled with forebodings. The grandmasters stroked their moustaches, surveyed the deadlock, and plotted their next moves.

10

The Intermission

EVER since the war began frustrated generals on both sides had largely blamed their failures on a shortage of artillery ammunition. In England these complaints had been to some degree justified and during 1915 had led to the famous 'shell scandal', one result of which was to raise Lloyd George to the Ministry of Munitions. (Winston Churchill assumed this post in July 1917; at the same time, Sir Edward Carson entered the War Cabinet and Sir Eric Geddes became First Lord of the Admiralty.) After the Somme the same outcry had arisen: If only the Allies —the French especially—had been supplied with enough heavy-calibre shells they never would have been stopped.

And on 2 September, 1917, in a report to the War Cabinet, Sir Douglas Haig grumbled again that his batteries had been limited in ammunition during August, and that this plus the terrible weather, neither of which was his fault, had affected adversely the first phase of his campaign. He hoped that both conditions would soon be rectified and expressed regrets that operations would not be resumed for about three weeks. But 'the best, if not the only, way to surmount the crisis and the temporary inaction of the French Army was to continue the campaign with all available resources'. Generally, however, his report implied that the August fighting had gone as planned. The Germans were demoralized. They had lost vast numbers of men. Valuable terrain had been captured. The Allies held a strong initiative. The spirit of his troops was still excellent. Casualties suffered had been reasonable, and only here and there had there been small setbacks.

Lloyd George was not impressed. Whatever else Sir Douglas may have thought of him, the Prime Minister could read a map and he could plainly see that a month of terrific fighting had produced almost no gain in ground. He also doubted Haig's other claims. He had lost faith in the campaign—not that he had much to begin with—quite soon after its disappointing start, and by now he was definitely alarmed. How was he, the Prime Minister of the Empire, to fulfil his mandate to win the war if Haig persisted in killing off the British army? 'Blood and mud,' he repeated dismally, over and over, 'blood and mud, they can think of nothing better.' Flatly before his associates he berated himself for having allowed the Belgian offensive to begin. As for this bland report from the field-marshal, Lloyd George considered it an insult to his intelligence.

Its tone was indeed reminiscent of a regrettable phrase once uttered by Joffre which had contributed to his downfall; the Frenchman had said that he was 'nibbling at the German line'. With the exception of Carson, who at this stage was fully backing the military, the War Cabinet was in an uneasy mood. Even Parliament as a whole, knowing nothing of Haig's earlier promises and less of what had really happened thus far, showed signs of doubt as to whether military affairs were progressing as admirably as claimed.

One reason for the uncertainty was the flood of rumours that had begun to engulf the home islands. Wounded soldiers returning to England told grisly stories, often exaggerated, of the condition of the battlefield, and the number of dead, captured and stricken. Like all bad news it travelled fast. Others who found ways of drifting away from the fighting zone and of circulating tales of disaster diligently did so, in the age-old manner of such men. The impression gained ground that British armies had suffered an inexcusable slaughter in Flanders and that the authorities were trying to hush it up; and these suspicions were not confined entirely to gullible or disillusioned members of the masses but to many in Parliament as well.

The same young women from the East End continued to walk

to and from Charing Cross in the same little groups, but they no longer sang their shrill, patriotic songs. Now they came silently to greet the ambulance trains and to watch the ambulance lorries load up and chug away with their never-ending loads of wounded men. Day after day—and mostly night after night, when it was deemed more circumspect to do so—the trains discharged their mutilated cargoes. Soon it was whispered that Britain had taken a quarter-million losses since 31 July. The first week in August people had believed that a great and inexpensive victory was being won. The first week in September the bubble inflated with hot air had already burst. While publicly the politicians and the Press made a fine show of optimism, Sir Edward Carson admitted that 'a great deal of very loose and mischievous talk about peace' was in the air.

The police and engineers went on strike. The whispering continued. 'Wully', it was said, was to be sacked. Plumer would be the new Chief of the Imperial General Staff. Haig was finished too. His successor would be Sir Henry Rawlinson. Robertson himself was depressed; and this was no rumour. He admitted to Colonel Repington during luncheon at the Bath Club that fighting conditions in the Low Country 'were pretty horrible', that the rain was giving Rupprecht plenty of time to reinforce his troops and to string up new masses of barbed wire. It was hard luck—'on Haig'. But, he added helplessly, what else was there to do but to go on? 'Haig thought that he was killing a lot of Germans.' Plainly Sir William was backsliding again.

On 3 September he wired Haig: 'General Foch arrives London ... to press British War Cabinet to agree to his sending 100 heavy guns from French First Army (Anthoine) to Italy at once; if, as I suppose, this will affect your plans, it is very desirable that you should come over and see War Cabinet.' The commander-in-chief needed no urging and arrived in England that evening.

The following day a meeting was held in Robertson's room at the War Office. Both he and Haig were in a difficult position. The War Cabinet had agreed to the offensive on condition that it would progress more or less as the general and the marshal had promised, and that it would be broken off if and when it showed signs of failure. How were they to evade their perfectly plain obligation to redeem the face value of the insurance policy they had sold their government in July?

Morosely Lloyd George summarized matters. The Russians were through. The French were recuperating. The Americans would not arrive till next year. The British had been stopped. The Italians had just started another offensive on the Isonzo and needed big guns. Therefore all operations on the Western Front should cease for the time being, and a hundred heavy pieces should be rushed to Cadorna.

Foch agreed. Bonar Law was, in Haig's words, 'as usual, very weak'. Carson and Smuts disagreed. Lord Robert Cecil of the Foreign Office stood aloof. The Premier would not back down. He insisted that the case was open and shut and kept referring to Haig's previous promises. Robertson—that impolite, intolerant, formidable, beloved hater of politicians—was unusually excited. He intended not to give an inch. When he spoke, all his h's disappeared. Concerning Cadorna's new effort that was to work wonders, he grated caustically (as so often in the past) 'I've 'eard different'. Haig refused to release a single gun or to abandon the initiative. Neither he nor Robertson argued that the first Flanders phase had been successful. They said nothing of the infinitely distant Channel ports, nor did they dwell upon the distasteful fruits of attrition. They merely emphasized that abandoning the offensive might allow the Germans to strike either the French or British an 'overwhelming' blow.

The military had a weak case, but again won out. For the record, Douglas Haig agreed to 'review' in his own mind, and perhaps some day with Pétain, the advisability of during some future month sending some guns to Italy. Meanwhile operations in Belgium would continue. But how long would Lloyd George continue playing Haig's game?

Sir Henry Wilson, now in charge of the Eastern Command, looked on sardonically and confided to his diary a series of biting comments:

This is unfortunate, especially as Haig is not going to do anything really serious at Ypres this year ... Haig, Robertson and Kiggell are running the maxim of superior forces at the decisive point, etc., into the ground. ... I believe that Lloyd George, knowing that Haig will not do any good, has allowed him to keep all his guns, etc., so that he can, later on, say, 'Well, I gave you everything. I even allowed you to spoil the Italian offensive. And now, owing to gross miscalculation and incapacity you have entirely failed to do anything serious except lose a lot of men.' And in this indictment he will include Robertson, and then get rid of both of them.

We do not know whether the Prime Minister was indeed plotting in this veiled fashion, but we learn that he had begun taking steps to reduce the flow of manpower to the Western Front where, in his opinion, Haig would only get them uselessly killed off anyway. In this indirect way he hoped to curb the commander-in-chief, even if he could not stop him altogether. Already 'Wully' was complaining that less than 8,000 drafts would reach France in September. Such skimpy rations would only replace 'normal wastage', in the rather repellent technical phrase, much less replace the abnormal casualties suffered in August and anticipated for subsequent stages of the campaign. Cyclists, clerks and other noncombatant personnel, already in Europe and beyond the clutches of the Prime Minister, were being 'combed' and rushed to the front. But this sort of thing had its limits, and by early September the fifty-two British divisions on the Western Front were each running alarmingly near an average of 2,000 men short.

From now until the end of the campaign there was to be a constant tug-of-war between the civilians and generals concerning the release of troops for duty in Belgium. Recruitments had fallen off almost to nil. Without volunteers, only draftees remained. But apart from youngsters gradually attaining military age, who could any longer be drafted? The rock-bottom requirement of the civilian economy had to be met. Lloyd George refused to weaken industrial capacity by calling up any more essential workers. Sir Eric Geddes, the new First Lord of the

Admiralty, even advised subtracting riflemen from Haig and putting them to work in the fields and factories. To this Sir Henry Wilson replied that he too wanted 'to take troops away from France during the mud months, not to grow cabbages here, but to beat the Turks'. Sir Douglas and Sir William would have none of this nonsense. They wanted all the men they had and at least 85,000 more. It was, they insisted, the only way to keep up the pressure and thus ward off a knockout blow against France.

This in turn raised a basic question late that summer, while the fighting died down and the war-lords wrangled: How weak *were* the French? Was it true that they were even incapable of defence? After all, five full months had passed since the Nivelle affair. Lloyd George conceded that they might be unable to mount a grand offensive, but he believed that they could surely hold their own on French soil. Pétain, ever gloomy ('*trop negatif, trop timide*', in Joffre's words), and perhaps trying cynically to keep Haig attacking, told the latter that he had not a man upon whom he could rely between Switzerland and the British right. Even Sir Douglas accepted this statement with reservations, though he was delighted to be implored to continue his offensive. *Someone*, at least, saw things his way. So weak was France in manpower and fighting spirit, Pétain continued, during his visit at British G.H.Q., that his government might even demand a separate peace rather than face another German attack. This remark Haig passed on to the War Cabinet. It was received doubtfully. Pétain, it was suspected, had rather a predilection for throwing in the sponge. Yet his assertions could not be altogether overlooked.

For there was no doubt that France was enervated that summer. Aside from her precise degree of military incapacity, which will for ever remain a matter of argument, it was well known that her civilian morale was lower than that of Britain. Even from as far away as Germany's triumphant Eastern Front Max Hoffmann writes in his diary 14 September: 'The news of the domestic situation in France sounds excellent. The country is sick of the war, and the accounts we get from responsible and impartial people in Switzerland are most encouraging, from our point of view.'

Matters had not been helped by a division of 17,000 Russian soldiers who had fought with Nivelle on the Aisne and then had been unwisely retained in France. Wherever they were stationed they preached revolution. An attempt had been made to ship them back to Russia, but Kerenski did not want them. In time they had become so bolshevik in sentiment, so troublesome, that it was decided to ask them to surrender, as though they were enemy troops. Only fifty-seven did so. The rest dug trenches and put up barricades. While the civilian population hurriedly departed, a final ultimatum was issued on 14 September. It was refused. Next day their food was cut off and they were encircled. On the following day they were attacked. After being defeated they were disarmed and shipped to ports on the Black Sea. The incident did its part to infect France with stop-the-war propaganda, not only in itself but because of the widespread publicity it received.

From September on, Haig used the argument of French weakness up to the hilt. How worthy it was, and how much of it he actually believed in his own heart, is a continuing riddle. Certainly Lloyd George thought little enough of Haig's opinion; he considered it a convenient device used for the purpose of furthering rash military dreams. He was fed up with the bickering. More and more his thoughts dwelled upon a supranational governing board which would run the Allied war effort from such a lofty, unassailable height that field commanders like Haig, Pétain and Cadorna would simply do what they were told, rather than fight on in solitary confusion, co-ordinating nothing, arguing incessantly with their respective chiefs and with one another, and getting nowhere. It was early this month that he first proposed an Allied Joint Council, to be composed of three members of each nation: the supreme civilian leader, one Cabinet member, one general. Painlevé and the British War Cabinet approved informally, and President Wilson evinced interest. Thus, tentatively and embryonically, the Council came into being.

As every Tommy knew, the Germans could make the rain come and go at will. Accordingly it had stopped early in the ⁻

month; and now there set in a period of brilliant, warm, dry days. Slowly the swamplike aspect of the Salient disappeared. Moving men, machines and mules stirred up a fine, whitish dust. Much water in the shell-holes evaporated, and from a distance they seemed dry as a bone. By mid-September only some hollows in the lower-lying ground remained waterlogged. To Australians the broad crest of the Ridge recalled the rocky, broken spurs of the Libyan desert where they had once trained. So hard became the thin upper crust of the ground that bullets often ricocheted on it.

These were perfect days for an attack. The Germans braced themselves, but their enemy did not come. On the 12th Crown Prince Rupprecht wrote in his diary: 'The Flanders fight seems actually to have ended,' though von Kuhl, his chief of staff, doubted that the 'stubborn British' had stopped for good. Rupprecht insisted 'the enemy was regrouping in order to attack at another place'. In this belief he was supported by several British prisoners who had lied splendidly; the Flanders offensive was over, they said, and the next attack would take place further south. On the 13th von Kuhl changed his mind and recorded his 'inmost conviction that the battle of Flanders is at an end'. It seemed almost inconceivable to the Boches that even the peculiar British would fight in the rain and rest in the sun.

The early September days dwindled. Splotches of green covered large portions of the sunlit Salient, a few flowers teetered in the breeze which drifted inland and even, in rare moments, smelled saltily of the North Sea. Some of the charred tree stumps put out a forlorn leaf or two: the most poignant note of all. For a fortnight the sky remained almost cloudless by day; and under the level stare of the sun the soldiers perspired and the birds hopped and twittered among the ruins of nature and the débris of man.

The Germans waited and wondered. Was this the end of the fight? Would Haig and his Tommies try again? 'They are paper tigers,' ran the ancient Chinese adage, 'fierce to look upon, but they melt in the rain.' Had they indeed melted?

There was astounding news along the British lines about the so-called 'Admiral', a middle-aged volunteer ambulance driver who had been allowed to tarry in the area wearing the badges of an Army captain and the crenellated rings of a Navy Lieutenant. Here he invented weird gadgets and bombs with which to mortify the enemy. Earlier he had devised a bullet-proof body shield, and to prove its worth had walked past Crossroads Farm and Forward Cottage in daylight, unfortunately forgetting that he had no flank cover and that he was in a salient. After recovering from his bullet wound he had invented and set a new booby trap into which he himself had just fallen—so flashed the spectacular report.

At the Hôtel du Sauvage in Cassel, last civilized stop on the way to Ypres, men thronged for dinner and wine at tables covered with real linen, while candles flickered against the dim walls, their shadows trembling delicately at the faraway rumble of the guns. Here reigned old Madame, and behind the desk sat Mademoiselle Suzanne, 'a dainty rogue in porcelain'; and seldom was it that the laughter, the singing, the tinkling of Madame's piano ceased. But only officers—and not those of the air force, who had proved too boisterous—were allowed in this pleasant rendezvous.

On the other side of the hill the Huns partook of similar fleeting interludes, similar pleasures, similar yearnings. And there were those who waited with longing for the lull to end and the war to be won. On 10 September one Helmut Zschutte wrote:

I am restless. I hate the kitchen table at which I am writing. I lose patience over a book. I should like to push the landscape aside as if it irritated me. I must get to the Front. I must again hear the shells roaring up into the sky and the desolate valley echoing the sound. I must get back to my Company . . . live once more in the realm of death.

Soon enough Corporal Zschutte would return to the realm of death, never again to leave it.

Time was running out, too, for Lieutenant-General Sir

William Birdwood's I Anzac Corps (1st and 2nd Australian Divisions) for these were the men selected by General Plumer to handle the coming main assignment. In the streams they fished with home-made hooks, shot at the fish with their rifles, and even set off Mills bombs to stir up the fish so that they could be caught. The villagers complained, and headquarters sternly ordered all such bombing to cease. Sports were organized almost every day after training. Again the tall youngsters from down under congregated in the towns and hamlets of France and Belgium, as hundreds of thousands had done before them. They ransacked the countryside for firewood (enough coal was never issued); chairs, sheds and ladders were liberated by the soldiers to heat their tea and bully beef, and countless were the suits for damage brought against the British army by the outraged Belgian citizenry. In the cool and peace of the evening the card players grimly waged their pasteboard wars for stakes ever more astronomical.

Occasionally fighting flared up, in accordance with Haig's instructions that the Fifth Army harass the enemy in the direction of Poelcapelle. The plan was to distract the enemy from the vast preparations under way by the Second Army. Accordingly two divisions attacked on 6 and 7 September, and one on the 10th. All three assaults neither won ground nor harassed the Germans, and about a thousand British casualties were suffered. In disgust Sir Douglas advised Gough to discontinue further such operations, and additional ones scheduled for three subsequent days were also cancelled.

The weather was ideal for flying. Twenty-six squadrons of the Royal Flying Corps were aloft day and night along the front of the Second and Fifth Armies; and slightly more than this amount had been allotted to the area by the German high command. Among the latter was Captain Manfred von Richthofen's dread 'Flying Circus', led by the phlegmatic 23-year-old killer who was to become the greatest ace of all. By the end of August he had already accounted (officially) for fifty-nine Allied planes, and one day early next month, soon after breakfast, flying a spanking-new bright-red Fokker triplane, he somewhat ingloriously nailed his sixtieth, an R.E. 8 observation model: 'I approached and fired 20 shots from a distance of 50 yards, whereupon the Englishman fell to the ground and crashed near Zonnebeke. It is most probable that the English pilot mistook me for an English triplane, because the observer was standing upright in his plane and watched me approach without making use of his gun.'

These were the halcyon days, days of glory for the greatest aerial heroes of the First World War; and above the Salient most of them fought duels the romance and terror of which will never be forgotten. Every day the human moles below peered up into the blinding sky and watched the virtuosi fight and die in their agile little machines: Albert Ball, he of the suicidal methods; Richthofen, the master; that impersonal killer, James McCudden; Billy Bishop, the Canadian sharpshooter; gay Ernst Udet; Mick Mannock, dogged and filled with hatred of Germans; the great Werner Voss; Hermann Goering; even sometimes the fabulous, brooding, deathly ill George Guynemer, France's greatest ace.

Overshadowed by these world-famous fighters flew the two-seater crews—pilot and observer—doing the less spectacular but vital photographing, observing, bombing, and artillery spotting. Throughout early September the Flemish air was peppered with planes in tight-knit formations of concentrated firepower; for the air war was no longer a potpourri of derring-do and life-and-death gambles but a crucial adjunct to the more desperate drama unfolding below.

The keynote of Plumer's plan can be expressed in the word concentration. The main attack against Gheluvelt Plateau would be conducted by four divisions. (Gough had used three.) The frontage of the attack would be 4,000 yards. (Gough's three divisions had been spread over 6,200 yards.) The ratio of mass, therefore, was more than two to one in Plumer's favour. Along the decisive front from Klein Zillebeke and Westhoek Plumer had almost 1,300 guns. (Gough had employed less than 900.) Almost half of Plumer's batteries were in heavy and medium categories.

(Gough's fraction was only a third.) Plumer's batteries were to fire three and a half million rounds before the actual attack and on the first day. (The density of Gough's fire was under a million rounds for the comparable period.) Plumer planned to capture the high ground in four steps, with about six days of meticulous preparation and consolidation between each. (Gough had vaguely figured on perhaps reaching the fourth German defence line, three miles away, in the first day or two.) In other words, Plumer hoped that his vastly greater power, concentration and planning would in three weeks pay out an advance such as Gough had envisioned for the first day alone.

All these differences are so remarkable and revealing that they call for little comment; though one might observe that Herbert Plumer and 'Tim' Harington intended to fight the battle of Messines again, while Gough had envisioned another Austerlitz.

The total front of attack would be eight miles. Studious arrangements were made for the almost instant relief of all primary attacking battalions. On the left the Fifth Army would, it was hoped, advance 1,000 yards toward Poelcapelle and Gravenstafel. To the right of I Anzac, the X Corps with two divisions would push south-east nearly a mile. Further south one division (the 19th) would hold up the right flank and attempt to proceed a few hundred yards toward Belgian Wood. All other divisions between this point and the Comines Canal would stay on the defensive; and while the French up north were to make a large uproar they too were to stand pat.

Thus, in effect, the entire scheme had been compressed—not only the basic drive toward the eastern highland, but the total front of attack—into a bull-like charge half as wide and twice as intense as that which had taken place on 31 July.

In all this there was the irreducible minimum of imagination, subtlety and surprise, and not a single tank would be used.

The bombardment began on 13 September. Each day it was turned on more heavily, and twice daily the barrage scheme was practised—deadly, earnest practice that inched across the German defence zone causing losses to enemy machine-gunners and leaving the remaining defenders wondering when the false alarms would prove to be the real thing. Any German doubts that a new attack was coming in the Salient were now ended. On 17 September Sixt von Armin's headquarters announced that it was, after all, imminent; but as yet these gentlemen did not know that the exact moment was to be 5.40 a.m. of the 20th—the very earliest, it was calculated, that an infantryman would be able to see 200 yards ahead of him.

On 18 September all attacking brigades of the Second and Fifth Armies regretfully left their training areas and moved up close behind the front. This was the day Bonar Law wrote to Lloyd George, who was in Wales:

> Treasury Chambers
> Whitehall, S.W.
> 18 September, 1917

My Dear Prime Minister,

   ... The only thing at all new is that, in speaking to Robertson yesterday, I said to him that I had lost absolutely all hope of anything coming of Haig's offensive and though he did not say so in so many words, I understand that he took the same view. I do not know when the next attack is supposed to take place but I believe it may happen at any time. It is evident, therefore, that the time must soon come when we will have to decide whether or not this offensive is to be allowed to go on. ...

> Yours sincerely,
> A. Bonar Law.

It was too late. The following day, with the sun setting behind the massed troops and sending streaks of pale light against the rising ground to the east, the final approach march began. Smoothly and silently the vast armies (squeezed together as they marched, to avoid casualties from long-range, probing shell-fire) moved across the open fields, leaving the roads clear for traffic on wheels. As the men trudged forward they were greeted by the usual comments from onlookers and those being relieved: 'There go the cemetery reinforcements!' and solemn warnings that 'there's a shortage of coffins up there'.

The very moment darkness set in, it began to drizzle. An hour before midnight rain was falling heavily and slowing everything down, especially in the soft, untracked fields. By now General Gough was distraught—he had become neurotic about rain, and with good reason—and rang up General Plumer. Stop the attack, he recommended. Plumer was equally worried but wanted first to confer with his weather expert and corps commanders. They in turn, after much indecision during which even the divisional generals were phoned for their views, told him that although the top-soil was muddy the rain was expected to stop. The consensus was recorded: 'Very difficult to form an opinion. Conditions not good but promising better things. Rain decreasing and wind rising. General opinion slightly in favour of continuation.' Birdwood was especially strong for carrying on. Plumer asked him to call Gough back and say that the attack would go on. At 12.10 the rain ended.

At 3 a.m. an Australian machine-gun officer lost his way in No-Man's-Land and, after a wild struggle, was captured by a German patrol. As they were taking him to the rear he was detected trying to destroy his papers; these were extracted from him and turned out to be the Second Army operation orders. The German 121st Division issued a tense report that 'about two Australian divisions are to attack on either side of the Ypres–Menin Road and about one kilometre south of the Ypres–Roulers railway. The date of the attack not definitely to be ascertained, but apparently for today'.

Enemy artillery was ordered to lay down 'annihilation' fire. A wireless alert was sent to all 4th Army divisions. Starting at 4.30 heavy fire opened up from German batteries against the starting positions of I Anzac. A shower of brilliant rockets soared from the enemy lines at 5.36. It was perhaps a coincidence, but one suspects that von Armin had somehow learned the exact time of Zero Hour. Four minutes later the barrage burst in all its brutal splendour, and in the swirling fog that had followed the rain the first British riflemen, 'like spectres out of the mist', fell upon the Teutonic defenders.

11

The Menin Road

THE date seemed an important one at the time: 20 September, 1917; and the event was given a grandiloquent name: The Battle of the Menin Road; and in truth it was the first measurable, big-headline victory since Messines, three and a half months ago. And like most other calculated advances thus far in World War I, it was essentially an artillery coup. Fully 1,000 yards in depth, the great barrage screened the infantry flooding into the greasy battlefield. The air saturated with drum-fire seemed to scream in pain, the mighty drone of the big shells high above blending with the screeching trajectory of the smaller projectiles below. Thousands of shells slammed against the Ridge, which appeared to burst into flames. Cherry-red patches flickered and fused along the enemy positions from No-Man's-Land well back into the rising ground where the heavier masses of German troops lay in wait. For miles along the opposing front yellow, white, red and orange flares pierced the sky. Within minutes, a greyish pall of smoke had begun drifting over the Salient.

To German eyes the oncoming British seemed maddeningly cool. Languid, unhurried, they trudged toward the Ridge in broad, straggling lines. Ant-like, they engulfed the extreme forward posts of the enemy as they went. Here and there a flame-thrower worked over a German target in a spectacle of solitary splendour. The khaki-clad Australians appeared the most disinterested of all, the most confident. Some carried their rifles on their shoulders. With sticks in hand, officers walked about and conferred.

When the British swarmed into an isolated German shell-hole or barricaded emplacement near the jumping-off line the defenders often panicked and yelled as they tried to escape, '*Die Tommies* . . . '*raus, 'raus, die Engländer!*' Inexorably most of these suicidal advance posts, already shaken by the unparalleled cannonade, were gobbled up. As the slow sweep continued, signallers worked feverishly to run their lines through the craters and mud. Stretcher bearers began to move gravely amidst the pandemonium. The Lewis gunners slipped and fell and swore, and their heavy, clumsy weapons often became choked with mud.

Further back, dense columns of supporting battalions shoved forward. The rear zone now swarmed with troops moving up front. Teams of little donkeys hauled at the guns and wagons, their dainty hooves slipping in the slime. Uncomprehendingly they laboured in the din, ears flapping and sad of eye, and seemed to wonder (like many a soldier) what they had done to deserve their fate.

From shell-holes, and while they walked, and from the jump-off tapes where the relief units awaited the signal which would send them forward, the men watched the drum-fire, fascinated by the innumerable petals of flame that flowered against the enemy lines. Anxiously they peered, not at the immediate front positions—they knew little opposition was left in this zone—but at the terrain further back where the danger really lay. Were the howitzers and field pieces scoring there as well?

The 75s belched in a hysteria of rage. New rearward batteries, formerly hidden and silent, now came into action. When a small copse was caught in a fury of shells the trees flew uprooted through the air like a handful of feathers; in a flash the area became, as in a magician's trick, as barren as the expanse around it. The artillery officers stood near their guns pensively, smoking cigarettes, instructing their men from large unfurled maps that flapped and crinkled in the brisk morning breeze.

Black rolls of smoke, like that which rises from factory chimneys, spread majestically and rolled skyward. As the riflemen disappeared into the haze and shell-holes a certain amount of confusion developed. Officers worked ceaselessly to locate and re-form their outfits. Occasionally toy-like silhouettes of Germans were outlined against the dirty sky; then, almost at once, they too were swallowed up again by the landscape. Here and there haggard men leaned stolidly over one of their wounded or dead companions, collecting his papers and identity discs.

The attack possessed a certain ghastly beauty, especially in the virulent pill-box area of the woods to the south where the explosions, the wretchedness of the ground, the density of attacking and defending troops, the madness of it all, were accentuated to a degree rare even for the Western Front. Here the air was dense with strands of hissing steel from the machine-guns ahead. As the men groped forward many fell, touched by an unseen wand. The remainder moved on rigidly, instinctively, gripped by fear. Over their heads aeroplanes whizzed like black hornets, strafing the enemy, and in return drawing clusters of anti-aircraft shrapnel that floated feebly above the battleground.

The barrage had made possible the contemplated advance. By nine o'clock the Australians had passed through Glencorse Wood. Later they entered Polygon Wood and swept over strong-points at Carlisle Farm, Black Watch Corner and Northampton Farm. They waited and rested for two hours before proceeding to their second objective. During this strange interlude one officer sent up bundles of newspapers and cigarettes. The riflemen turned the pages and smoked, like gentlemen of leisure, while the shells roared back and forth over their heads. Then they tossed aside their cigarettes, picked up their guns, and went forward.

Many deeds were performed, all monotonously similar and astoundingly heroic . . .

Lieutenant Colvin and his platoon cleared one dug-out after another, and he alone took about fifty prisoners.

Private Inwood invaded a strong-point, killed several Germans, and captured nine.

After Lieutenant Glanville worked his way up to the entrance of a pill-box, nine Germans emerged, and in so doing were all killed by the Lieutenant's men.

Lieutenant Birks rushed a machine-gun nest single-handed and killed the entire crew with one bomb.

Corporal Egerton volunteered to neutralize a stubborn German block-house, dashed in under heavy fire, shot three Germans, and came out with twenty-nine prisoners.

When an Australian officer was shot through the head in trying to take a pill-box from behind his men swarmed forward, and though these Germans too tried to surrender, the former 'went mad', so it was told, and 'filled the place with bombs until, growing tired of the killing, they allowed a remnant—an officer and forty men—to go to the rear as prisoners'.

One section, having run into some old concrete artillery shelters, was in the process of eliminating their garrison when a German emerged with his hands up. Another, behind him, fired between his legs and wounded a sergeant. An Australian Lewis gunner yelled, 'Get out of the way, sergeant, I'll see to the bastards.' He fired bursts into the crowd until almost every German was dead or wounded.

By early morning the 'Diggers' were digging in and a 2nd Australian Division captain was reporting:

> I have just returned from a tour round the whole of our country and everything is absolutely *très bon*. 9th [Bn.] just a bit disorganized . . . but all right now. They are getting no machine-gun fire from the enemy on the very front line, and will quite easily take the two final objectives and then will have enough men there to hold all the German divisions on the whole front.

That afternoon, 20 September, 1917, the Battle of the Menin Road virtually ended. The main attack had gone practically according to plan except for a single hold-up at Tower Hamlets, a mile west of Gheluvelt. The average gain, from the Comines Canal on the south to the Ypres–Roulers rail line, was about 900 yards. Gheluvelt itself was now only a half-mile away. The gain along the Menin Road was a full mile. Gough's Fifth Army had also proceeded according to instructions except at the extreme north toward Poelcapelle and in the centre in the direction of Gravenstafel, where checks had occurred. During the fading sunlight German counter-attacks started, but nowhere were they successful.

Over 3,000 prisoners were taken. Total British casualties were 22,000. On the other hand, writes an official historian, 'the losses on the two sides were about equal, or the British loss even slightly in excess of the German'.

Who had won? The British line had been shoved forward in general half a mile, and gloomily the German official history states, 'The new English method of attack had proved its effectiveness.' Yet in Paris Lord Bertie, Ambassador to France, summed up in his diary a broader view: 'We have done a good offensive which is much appreciated. But will it lead to anything really important?'

It is a commentary on the way of thought of Haig and his officers, after three unbroken years of heartbreak, that they were electrified by the day's action and spoke as though it were the beginning of the end of the war. Knowing nothing substantial concerning enemy casualties, they jumped to remarkable conclusions and came to believe that they had slaughtered the Boches wholesale. About the disappointing bag of prisoners they said, 'We are killing the enemy, not capturing him'. (In all this one discerns the hand of General John Charteris.) Though it later developed that British losses exceeded those of the Germans, and though the average gain in ground was little more than the length from tee to green of St. Andrews' Long Hole which Sir Douglas had played so often, the Battle of the Menin Road was labelled and filed by the British high command as an outstanding victory.

But the problem was not whether it was, in fact, a decisive triumph, or a small victory, or an equal encounter, or what it really meant in terms of ultimate victory. The question at General Headquarters was merely whether this conquest, this hammer blow, could be repeated the following Wednesday—26

September—preparations for which were even now under way from St. Julien on the north to the newly occupied ground just west of the Gheluvelt ridge.

Mr. David Lloyd George could not have been less entranced. For one thing, he believed hardly a word of General Charteris' Intelligence summary concerning the alleged victory. For another, he was furious over the latest development from Italy. On the day after the fight Cadorna had dispatched a note to his Allies expressing his regret that his present offensive was to be curtailed, and that the Italian armies would have to go over to the defensive. His reason (it developed a month later that it was an ominously good one) was that he feared a heavy attack reinforced by German troops drawn down from the Eastern Front. Another reason, which he did not state, was that his own offensive was faltering. In any event, the British Prime Minister was much perturbed. Cadorna had promised continuing attacks and for weeks had been boasting about his magnificent accomplishments. The British high command also came in for its share of scorn from 10 Downing Street. Note what has now happened, Lloyd George pointed out, because of the fact that Haig and Robertson had refused to support Cadorna even with guns. Naturally the man had to stop attacking. What else could he do without mortars and heavy artillery? Everybody knew that the Italian Army was rich only in field pieces, but thus far Haig had consented to deliver the grand total of one 9·2-inch howitzer to that front.

Robertson being in London and Haig in France, the former had to take the brunt of the Prime Minister's onslaught. A couple of tempestuous days ensued during which, 'Wully' wrote to Sir Douglas on 24 September, the civilian's mind had been 'very active':

> I have had to knock out a scheme for operating in the Aden hinterland involving the employment of not less than a division. I have also had to destroy one for landing ten divisions at Alexandretta, all of which would have had to come from you. Further, I have had to fight against sending more divisions to Mesopotamia. Generally, all round, I have been quite successful, although the expenditure of

energy which ought to have been otherwise employed has been a little greater than usual. The whole Cabinet are anxious to give the Turk as hard a knock as possible this winter; they have heard that he is sick of the whole business . . .

Haig was also sick of the whole business. Would there be no end to Lloyd George's mad schemes to undermine him on the Western Front? The commander was visited by Mr. Gardiner, editor of the *Daily News*, who told him that the Prime Minister 'never reads anything or thinks seriously'. Haig listened with sour pleasure and in his diary that evening exclaimed, 'How unfortunate the country seems to be to have such an unreliable man at the head of affairs in this crisis. I thought Gardiner much above the usual newspaper man who visits France.'

For his part, Lloyd George considered it a calamity that Sir Douglas was at the head of affairs in France and Belgium. It was his dream to fire the man. But how? A frontal assault was impossible, nor was it in keeping with the Prime Minister's methods. Were Haig to be summarily dismissed, Robertson would quit in sympathy and the entire country, Parliament, even the War Cabinet would hit the ceiling. Firing Haig would also imply that the Empire was losing the war, would encourage the enemy, and was certain to strike a heavy blow at Allied morale. No, he could not remove Haig and Robertson outright. He would have to find another way. He began in September to put his mind seriously to the problem.

He visited Haig at his French château around this time and writes:

I found there an atmosphere of unmistakable exaltation. It was not put on. Haig was not an actor. He was radiant. He was quiet, there was no swagger. That was never one of his weaknesses . . . the politicians had tried to thwart his purpose. His own commanders had timidly tried to deflect him from his great achievement. He magnanimously forgave us all.

Sir Douglas and his staff told the Prime Minister of the wretched calibre of German prisoners now being taken—proof that the

enemy was scraping the bottom of his barrel. Lloyd George asked
to see some of them. The officers hesitated. Would he not prefer
to drive to Vimy Ridge for a fine view of the enemy lines?
Lloyd George replied in the negative, and since there was no
stopping him, G.H.Q. surreptitiously phoned one of the Fifth
Army corps headquarters and gave instructions to remove all
able-bodied prisoners from the compound before the Prime
Minister arrived. When he got there he was forced to agree that
'the men were a weedy lot. They were deplorably inferior to the
manly specimens I had seen in earlier stages of the War.'

Lloyd George's contempt for the military was graphically
expressed in this short trip to the Fifth Army. He did not tell
General Gough he was coming, and the latter became aware of
his distinguished visitor only by catching sight of him pass by his
window, accompanied by General Charteris. Sir Hubert was
astounded, sent an aide to find out why Lloyd George was there,
and was told that it was for the purpose of examining prisoners.
The civilian did not condescend to drop in, and the general let
him continue on his way.

The ostensible purpose of the trip was to get Haig's personal
views, which were duly delivered: 135 of the 147 German
divisions on the front were broken by their losses. The offensive
was making good progress. The British troops were 'elated and
confident'. The Germans were depressed. It was beyond question
that the attack had to be continued up to the limit, especially
since the enemy's manpower, at its present rate of annihilation,
would run out by the following spring.

'Then', in Lloyd George's words, 'came the usual stuff from
the Charteris stillroom', except that the latter placed the number
of German divisions at 179, of which 154 were classified as inferior
and getting worse. The Prime Minister considered the appraisals
of both Haig and Charteris fantastic and implied that they were
nothing but propaganda:

> G.H.Q. could not capture the Passchendaele ridge, but it was
> determined to storm Fleet Street, and here strategy and tactics were

superb. The Press correspondents at the front were completely enveloped and important publicists and newspaper proprietors in this country were overwhelmed. Lord Northcliffe had, ever since 1916, been the mere kettledrum of Sir Douglas Haig, and the mouth organ of Sir William Robertson.

But such a view contradicted what he had said earlier. Haig did sincerely believe that he was on the verge of shattering the enemy front. Immaculate in his service khaki uniform, his field-boots glistening like a mirror, gesturing stiffly with his forearm, the field-marshal tried hard to prove his point. The Prime Minister listened politely but was not convinced. He returned to London more certain than ever, as he remarked vulgarly to Robertson, that he was 'backing the wrong horse'.

Autumn arrived that week and bathed all of Western Europe in sunlight and warmth. It was proving to be one of the driest Septembers on record; but as the beautiful days crept on Haig's offensive appeared stalled no less than in August. Feverishly work continued for the attack of the 26th. The artillery made its forward moves. Sir Douglas issued his final orders for the second step of 1,200 yards up the Gheluvelt plateau, to include the capture of the entire Polygon Wood and the town of Zonnebeke.

On the 25th, behind a vicious barrage, the supposedly shattered German Wytschaete Group surprised the 33rd Division with a heavy attack between the Menin Road and the edge of Polygon Wood, drove it back, and exposed the southern flank of the Australians directly above them. Coming when it did, the enemy move was most embarrassing and threatened to dislocate Plumer's thrust intended for the following morning. While Rupprecht knew it was due, the success of his own stroke led him to believe that the British would have to hold off for a few days. He left for Munich on personal business. But immediately after the Crown Prince's departure it was learned through English prisoners that Haig was, after all, going to attack on the morning of the 26th. All German front-line divisions were placed on the alert. A special artillery concentration was organized.

The Battle of Polygon Wood took place as scheduled, after

14

a frantic last-minute patch-up job to repair the damage and timing caused by the German stroke of the preceding day. In general along the five-mile front all objectives were obtained. Most of Zonnebeke village was captured, Polygon Wood was almost completely cleared and occupied, and I Anzac and V Corps pushed forward for an average gain of 1,000 yards. British losses in infantry and artillery personnel were 17,000, very nearly the same as the German. Throughout this day and the next the enemy counter-attacked, but gained not a yard of the ground they had given up.

The two attacks of 20 and 26 September annoyed Generals Ludendorff and Rupprecht. Their losses, too, had been considerable, and it was becoming difficult to reinforce their lines through the west Belgium rail bottleneck. It was not a matter of the lack of troops—they had at least a million fighting men in or near the Salient, and there was no end to the divisions available from Hoffmann's front—but it was a problem to keep them flowing into tactical position during periods of incessant combat. On the 24th the Crown Prince had noted in his diary: 'It is to be hoped that another attack will not follow too quickly, as we have not sufficient reserves behind the front.'

Erich von Ludendorff begrudged the enemy his small gains and the fact that he had 'managed to adapt himself to our method of employing counter-attack divisions'. The trouble was that the German technique of elastic defence had the defect—more psychological than anything else—of almost automatically surrendering the thinly held advance zone. The German high command decided to make some changes. In the future they would strike back the day after a British assault, instead of throwing in their *Angriff* divisions piecemeal from the beginning. Therefore their front-line defenders were allotted more machine-gun crews, in a partial reversion to the pre-war German motto: 'One line and a strong one.' The importance of these minor alterations was not great, but they did reflect German irritation over the incessant denting of their front starting with the Messines affair sixteen weeks ago.

Yet one may wonder whether the customary pessimism of the Bavarian Crown Prince and the Quartermaster General was warranted here. It can hardly be said that the British had burst out of the Salient since 31 July. At the point of furthest advance —toward Zonnebeke—the gain was three miles. Elesewhere it was a good deal less, and in some sectors on the extreme flanks the line had hardly been carried forward at all. The Salient was now a different one, indeed a deeper one, but essentially it was still a salient transposed slightly to the north-east. What of the Ridge? In this respect, too, the Germans stood fairly well despite the violent pounding to which they had been subjected. Only the bottom third of the arc had been wrested from them, and they still held the long seven-mile sweep of elevations from Gheluvelt through Broodseinde and Passchendaele to the outskirts of Westroosebeke. 'Counting heads', they had taken a heavy toll of the British and French, though Ludendorff did not know that to date the ratio of casualties was five to three in his favour.

Many an English dream had faded since July. The Channel ports of Ostend and Zeebrugge no longer beckoned; they lay quietly in the German embrace. Near Nieuport Lord Rawlinson and his army fretted and squatted and waited for the command which they now suspected would never come. In the Thames and the waters of the North Atlantic Admiral Bacon's ships and sailors carried out other tasks and thought no more of amphibious landings. On the flanks of the Salient the cavalrymen and their steeds rested; no gap had been opened for them to pour through. Even the Ridge itself, which Sir Hubert's legions were to have overrun many weeks ago in the early stages of the campaign, still commanded most of the Allied positions lying in the shallow bowl below.

Sir Douglas was forced to concede all this. But, he asserted, the fundamental strategy was to wear the enemy down; and he claimed and perhaps believed that he was doing so. Mr. George Bernard Shaw was one of many doubters:

The war dragged on; and I sedulously assured everyone who discussed it with me that it would last thirty years; for the war of attrition, as it was called, attrited both sides impartially, the great offensives always petering out just before their consummation, and the momentary successes producing no more decisive results than the tediously protracted failures.

Such an attitude was to be expected of Mr. Shaw, that communist, but one is more surprised to find Sir William Robertson writing Haig on 27 September in much the same vein:

> My views are known to you. They have always been 'defensive' in all theatres but the West. But the difficulty is to *prove* the wisdom of this now that Russia is out. I confess I stick to it more because I see nothing better, and because my instinct prompts me to stick to it, than because of any good argument by which I can support it.

What bothered Sir William was a feeling, which he never quite crystallized into words, that the Third Battle of Ypres was only a fragment of the same old siege-war mosaic. Nothing had really changed. During the first half of 1915 the French had attacked incessantly in Champagne and Artois. Late in 1915 the British had attacked day after day at Loos, and the French had again attacked week after week at Champagne. For four months in 1916 the Allies had attacked on the Somme. In early 1917 Allenby had attacked interminably around Arras, and Nivelle on the Aisne. All these operations had cost the attackers far more than the entrenched defenders, and they all bore a disquieting resemblance to what was now going on in Flanders. No rational person—and Robertson had more than his share of brains—could fail to notice the similarity.

The high command had gradually shifted their perspective from the forest to the trees. If it cost them 20,000 men to advance 1,000 yards they consoled themselves with Intelligence estimates which proved that the enemy had lost even more. It did not seem to occur to them that General Charteris could not possibly know the enemy's casualty figures, nor that such victories were essentially Pyrrhic, nor that tales of woe from Ludendorff and captured privates did not really indicate an enemy breakdown. British prisoners also complained, and so did many a British general on occasion; but the German warlords were more sophisticated than Haig and paid them little heed. The enemy seemed more capable of facing facts. After the war Captain Liddell Hart, the military analyst, in his essay 'Two Appreciations' demonstrated incisively the difference between Haig's wishful reasoning and the cold realism of the German Supreme Command's Operations Section. G.H.Q. in France had a tendency to resent negative facts and adverse opinions. With their eyes riveted on the little Salient in Flanders they ignored the slings and arrows of outraged amateurs such as Winston Churchill, who pointed out: 'A policy of pure attrition between armies so evenly balanced cannot lead to a decision. . . . Unless this problem can be solved satisfactorily, we shall simply be wearing each other out on a gigantic scale and with fearful sacrifices without ever reaping the reward.'

And, concerning the new goddess of attrition that had sprung into being Minerva-like that September, Lloyd George had this to say:

> Our men advanced against the most terrible machine-gun fire ever directed against troops in any series of battles, and they fell by the thousands in every attack. But divisions were sent on time after time to face the same slaughter in their ranks, and they always did their intrepid best to obey the fatuous orders. When divisions were exhausted or decimated, there were plenty of others to take their places.

Haig insisted that this time the Germans really were crumbling. The operations of 20 and 26 September had turned out splendidly. Another one was set for the first week in October. Who could deny that it would be equally successful? The problem was to define the word 'success'.

The countless human moles that made up Haig's armies could hardly agree that they were winning the war. To them the passing days were a crazy-quilt of blood and thunder; 31 July, 16 August, 20 September, 26 September were not isolated battles; for between these dates local attacks occurred (or were endured) again and again. The front-line soldiers saw no victory, no end to the war. At times they were exhilarated by a tiny creep forward; a day later they sensed that peace and normal existence were as far away as ever. They understood, if the high command did not, the enduring superiority of the defence and the true meaning of the impersonal concept of attrition. They knew that only the rats grew fat on attrition; they were everywhere throughout the Salient, so glutted with the flesh and blood of soldiers that they hardly bothered to move aside—'loathsome, bloated creatures, half-blind and as big as cats'. When *The Times* reported that 'we have broken, and broken at a single blow, in the course of some three or four hours, the German system of defence', not one British or German rifleman could possibly have known that the reference was to the incident at Polygon Wood.

British morale had begun to dip, and this was reflected in the increasing number of arrests and executions for desertion. Philip Gibbs, the Press correspondent, writes:

> . . . about a young officer sentenced to death for cowardice (there were quite a number of lads like that). He was blindfolded by a gas-mask fixed on the wrong way round, and pinioned, and tied to a post. The firing-party lost their nerve and their shots were wild. The boy was only wounded, and screamed in his mask, and the A.P.M. had to shoot him twice with his revolver before he died.

And he continues to say that he encountered more and more 'deadly depression' in the ranks, among men who could see no future except more bloodshed. They feared what was to come, they cursed the luck that had brought them to Flanders while other more fortunate fellows were in Palestine, on battle cruisers in the Atlantic, at desks in London, playing at war in Greece, counting boots and cartridge cases at French ports, or a hundred other cushy places; and above all they hated the Salient with a despair reflected even in the place-names: Suicide Corner, Dead Dog Farm, Idiot Crossroads, Stinking Farm, Dead Horse Corner, Shelltrap Barn, Hellfire Crossroads, Jerk House, Vampire Point.

The scene in No-Man's-Land during these final days of September was indeed a chilling one. The one-time barns were litters of rocks and mouldering timbers. The Ridge was a faint, feature-less rise that hardly disturbed the endless expanse of rubble. Farms were deserts. Woods were empty fields marked by what seemed to be a few short poles stuck into the ground. In many places weeds tried to grow among the gravel, between the shell-craters, and around the faintly protruding concrete block-houses. But while the landscape was not a thing of beauty, it was at least dry; and from a strictly military standpoint it was capable of supporting men, horses, guns and tanks. It was the British high command's intention to capture more of this wretched lowland with Plumer's next 'bound'.

The spectre of rain pressed against the brains of the British generals and filled them with a sense of urgency. They had been abnormally lucky in September, just as they had been unlucky in August; but their luck could not hold up indefinitely. Sir Douglas Haig, however, seemed less worried than other officers about the race against time. On 28 September he conferred with Generals Gough and Plumer concerning the forthcoming operation and explained how, after the probable collapse of the enemy's resistance, the reserve formations, the tanks, and the mounted cavalry were to rush in pursuit and turn the enemy's flank. He asked Gough and Plumer by what tactical methods they intended to do this, and what their material requirements would be.

The two army commanders were rather taken aback. Gough thought that Haig's views were 'somewhat optimistic', and though he too was encouraged by recent events he doubted whether they could actually plan on pushing ahead with un-limited objectives in view.

Plumer questioned Haig's estimate that German casualties thus far had exceeded the British 'not improbably by a hundred per cent', nor did he see eye to eye with him concerning large-scale exploitation of purely siege assaults.

Both generals then responded in writing to their chief's exhortations. They rejected the idea of a break-through and suggested that, in any event, the Ridge would have to be captured first. Gough could not understand, he explained politely, how step-by-step methods which would leave the enemy's artillery intact could suddenly lead to conditions of open warfare.

On 2 October the three generals met again. Haig back-tracked slightly, but still insisted that they should be ready to plunge forward if the opportunity arose. It was decided to bring ten more divisions to the Salient front, and five new tank battalions. The attack would take place at dawn on 4 October. Gheluvelt, that exasperatingly tough nut, would be by-passed; and the main effort would be made further north by I and II Anzac Corps, their targets Broodseinde and the Gravenstafel spur respectively, both roughly a mile away. As for the Fifth Army, still further up the line, its objectives were more limited and included the ruins of Poelcapelle and certain modest heights.

While Plumer and Gough were not as sanguine as Haig, they too felt certain stirrings of hope. The last two moves had, after all, acquired the intended ground. Perhaps the next one would also do so, and perhaps—if the weather held up—more of the same kind of gains might follow. While other individuals, high and low, considered a major triumph out of the question in Belgium that autumn, most British generals thought otherwise; and the atmosphere at the highest levels of command was redolent with impending glory.

Early on 3 October Haig's weather prophet announced that rain was coming, and scarcely were the words out of his mouth when a fine drizzle began to fall. The assault brigades began their approach march, the Australians leaving Ypres through the remnants of the Menin Gate. The sun sank gloomily, for by now brisk, sporadic showers were falling and the sky was overcast with low clouds running hard to the north-east before winds of gale force.

Across the North Sea another moonlight raid had just taken place on London, causing much commotion and some damage. As usual, thousands took refuge in the tube stations—among them, the *Morning Post* reported, 'swarms of aliens' who 'push

women and children aside and generally act like brutish beasts'.
Several dozen people were killed by the bombs; in the euphemisms
of the day they were 'knocked out', or 'went out of it'.

There in that far-off land the shortage of butter was causing
much indignation. The restaurants were thronged, and endless
queues outside the music halls were the despair of nearby shop-
keepers. The cinemas rolled in customers and wealth, and servicemen on leave (reported the *Nation*) rushed after 'purchasable
satisfaction, and the Bishop of London utters his voice in vain'. A
horrid rumour spread that some kind of a khaki uniform was
being considered for all war workers, a term which by September
1917 included practically everyone.

Meanwhile Sir James Barrie's play *Dear Brutus* was playing to
enthusiastic audiences, and so was Henry Arthur Jones' new
production, *The Pacifists*, which berated all those who pursued
an ignoble peace. The sensational trial of Lieutenant Malcolm
had just ended with his acquittal for murdering Count de Borch
who, during the lieutenant's duties at the front, had tried to
seduce his wife; and the joyous echoes over the jury's decision had
not yet died down.

Alone in his quiet room at the War Office, that day in London
before the attack, Sir William Robertson scrawled out a glum
message for transmittal to Field-Marshal Haig. It was to the effect
that the War Cabinet had 'approved in principle' of the British
army taking over more front line from the French, and it meant
that the civilians had finally given up hope that the Third Battle
of Ypres would accomplish anything. 'Wully' knew what
Haig's reaction would be, especially since the latter had not even
been consulted. Now it was more important than ever for the
future of the campaign—from Sir Douglas's point of view—that
tomorrow's great battle should be a winning one, an absolutely
decisive one, unmistakable proof that he was on the right track.

12

Haig's Decision

O F the three blows delivered by the British and French starting 20 September, that of 4 October was the largest and presumed to be the most telling; and after its conclusion the air was filled with groans, both from German wounded and from the German high command. Ludendorff grumbled that 'we only came through it with enormous losses. It was evident that the idea of holding the front line more densely . . . was not the remedy.' The German official historian summarizes: 'The new battle scheme had not stood the test on the 4th October.' Prince Rupprecht's chief of staff wrote: 'Crown Prince Rupprecht found himself compelled to consider whether . . . he should not withdraw the front in Flanders so far back that the Allies would be forced to carry out an entirely new deployment of Artillery.' Another enemy monograph referred to the Battle of Broodseinde as 'The Black Day of October 4th'. Foot Guard Regiment No. 5 considered it 'the worst day yet experienced in the War'.

On the other side of the hill, British comments were joyous. In his diary Haig speaks of 'a very important success'. Even more cheery than usual, Charteris thought that the Germans had been so mangled that they possessed 'few more available reserves'. He turned to Harington and exclaimed, 'Now we have them on the run—get up the cavalry!' The Australian official historian writes: 'An overwhelming blow had been struck, and both sides knew it.' For the London Press Philip Gibbs reported, 'It had been a bad defeat for them and they did not hide their despair.' British officers claimed a record number of dead Germans littering the captured area. New Zealanders spoke of unusually heavy casualties dealt the enemy and boasted that their division alone had taken 1,159 captives. General Plumer called it 'the greatest victory since the Marne'.

All this seems to indicate a triumph beyond argument or carping, despite the deteriorating weather.

Yet an examination of the map shows, that the physical gains were even smaller than in the two previous attacks. The ex-towns of Gravenstafel and Poelcapelle were captured (the latter not entirely), the remnants of Polygon Wood were occupied, Broodseinde was taken, and so was the remaining half of Zonnebeke village. One mile in the centre was the point of furthest advance. Averaging out the gains over the entire front from Tower Hamlets to the Ypres–Staden railroad, one learns that the dividend was some 700 yards. The price of this investment was nearly 26,000 casualties, half of whom were killed or missing. And this figure does not include scattered losses suffered by the French in the north.

The Germans had been hurt no worse; and despite the complaints of their commanders that they were still finding it hard to fling reserve divisions into crucial sectors exactly when needed, their defensive wall was intact. They had, however, lost more of the Ridge, especially around Broodseinde. They had taken a terrific battering which they could ill afford, for the legions of America would soon counter-balance the Russian defection. They had given up 5,000 prisoners as compared to the British 3,000. Yet, all in all, one cannot fully accept the view of British officers who thought they had handed the enemy a crushing defeat.

A further inspection of the official map shows that along half the front of attack objectives were not quite reached. The New Zealand historian admits that Broodseinde was only a partial success, since German counter-attacks on the extreme right flank had regained most of the ground which the 5th and 21st divisions had initially won.

The Boches showed little sign of any deep-seated demoralization around mid-day, when both Plumer and Gough attempted to exploit their gains. After a few hours of trying without avail to get their attacks rolling again, both generals gave up and turned their attentions to the more negative business of merely warding off enemy counter-strokes. The victory, if one cares to interpret it as such, thus fizzled out as soon as the British tried to fan the flame.

'Long ere now it had become but too clear that the strategic aims of the Ypres offensive were incapable of realization,' writes one authority, and he blames the worsening weather and the 'brave and skilful' enemy for the meagre fruits of Haig's programme.

But had it never rained in Flanders in the autumn, and had not the Germans always been brave and skilful? The front-line soldiers muttered about the Germans' unusually powerful show of artillery. But the Royal Flying Corps, the eyes of the guns, had been grounded all day because of the high winds (a serious flying factor in those times), the rain, and the low clouds.

In his dispatch to the King, Sir Douglas, after pointing out that one of the most important segments of the Ridge had been taken, proceeds as follows:

> The year was far spent. The weather had been consistently un-propitious, and the state of the ground, in consequence of rain and shelling combined, made movement inconceivably difficult. The resultant delays had given the enemy time to bring up reinforcements and to organize his defence after each defeat. Even so, it was still the difficulty of movement far more than hostile resistance which continued to limit our progress, and now made it doubtful whether the capture of the remainder of the ridge before winter finally set in was possible.

And lamely he continues:

> On the other hand, there was no reason to anticipate an abnormally wet October.

But these words were written in retrospect. On the day of the attack he, as well as his fellow generals, was exultant. It seemed to them that they could continue their progress indefinitely.

Haig decided to move up the next attack by forty-eight hours and was annoyed when General Anthoine told him that he could only advance the schedule by one day. Always prudent, General Plumer suggested mildly that perhaps they had only encountered forward units of the enemy defence as yet; he too, however, thought affairs had gone wonderfully up to 3 p.m.; and Gough was also in favour of shoving on with all possible speed.

There was an air of suppressed excitement that afternoon at G.H.Q. Two miles on the average had been gained in two weeks. A calmer observer might have reasoned that at this rate Berlin could not be reached for nine years; but the generals were not calm. Tensely they projected their gains in ground westward towards the Channel, they told each other of the decay of enemy morale, they computed his present and eventual gigantic losses in men. They felt that if the weather held up (and what could be more sensible than always to concede the possibility that it might not?) British troops faced the possibility of a really big success.

General John J. Pershing sent Haig a message congratulating him on his gains, which 'give a striking answer to weak-kneed peace propaganda'.

From London Lord Derby wrote to him; '. . . congratulations on your great successes. You cannot imagine how it has bucked up everybody here.'

And Sir Douglas, in his grave and impassive way, was the most exhilarated of all. He could hardly wait for the next attack and, as we have seen, he had impatiently advanced the date upon which it would take place. He decided not to send Gough the Canadian Corps of some 60,000 men. They despised this officer for the way he had driven them at the Somme last year; and in any event Plumer was spear-heading the present drive and needed them more. On the afternoon of 4 October, while heavy fighting continued, hurried planning got under way for the blow scheduled at dawn, 9 October.

Colonel Repington was in France that week, and he too thought Haig's offensive might as well keep going on the same old lines, though his views were more cynical and far-reaching:

Since nations counted money no more than pebbles on a beach, and all would probably repudiate in one form or another at the end of the war, there seemed no reason for stopping, especially as so many people were growing rich by the war; the ladies liked being without their husbands, and all dreaded the settlement afterwards, industrial, political, financial and domestic.

So among everyone but spoil-sport civilians like Lloyd George and certain French officers there was a willingness to continue the big push. Perhaps Haig was right, after all. Perhaps it was natural for the generals to congratulate each other and for their staffs to work out brilliant new assaults. But only the weather refused to co-operate; and while it was true that 4 October was a turning point in the Third Battle of Ypres, it was not of the sort that the buoyant generals had in mind.

It had been drizzling and gusty all morning during the main attack, but at noon conditions took a turn for the worse. Now the wind shifted slightly to a northerly quarter and heavy showers broke. For three days it rained. On the 7th the showers changed to a heavy drenching downpour, and after a meeting Charteris suddenly made this personal note: 'Unless we get fine weather for all this month, there is no chance of clearing the coast. . . . Most of those at the conference would welcome a stop.'

The rain created extreme problems in the frontal zone. For one thing, the duckboards only reached up to the previous line. Beyond that it became almost impossible for anything or anybody to move. Carrying parties, trying to get supplies to the new forward positions by working their way through the untracked morass, were soon exhausted by their labours. The system for evacuating casualties collapsed. In captured pill-boxes the badly wounded men lay, while those less hurt crouched outside on the muddy ground, exposed to the weather and shell-fire. The majority had to be left unattended for the better part of a day. Ambulance cars kept careening off the slick tracks and over-turning into the shell craters on either side. Even the horse-drawn ambulances skidded and crashed, at least one of them with a full load of wounded troops inside.

The more it rained the more it became a puzzle how the light artillery was to be moved up. Some battalions ran completely out of duckboard planking. Soon the heavily trodden mule paths were in ruins. Water lapped at, and often covered, the duckboards; inch by inch the crests rose in the shell-holes where many thousands of riflemen held on, chilled through and utterly soaked. Far away in Paris Marshal Foch, temporarily stripped of his field command and surveying the military scene from his lofty but impotent status as chief of the French general staff, said when interviewed, '*Boche* is bad, and *Boue* is bad, but *Boche* and *Boue* together—ah!', and he raised his hands in a warning gesture.

There was much unhappiness among the tank people. They had been squandered in small packets here and there for the past two months and had accomplished precious little. Their casualties had been severe, and they were sick of being wasted under hopeless conditions. They felt that they held the key to victory on the stalemated Western Front, for there was no way around and they alone were capable of breaking through; and they insisted that their formations be employed only on dry ground at a time and place of their own choice. The revolt was accepted without much concern at G.H.Q. In relief, armoured commanders settled down to examine microscopically the British front for a sector they could later exploit; and, as we shall see, they found one.

After the battle and counter-attacks of 4 October a relative peace descended upon the Salient. The rain came and went; but mostly it stayed—hypnotically, almost caressingly murmuring as it splashed into the saturated, semi-liquid ground, tapping ceaselessly against the steel helmets of the warriors. Tea, bread and jam were served for breakfast, and further back the soup kitchens did a thriving business. As the fighting died down, salvage crews scoured the area for arms and equipment that might be used to fight another day. Redcaps directed the men to the rear along roads and trackboards that led into open fields where bivouac sheets were raised. For two days despondent stragglers kept shambling in. Each night, in silence, rum was issued and the companies settled down as best they could. And up ahead less fortunate people brooded in the flooding craters, weapons at hand, unable to sleep, almost under the muzzles of enemy machine-guns a few hundred feet away. These at the moment were the least insurable men on earth: the extreme front-line infantry soldiers of Great Britain, clinging to the outer rim of the most lethal battle zone in history. And as they did so they pondered two questions—Were the Huns coming? When would they be put back into reserve?

The meeting held at the commander-in-chief's French château on the evening of 7 October was a far cry from that glad occasion three days earlier. The heavens had thrown cold water upon the Salient and upon the spirits of two of the conferees; but the third, Sir Douglas Haig, was as grimly determined as ever to proceed with the attacks scheduled for the 9th and 12th.

He started by asking Generals Plumer and Gough to state their views. They responded flatly that the campaign should be stopped. Haig refused to do so, and one wonders why the conference was called; but since the decision made here was one of the most serious in the annals of the war it may be pertinent to consider his motives. By any normal standard, the campaigning season was over. Haig certainly knew that proper preparations, rested troops, and full artillery coverage were no longer possible. His armies were groping and floundering. With the Westroosebeke ridge now barring their way even to Passchendaele, it seemed that only two rational possibilities existed, both of which meant that the field-marshal would have to abandon his strategic plan sold to the civilians in London many weeks ago—first, to stop where they were and simply try to hang on for the winter along a very bad line; second, to retreat to a decent line. The latter was more logical, but nightmarish. Not even Gough and Plumer could face up to the prospect of writing off nearly 200,000 casualties (the total since Messines) and going back where they had started from, or even further.

Walking on tracks over the
Zonnebeke Marshes; October, 1917

A trench near Westhoek;
October 17, 1917

Bogged down; October 1917

Near Pilckem; October 10, 1917

After the Somme, Joffre had said coolly to another officer, 'I shall be sacked, you shall be sacked, we shall all be sacked.' The uproar that would take place if the British armies should retreat, as though admitting failure, was one that the generals absolutely refused to consider. Haig insisted that they at least try to capture more of the Westroosebeke–Passchendaele sector of the Ridge. If they could do so, he argued, they could then overlook the valley of the Steenbeke (for whatever value that depressing sight might be worth), and the men would be able to rest on higher, dryer ground for the winter.

And there were other reasons. One which requires no comment was that capturing the Ridge would 'tranquilise public opinion'. Then there were the French. It had been decided in London on 25 September to have Haig take over six divisions of their line. The idea was that spreading out his armies more thinly would keep him from attacking. But Haig turned the scheme upside down. If the French were so weak, he explained, that they could not even hold their assigned frontal breadth, then it was essential to keep attacking so as to save *them* from attack. It was the same tune in a different key. Furthermore, Pétain had promised to deliver a strong attack at Malmaison on the 23rd. To some this might have seemed a contradictory note, but Haig looked upon it as still another call for continuing the teamwork at his end.

Italy, too, was a factor. All signs pointed toward a combined Austro-German blow at Cadorna's front in the near future. Haig would not agree to reinforce that line. Rather, he insisted, the best means of co-operation was to keep Ludendorff busy in Flanders.

As for the weather, he had hopes that it would soon change for the better. Concerning the terrain, it was 'not yet impossible'. To delay would only give the Boches extra time to strengthen their defences. Sir Douglas had an answer for everything. The campaign would continue, and when it would end nobody could any longer guess. There were many who now considered Haig obsessed by a conviction that he could defeat the Central Powers single-handed. Memoranda summarizing his attitude, delivered

15

to Robertson and the War Cabinet next day, seem to lend some
weight to that growing contention.

He would refuse to take over more of the French line, and would
'adhere resolutely to that refusal, even to the point of answering
threats by threats if necessary'.

He claimed that the French were not capable of a serious
military effort, but appraised them as 'staunch in defence' and
'may be estimated as fully equal to an equivalent number of
German divisions'—a rather astonishing admission, for it seemed
to undermine his own basic argument for the Flanders offensive.

He asked for more drafts to replace his wastage and that the
War Cabinet should have faith in the outcome of his plan.
Neither request was granted.

He felt that Russia would stay in the war and would continue
to contribute the same number of divisions as at present. Two
months later the Russians collapsed.

He claimed that the Germans would only be able to place
179 divisions on the Western Front in 1918 as a result of their
losses in the present campaign. The number turned out to be 210
—a difference of some half a million men.

He felt that the enemy was collapsing and might soon 'gladly
accept such terms of peace as the Allies might offer'—provided,
of course, that the pressure in Belgium were kept up.

For the sake of argument he admitted that Russia might
break down, but that even so Germany could only transfer 'the
32 more efficient divisions' to the west. But Germany had
already switched to Rupprecht's front more divisions than Haig
had envisioned 'at the most'. By the following April they had,
in fact, brought down 300,000 more men than Haig had estimated.

He said nothing about a possible German offensive, even aided
by Hoffmann's divisions, which might some day counteract his
own. The following spring Ludendorff went over to the attack
and smashed through Haig's line.

He predicted that if Russia dropped out the pressure on Italy
might increase, but that the latter 'should still be able to hold her

ground unaided'. Sixteen days later the Italian army was crushed at Caporetto.

There was to come a time when Haig would throw open the door of his room of dreams and enter the grey corridor of reality; but that day was six months distant. Meanwhile the War Cabinet and even 'Wully' received his assurances uneasily. They had that tone of dull, relentless optimism which over the years they had come to associate with the man. As for Broodseinde, the civilians did not believe it was a great victory. Lloyd George sarcastically called it 'still another smashing triumph a few hundred yards ahead'. Haig had cried wolf once too often. The politicians were generally convinced that his offensive was buried in a sea of mud, nor were they impressed by *The Times*' claim that 4 October had seen 'the most important British victory of the year . . . the particular task which Sir Douglas Haig set his armies has been very nearly accomplished'. Next day *The Times* went even further. Now, in truth, 'our object is already secured'. The British armies were said to be in sight of Bruges, and the corres- pondent praises the marshal's 'calm, unhurried persistence which compels the admiration of the world. . . . With each successive stride the arrangements grow more exact, the results more certain, the losses lighter.'

And Philip Gibbs in his report the day after the battle evoked even more thrilling vistas:

> One of the prisoners, a professor . . . thinks 'it will not be long before Germany makes a great bid for peace by offering to give up Belgium. By mid-winter she will yield Alsace-Lorraine; Russia will remain as before the war, except for an autonomous Poland; Italy will have what she has captured; and Germany will get back some of her colonies.'

Marshal Henri Pétain, for one, was less sanguine and to Colonel Repington said that: 'Charteris killed off the Germans too quickly . . . he and Davidson egged on Haig to believe that he was winning the war.' And he remarked of the British generals that they were 'very tenacious of their ideas, kept a straight course, but ran in blinkers'. He held his hands up to his eyes to show Repington what he meant and added that he could not consider the Flanders attack good strategy—this despite the Frenchman's own incessant pleas to Haig to keep the campaign rolling.

Nor was Pétain alone in questioning, on the basis of original strategy, Haig's 7 October decision. For one thing, the submarine menace was subsiding. From the beginning many had derided the alleged need for recapturing the Belgian ports. Now the dispute was academic. In April one quarter of all British merchantmen leaving the United Kingdom had never come back; but the convoy system (resisted heretofore by the Admiralty and put into effect at the insistence of Winston Churchill) had started the following month and had worked wonders. The April losses of 874,576 tons were cut to 351,105 in September, only 1 per cent of which was in convoy. The sinkings were lessening month by month and would surely continue to do so. Therefore the naval significance of Zeebrugge and Ostend had become quite negligible.

Over the months, and under the wise tutelage of Henri Pétain, the French army had largely recovered its willingness at least to resist. And while it was conserving its strength it was, in 1917, inflicting nearly as many casualties as the British upon the enemy in the west.

What of the United States? Haig had not considered the entry of that country when he had first formulated his plans, but by October the new giant had been in the war for six months. Her weight would soon be felt and would make eventual victory certain. Already nearly 100,000 Yanks were in France; and this number could if necessary be increased to five million—and, behind the men, the wheels of the greatest industrial establishment in the world were revolving ever more prodigiously.

In his published papers Haig refers to America only once during the Flanders fighting; on 10 June his diary reads in part: 'There must be no thought of staying our hand until America puts an Army in the field next year.' The marshal's utter indifference to U.S. power (he was at heart militarily indifferent to all Allied nations but his own) must be rated one of the strangest phenomena of the campaign. Now, four months after the above entry, various invoices were coming due.

Haig had promised the politicians that he would close down the offensive as soon as it showed signs of foundering. It was doing so. He had sworn that the French would co-operate in strength. They were not. He had assured Lloyd George that his campaign would be predicated upon achieving decisive results before the notorious Flanders weather broke. The results to date were meagre, and the weather had broken with a vengeance. The German line showed no sign of cracking. The amphibious plan involving Rawlinson's Fourth Army and the Royal Navy had been finally and quietly shelved. The British cavalry was marking time; there was no opening for them, nor could they operate in mud. Russia's virtual collapse meant unending new reserves for employment on the Western Front. Italy needed help. The element of surprise was irretrievably gone. Haig's own generals wanted him to stop. The politicians had lost their last vestige of faith in his campaign. The morale of his own armies was sinking into the swamps of the Salient. What Haig still hoped to achieve, that day of decision in early October, and what he was trying to prove, are perhaps questions more appropriate to a psychiatrist than to the student of military science.

German diplomacy was currently in the hands of the brilliant young Baron von Kuhlmann, who as Foreign Minister had decided to make another try at a negotiated peace and in September had established contact with Great Britain through neutral offices in Madrid and Brussels. These overtures were formal and serious, and aroused much alarm among the Allies. Among other things, von Kuhlmann offered to return Alsace-Lorraine to France, to restore Serbia to her pre-war status, to make territorial concessions to Italy and colonial concessions to Britain, and to clear completely out of Belgium. Monsieur Painlevé was dismayed. If the terms were genuine, as they appeared to be, how could his nation be induced to go on fighting?

Lloyd George was uninterested in general principles. He wanted a military victory, so that peace terms could be dictated to the Central Powers rather than negotiated. For once he and Haig were in accord. The latter put his views in writing. They were to the effect that Germany would be defeated even if Russia left the war, provided that he were given all the men and munitions he needed in Flanders, and that 'accepting an unsatisfactory peace' at the moment would lead to dire consequences in the future. The ambassadors of Great Britain, France, America, Japan, Italy and Russia convened in Paris on 8 October and drafted a somewhat evasive reply to the irritating German minister which, however, indicated a willingness to discuss matters further. Unfortunately von Kuhlmann backed off from his previous pledge concerning Alsace-Lorraine, and the episode led to nothing.

The fact is that Lloyd George, despite his disappointment over Haig's military progress, was really in no great hurry. Like Pétain, he was waiting for the Americans and the tanks. Meanwhile he urged the War Cabinet on 5 October to back his request for an offensive in Palestine. That evening he sent for Sir Henry Wilson, and a discussion followed which the latter summarized in his diary:

> Lloyd George is mad to knock the Turks out during the winter . . . his difficulty being that Haig was hostile (which he thought natural) and Robertson was mulish, which he thought maddening. He wanted to know my advice. I repeated . . . that, if a really good scheme was thoroughly well worked out, we could clear the Turks out of Palestine, and very likely knock them completely out, during the mud months, without in any way interfering with Haig's operations next spring and summer . . .

> Lloyd George has no illusions about Haig's 'victory' of yesterday. At the same time I again insisted on Lloyd George giving Haig *all* the men and guns that he possessed, up to the time of the mud, to which he agreed. The fact is that Lloyd George is profoundly dissatisfied, but does not know what to do.

But 'the time of the mud' had already and quite definitely arrived, and the Prime Minister was at least clear on what not to do. He still hoped to curb Haig indirectly—by withholding drafts, by extending and thus thinning out his front, by shifting emphasis to the Holy Land and thus killing time rather than Englishmen, and by denying him the moral support of the War Cabinet. But all this was a slow process, and in the interim Haig was pushing his offensive with feverish haste. The tortoise had too much of a start and could not be caught by the hare.

And though Haig still stood fairly well in the estimate of many members of Parliament, Robertson's star had begun to decline. Unlike the former, who was literally and figuratively remote, 'Wully' was too close to the politicians for comfort. They resented his never-ending demands for more men to be sent to the charnel houses of France and Belgium, and they reacted in natural fashion to his plain contempt for politicians. They felt, in Winston Churchill's words, that Sir Douglas at least 'acted from conviction; but Sir William Robertson drifted ponderously'. Mostly he backed Haig with passion, but often and in public he questioned whether endless battering at the Ridge was truly worthwhile. The civilians had begun to wonder whether the chief of staff really knew his own mind. His egregiously poor manners did not help. And, as Haig's campaign proceeded down the muddy road to extinction, the career of Sir William followed in kind.

In Flanders prospects were a shade brighter. The rain ceased on the evening of the 7th, and a flurry of activity ensued. Plumer phoned Birdwood, commanding I Anzac Corps, and asked his opinion. Birdwood still thought the attack should be cancelled. He was overruled. Charteris was galvanized into a new fit of elation: 'With a great success tomorrow, and good weather for a few more weeks, we may still clear the coast and win the war before Christmas.' Gough rang up to say that Lieutenant-General Cavan (XIV Corps) was in favour of attacking as planned, but that Lieutenant-General Maxse (XVIII Corps) was opposed. Haig was brought a message from the Frenchman, Anthoine.

It was not enthusiastic; according to the Scot's diary that evening —'a very mean document. He is evidently keen to save himself and to place risk of failure on me. I am ready to take the responsibility and have ordered him to carry on and do his best. The French seem to have lost their chivalrous spirit, if it ever existed out of the story books!'

General 'Tim' Harington, that guiding spirit of Plumer's Second Army, held a conference with the war correspondents. His army was invincible when it came to limited, step-by-step attacks, he assured them; and tomorrow would be the same story as in the past. He said he was not concerned with certain lugubrious views emanating from the Fifth Army. His officers were determined to attack. He still hoped to fling the cavalry through the gap. The sandy crest of the Ridge, he claimed, was 'as dry as a bone'.

But this was said when it was raining again, and raining heavily. The newspapermen listened to the general with alarm; had he too lost his perspective? One of those present recorded his impressions in a despondent passage:

> I believe the official attitude is that Passchendaele Ridge is so important that tomorrow's attack is worth making whether it succeeds or fails. . . . I suspect that they are making a great, bloody experiment—a huge gamble. . . . I feel, and most of the correspondents feel . . . terribly anxious. . . . The major-generals are banking on their knowledge of German demoralization. . . . I thought the principle was to be 'hit, hit, hit, *whenever the weather is suitable*'. If so, it is thrown over at the first temptation.

It was not so much that it rained but that it seemed to rain, by a maddening coincidence, nearly every time an attack was due. If only the beautiful weather earlier that day had persisted!

13

The Slough of Despond

SOME fifteen hours before Harington's uneasy Press conference, along the disjointed line of shell-craters and shallow ditches which constituted the new British front line in Flanders, a balmy and brilliant autumn day had been born. And the sight which greeted the front-line men that sunny dawn of 8 October was impressive indeed. Thousands of shell-holes, many of which overlapped each other, were at least partly full of water and many of the smaller ones were already overflowing. The canals, the 'bekes', the intricate system of drainage ditches torn by months of shelling were everywhere spreading their waters horizontally throughout the low-lying and level plains, for the molasses-like top-soil could neither absorb it nor allow the water to sink through. All these conditions were especially prevalent in front of the Fifth Army lying to the south of Houthulst Forest, where the surface was almost pure clay at an altitude of sea-level. Looking northward from the front afforded an unusual view indeed. One observer

... through what might have been a porthole of a ship . . . saw as still a sea as any sailor gazed on . . . watched the blessed sun dawning on still another sea of mud. And that too was beautiful! Sunrise, gold and orange fading into an ultra violet that the eye could not discern, and under it mud and swamp and brimming shell-holes, all reflecting the gaudy colours of the sky . . .

That morning of the 8th a strong wind came up, and hopes lifted; but by late afternoon the rains had begun again in torrents worse than before, accompanied by an icy wind that screamed across No-Man's-Land, lashed the rain into horizontal sheets, and turned the Flanders plain into a frenzy of little waves. Field-Marshal Haig's forecasters had correctly predicted no immediate end to the storm, and by dusk it had settled down to an ordinary downpour. It was now that the assault brigades started their march to the jumping-off line.

The attack that would begin the following morning at 5.20 was to be a double blow with objectives of roughly a mile each. The major task was assigned to General Plumer's Second Army. The II Anzac Corps, composed of the 49th and 66th divisions, would advance along two parallel spurs towards the flattened village of Passchendaele. The corps commander, Lieutenant-General Sir Alexander Godley, had allotted two brigades from each division for this purpose. There was no chance of the sections offering each other flanking support, because between their respective ridges lay the valley of the Ravebeke; this was described in an Intelligence summary as 'saturated ground. Quite impassable. Should be avoided by all troops at all times.'

Below II Anzac stood I Anzac Corps, Lieutenant-General Sir William Birdwood commanding, an officer who deeply mistrusted the coming operation but because of his minor role in it had decided to say nothing of his opinions to Haig or his staff. From here the 2nd Australian Division had been designated to furnish a flank for the 66th. Operating from around Broodseinde, its advance was to be in the nature of a small, shallow smoothing out of the line. Simultaneously the 66th would advance to the first cottages of Passchendaele, about half a mile short of the ruined church. And finally the 1st Australian Division to the south would provide a tiny diversion, using less than a hundred men, of whom more will be said later.

The Fifth Army to the left under General Gough had been assigned a far more modest task from the standpoint of material gain: they were merely to proceed almost due north through Poelcapelle and stop near the outskirts of Houthulst Forest. This flat, low-lying 600 acres of broken stumps and wreckage—once a

Allied Front Line: 9 October, 1917

forest—was really a swampland now. In appearance it resembled a large junk-heap. It possessed a minimum of tactical value, and the Germans had made no serious attempt to fortify its approaches.

Two British corps would advance in that direction—one brigade each from the 11th and 48th divisions, XVIII Corps, under Lieutenant-General Sir Ivor Maxse; further north five brigades total from the 4th, 29th and Guards divisions, XIV Corps, Lieutenant-General the Earl of Cavan commanding. These units were to be assisted on their left flank by the First French Army under Anthoine.

It cannot be said that the offensive of 9 October involved any striking innovations. Rather it was in the established tradition of the Western Front: masses of artillery would pour forth a prior bombardment which would in theory stun and disorganize the front-line troops of the enemy, knock out his machine-guns, cut his wire entanglements, neutralize his opposing batteries, and (incidentally) eliminate any possibility of surprise. Afterwards the infantry would advance behind a creeping barrage and occupy the ground. As for tanks, there would be none in action this day; there was no chance at all that these feeble, primitive Mark IVs could make progress through the gluey battleground.

Provided that the shelling were heavy enough, the past history of the war had proved that methodical operations like these did work successfully, up to a point. The system had even been dignified by a little formula: average depth of advance equals width of assault divided by two $(D= W/2)$, assuming artillery of maximum density and that this intensity of fire could be maintained all along the attacking front. On 9 October that front, from the French near the forest to the Australians just south of Broodseinde, would be eight miles wide and the theoretical advance would therefore be four. Needless to say, this was neither assigned nor anticipated. However, it was hoped that a little more of the ridge could be bitten off to the south and that Poelcapelle could be wholly occupied by Gough's brigades. And then, if further advances of even a few hundred yards could be attained near the forest by Plumer and the French, all this would add up to a small achievement that might be capitalized on in drier weather for capturing the entire Passchendaele–Westroosebeke–Staden ridge.

Thus the operation that took place on 9 October was minor, routine, and conservative in its aims. About 31,000 British troops would participate in the direct attack, and 6,000 French. On the other side of No-Man's-Land the German Fourth Army lay in wait, a hundred yards away in some places (such as in the village of Poelcapelle held jointly by both sides), fully a mile away in others. As for the British front, it was nothing more than a collection of joined shell-holes. The only trenches, so to speak, were messy affairs that joined the crater-pits, and they could only be dug about two feet deep, at which point permanent underground water was reached. The biggest holes were used for battalion headquarters. Lesser holes were occupied by company headquarters. The smallest holes housed one or two forlorn men.

Let us now unravel what happened to the six attacking brigades of I and II Anzac Corps, Second Army.

The 66th (2nd East Lancashires) was an untried division that had arrived in France a few months previously. Since this was to be its first serious test it had been assigned a front along which there was no enemy barbed wire—this, at least, was the understanding of Second Army Intelligence. In view of the inexperience of the unit and the lamentable ground conditions Plumer's Chief of Staff, Harington, had suggested assembling the men about two and a half miles from the front and starting them on their march at 7 p.m. Conservatively assuming a rate of half a mile per hour they would arrive at the jumping-off tapes at midnight, and would be able to rest for five hours before zero hour. The 49th Division started from its assembly area east of Ypres at the same time. Nine thousand drenched troops began their forward march at dusk in full battle order—water bottle on the right hip, haversack moved rearward, an extra fifty-cartridge bandolier over the right shoulder and under the left arm, and a Mills bomb in each side pocket.

Grave difficulties were immediately encountered. The engineers had not been able to improve the infantry's sorry duckboard tracks beyond marking them with tapes and lamps (it had been deemed more essential to make roads for the heavy guns) and by nightfall conditions were such that the men could barely walk. The boards were now coated with slime, or submerged, or shattered every few yards. The heavy-laden troopers (60 lb. of

clothing, equipment, and weapons were carried per man) kept
slipping and colliding. Many toppled into shell-craters and had to
be hauled out by comrades extending rifle butts. And falling into
even a shallow hole was often revolting, for the water was foul
with decaying equipment, excrement, and perhaps something
dead; or its surface might be covered with old, sour mustard
gas. It was not uncommon for a man to vomit when being extri-
cated from something like this.

Worse yet, the 66th encountered unexpected swampy areas
in the direct and unavoidable line of march. Here it was necessary
to walk in liquid mud at least knee high—the kind of autumn
terrain in this area well known to Napoleon, whose remark,
'God—besides water, air, earth and fire—has created a fifth
element—mud!' was well known throughout the Salient.

Throughout that wretched evening the wind slapped the rain
against the numbed faces and hands of the wading troops. By
midnight, five hours later, only a little more than a mile had been
covered. Everyone could now see that it would be touch-and-go
whether the 5.20 attack would be mounted on time. One thing
was certain: the right-hand brigade (197th) could not possibly
make zero-hour, and staff officers were sent forward with
instructions to get all able-bodied men to the front in time and
let the stragglers jump off whenever they arrived—a remarkable
arrangement made necessary by circumstances. (As it later
happened, the bulk of the outfit arrived twenty minutes after the
attack had started, whereupon without pause the men fixed
bayonets and kept walking.) One junior officer, lurching back
along the greasy duckboards with his head bandaged, said to a
reporter:

Ah doan' know what our brigade was doin' to put us in after a
twelve hours' march—twelve hours from beginning to end. We
had no duckboards like these—we plugged through the mud. We
didn't know where the tapes were, and by the time we arrived
there our barrage had gone on half an hour. The men were so done
they could hardly stand oop an' hold a rifle. We didn't know where
our starting position was, but we went on after the barrage. I'm

sorry for the Australians, and it was our first stoont too. We're a new division, ye know.

Meanwhile the 49th (1st West Riding) Division had been encountering similar problems. Both of its brigades barely made it on time, and the men that arrived at the jumping-off tapes (the tapes themselves were studded with aluminium discs to keep them from sinking under the mud) could hardly be recognized as civilized creatures. From head to foot they were daubed with slime. Their faces were clay-white like those of corpses. Many had tied strips of sacking around their boots. In the words of one correspondent they looked 'like men who had been buried alive and dug up again'. In the inky darkness and driven rain they had been able to see scarcely a yard in front of them. Meanwhile the Germans were shelling the roads, mostly with their heavier guns, causing hundreds of casualties. Every man fell not once but a score of times en route.

'Where are you, Bill?' one soldier shouted.

'I'm bogged. For God's sake, give me a hand, old lad!' The troops splashed and slogged towards the front at an average speed of 400 yards per hour.

One man recounted: 'My pal Bert fell in deep and then sank further in. "Charlie!" he cried. Two of us, and then four, tried to drag him out, but we slipped down the bank of the crater and rolled into the slime with him. I thought we should never get out. Some men were cursing and some were laughing in a wild way, and some were near crying with the cold. But somehow we got on.'

As one company in the 49th worked its way along the track a young subaltern recognized an onlooking friend. 'Our turn now', he said without smiling. 'Bye-bye.'

Moving shells to the advanced field batteries was a difficult chore. It could only be done by mules; and they too required about eleven hours to arrive at the battery sites, except for those which slid off the planks and suffocated in the bottomless mud on both sides. In one official history there is a picture taken during the day, captioned 'Bogged', of a mule in a shell-hole. His hindquarters are deep in the mud; only his head and shoulders protrude. In utter despair his head rests in the mud, eyes half closed. Many mules had panicked, had fought merely to stand on visible portions of the planking, and could be made to move only with much coaxing and punishment. And most shells that did arrive at the batteries were covered with mud and had to be cleaned, one by one, before they could be fired.

As for the guns themselves, it is not known to this day what proportion of the Allied light batteries got into action that morning. From what ensued one might guess no more than a third of those assigned. The main trouble was that the gun roads had not been adequate. Again the mules and pack horses had scrambled aboard any part of the tracks before they were finished. And very few of the gun platforms themselves could be properly laid in position; they either sank under the mud or simply floated away on the surface water in the manner of an episode in *Alice in Wonderland*. A few of the light pieces were supported in one make-shift way or another, but most were left up to their axles in mud while their helpless crews awaited the signal to open fire. With each shell thrown, the recoil forced them deeper, often up to their muzzles. Their barrels began pointing upwards at increasing angles. Accurate aiming was impossible, and the range of many guns was so reduced that they could not reach the enemy lines. So although the heavy artillery well back was able to operate as per schedule, the preparatory 18-pounder bombardment before 5.20 was exceedingly feeble as a whole. Would this be true of the covering barrage also? That question began to loom larger as the hours passed.

To the north, XVIII Corps' two attacking brigades were also trying to get up to the front. And it was fortunate that these 4,000 men had started early the previous afternoon, for they needed fully fourteen and a half hours to arrive. In the pre-dawn morning many fell asleep during rest periods and had to be prodded awake and pushed forward by their officers.

Cavan and his XIV Corps had better luck—their terrain was

A Mark IV tank; October 12, 1917

Ypres; October 27, 1917

Polygon Wood; November 1917

Remus Wood; November 1917

not so badly torn up—and this collection of five brigades arrived at the tape-lines well in advance, as did the French to the extreme north-west of everybody.

So now by that morning in Flanders, 9 October, 1917, almost all Allied troops had in one manner or other splashed up to their assigned positions. Bayonets were fixed. Pale and silent, the infantry kneeled in their shell-holes or lay nearly prone in shallow oozing trenches awaiting the beginning of the covering barrage. There was some whispering of final arrangements. Everywhere platoon officers slithered along the tape and repeated, 'Wait for the whistle now, boys, and keep in touch.'

There were some whose nerves gave way, or who developed diarrhoea, or whose legs collapsed beneath them in fear. The advance would have to go on without such as these. They would be dealt with later. Cases involving commissioned and non-commissioned officers posed a problem of leadership. Somebody would have to lead. Hurried consultations took place, and these occasional difficulties were ironed out. In one instance (Lancashires of the 66th Division) a corporal went to pieces and an ex-corporal was ordered to command the section. He refused. A squabble developed, and the platoon officer himself had to take over.

The rain continued. And from thousands of pill-boxes and other observation posts German eyes surveyed the wasteland and the enemy front. Almost untouched by the futile bombardment, suspicious of certain signs of an impending attack, quite rested, the German Fourth Army patiently waited for what was to come.

When the barrage exploded at dawn—none too convincingly—the Second Army advanced, followed later by stragglers from the 197th Brigade. Immediately it was found that Intelligence had erred in assuming that no wire existed in front of the 66th Division. Two continuous belts of dense entanglements did in fact bar the way. The prior bombardment had been too weak to break it up, and had left enemy personnel almost untouched as well.

As the British walked forward the classic drama of the Western

16

Front was again enacted, in this instance even more graphically —the scene that will for ever haunt Western civilization—for as they did so the rain perversely stopped and in perfect visibility German machine-gunners began to play upon the advancing waves of men, their bullets lashing and spurting from the pill-boxes and from behind parapets. In the flame and clamour and greasy smoke the British slogged forward deliberately, almost unhurriedly. They moved from crater to crater, but even in the craters they were not safe, for the German gunners streamed bullets against the edges of the holes and wounded many men lying near the rims. As the British walked, some seemed to pause and bow their heads; they sank carefully to their knees; they rolled over without haste and then lay quietly in the soft, almost caressing mud. Others yelled when they were hit, and grabbed frantically at limbs or torso, and rolled and tumbled. In their fear of drowning beneath the slime they tried to grip the legs of their comrades, who struggled to break free.

The first wave almost melted away, the second one splashing forward also seemed to dissolve, the third wave melted into the chaos of the first and second, and later waves blundered into the remnants of the others. By now the remaining troops of the Second Army, exhausted and soaked, had dived panic-stricken into the shell-holes of No-Man's-Land. There they waited for instructions, or more supporting artillery, or nightfall; but as for advancing, there would be no more of that.

The stretch of uncut wire had stopped the inexperienced 66th and would have stopped anybody. Many of these newcomers to war had tried to pick their way through it. As they struggled to free themselves, German machine-guns worked them over. Their limbs jerked when the bullets smacked home. Some ripped off their clothes and when killed were almost naked, and often they were accompanied in death by friends trying to help them get loose. The great trouble was that the artillery had failed not only in its pre-dawn bombardment but in the creeping barrage that opened up at 5.20. If aircraft—eyes of the artillery—had been able to operate effectively matters would have been improved, but the

high winds, rain, and clouds had made practically all air operations
impossible. A few single-seater fighters did get under the low
ceiling to attack the German trenches and batteries, but not
enough to help appreciably.

Germans were killed by British guns that day, but due to the
pinning down of most of the Second Army at the outset it was
reported that not a single enemy soldier was found dead of shell-
fire on the battlefield: '. . . there was no curtain of fire at all,
and it was impossible to see where the edge of the barrage was
supposed to be'. The few field pieces in position to cover the
advance were worked with extra fury by gunners mostly stripped
to the waist despite the cold wind. The noisy little guns rattled
and roared without let-up. The approaches to the gun positions
were a litter of dead horses, refuse, scattered shell casings, live
ammunition, stranded wagons.

By superhuman heavings some of the bogged-down guns were
twisted around and fired from where they lay. Meanwhile efforts
were still being made to get more 18-pounders up near the front,
and sometimes it was actually possible for a failed or knocked-out
gun to be replaced. Casualties to field gunners were severe that
morning, for when the rain stopped the Germans could clearly see
the exposed British batteries in action below, and turned their
guns on them with devastating effect. And, finally, the weird
or non-existent gun platforms caused parts of the barrage to fall
short. One battalion of the 66th found itself under protracted
bombardment simultaneously from enemy and friendly artillery.
Afraid to move in any direction at all, the men huddled in craters
and waited for at least one side to leave them alone. And, as one
historian reports, 'similar occurrences were noted by other
units . . .'.

An unfortunate feature of the artillery débâcle on 9 October
was that the British high-explosive shells either failed to detonate
in the mud, or, if they did so, were smothered so deep under the
surface that their effect on the enemy was minimal. (While this
was true of German heavy artillery also, the British did need their
own big guns far more than the enemy that day.)

Yet for a few hours there had been some isolated gains. The 198th Brigade had jumped off exactly on time, its left flank on the flooded Ravebeke, its objective 700 yards short of Passchendaele. Scarcely had the men been slowed down by several water-filled, unexpected derelict trenches, when they were caught in enfilade by machine-guns working from pill-boxes a few hundred yards away. The men flopped into craters and awaited developments.

At about this time the overdue 197th troops began their attack along drier ground to the right, and made some progress up the main ridge. Around eleven o'clock one officer's patrol actually entered the outskirts of Passchendaele itself, found that section of town deserted, and after a few wary moments retired to their companies. By now, in fact, advance units of this brigade had already reached their 'red-line' objective. Then these men discovered that they possessed no support on either flank. They swung back on both sides as a precaution. Those in the centre observed the men on their right and left withdraw, assumed that for some reason the entire brigade had been ordered to retreat, and did the same. This was about 1 p.m.

Thus the one brigade which had managed to carve out a respectable gain, and more, of higher ground was now back in contact with the stationary 198th and with the 2nd Australian Division to the south-east.

What had happened to the Australians who had been assigned the simple task of merely flanking the 66th near Broodseinde? By late morning the commanding officer of the 66th, Major-General H. A. Lawrence, was complaining bitterly that the Australians had not yet appeared, as far as he or anyone could see, and he was right. The reason goes back several days. Both attack brigades of the 2nd Australians had foolishly been pressed into laying cables and plank roads during the 6th, 7th and 8th. Each evening they returned to find their crater homes full of water, and there they had slept. Their historian reports that 'under such treatment the 6th Brigade, and the 7th also, simply faded away. Hundreds were evacuated through exhaustion, hundreds more with incipient "trench feet". By 9 October the

6th Brigade was down to 600 available men, and the 7th to 800', and it was suspected that there had been a certain number of desertions.

This abbreviated division had been stopped cold by German infantry in shell-holes. Observing large enemy reinforcements moving up, the Australians read the writing on the wall and withdrew another half mile.

As for the 49th Division further north (the left unit of Plumer's army) its attempt to advance was marked by one mishap after another. First was the Ravebeke, a little canal shown on maps to be only five feet wide. Today it had spread to 150 feet, with water waist-high in the centre. One of the two brigades (except for a few men) never did get across. This left the 146th Brigade. These men crossed further north and advanced several hundred yards, whereupon they were staggered by shrapnel and heavy machine-gun fire from pill-boxes on the higher ground ahead. Messenger pigeons released to bring word back to headquarters were so terrified by the din that they fluttered about and refused to leave their bearers. Next the British encountered 100 feet of low barbed-wire entanglements which lay intact across the entire line of advance. Even each pill-box was encircled by an apron of wire. The men took pot-shots at the apertures and tried to formulate a plan of attack. Lewis guns rattled tattoos around the loopholes. Sometimes a man charged forward; in most cases he was hit long before arrival. Other bombers actually arrived at the emplacements and crouched down by the apertures. One has been described:

Suddenly his helmet seems to be knocked off by an unseen hand. We wait to see his arm swing up and deposit its messenger through the little slit; instead it sags limply while blood commences spouting from his neck. His face has disappeared, leaving him practically headless in a kneeling position, one hand resting on the concrete wall, the other hanging down still clutching the bomb—so near and yet so far.

And in some cases (though this was a particularly futile day for the 49th) an attacker did get through, and did drop his Mills bomb into the pill-box, or accepted the surrender of the inmates, or killed them one by one as they emerged with their hands up, shouting 'Kamerad!'

And finally what one reporter calls 'the main resistance' was met in the form of rifle and light machine-gun fire from hundreds of shell-holes scattered through the zone of attack. Eleven men in one platoon of Yorkshiremen were shot down by one German sniper. A special party was detached to find him, but failed. By ten in the morning an impasse had been reached; the German 16th Rhineland Division was master of the field.

Back at division headquarters Major-General Perceval paced and fretted. What was the reason for the hold-up? Reserve troops were sent forward to get the attack moving. Something resembling a traffic jam seems to have occurred on the Graven-stafel spur west of the Ravebeke, where the assault had collapsed. There was much hole-to-hole milling around, indecision, and cynical waiting, while groups of officers, N.C.O.s, messengers, and telephone men crouched in the sloppy craters and argued over what was to be done next. Some units were stubbornly ordered forward into the same trap as their predecessors, and were similarly handled by the enemy, but local officers stopped most companies from trying to advance, despite orders from higher up and further back. And as the interlude dragged on the men's water began to give out, water parties were ordered up, and there began to be much stealing of water canteens from the corpses underfoot; for war is a thirsty business even in rain and swamps. By early afternoon both brigades had returned exactly to where they had started from.

When this withdrawal of the 49th Division became apparent to the officers of the 66th on the former's right, the latter also retired slightly, so as not to protrude, and to avoid being enfiladed by the same enemy machine-guns and light field pieces which, from the north of the Ravebeke, had harassed and decimated II Anzac Corps all day long.

German counter-attacks were few and small. There was really

very little for them to counter-attack. The Second Army's original meagre objectives were in no sector reached or even approached. The 49th Division had suffered 2,585 casualties and had not advanced at all. The 66th Division had lost 3,119 men, had attained 500 yards of No-Man's-Land, but had not even dented the main enemy positions on top of the ridge. The 2nd Australians had received 1,253 casualties and had not advanced their line.

One more bit of action completes this day's story of the Second Army. It will be recalled that the 1st Australian Division on the extreme right of the line was to furnish a diversion in hopes of tricking the enemy into broadening his artillery fire somewhat away from the attacking front. To accomplish this, eighty-five men had raided Celtic Wood—an area south-east of Broodseinde alive with pill-boxes—exactly at zero hour, 5.20 a.m. What the men lacked in experience they possessed in enthusiasm. Briskly they entered the edge of the wood; at once they came under attack from the 448th German Infantry Regiment. Fourteen unwounded Australians returned. To this day nobody knows what happened to the missing men. They were never heard of again. Their names were never listed as prisoners by the Germans. The German regiment never reported the attack in its records. After the war the Graves Commission found no trace of their bodies. Australian stretcher-bearers carrying Red Cross flags who tried to enter the wood in search of survivors were themselves shot down. Thus ended the efforts of the Second Army in the fields of Flanders 9 October, 1917.

Some miles to the north-west the Fifth Army under General Gough, flanked by the French under General Anthoine (that enormous, genial Santa Claus of a man), were simultaneously carrying out their end of the day's bargain. Let us sketch briefly the fortunes of the various divisions concerned.

First in line, just above Plumer's people, stood Major-General Fanshawe's 48th (1st South Midlanders), one of the two divisions in Maxse's XVIII Corps. Opposed to this was the crack German

16th ('Iron') Division with instructions to cover and hold the Passchendaele high ground at all costs. Fresh, rested, outstanding in quality, this latter unit had advanced its machine-gunners during the night to shell-holes so close to the British jumping-off tapes that the barrage of the latter fell far behind them. When the British advanced they were, as a result, surprised almost instantly by sheets of bullets that forced them back to their starting lines. And here, for all practical purposes, was where they spent the day.

Next came the 11th Division. Exhausted by the fourteen-hour march to the front, the Yorkshiremen were only able to capture the remaining half of the long village of Poelcapelle that had formerly been in German hands. In this wreck of a town there was savage fighting, especially around the brewery held by fanatic German machine-gunners. In these operations, and to buy this one victory, Maxse's corps paid over 2,300 men.

XIV Corps under the Earl of Cavan was more fortunate. His 4th Division, attacking along an 800-yard front with one brigade, advanced precariously a quarter-mile on atrocious ground, but none the less advanced, and might have gone even further had it not been that Maxse's men on the right were unable to get past Poelcapelle. So after losing about half its men in casualties the brigade consolidated its position where it was, a little to the east of that town.

The central division of this corps was the 29th, attacking directly toward the south rim of Houthulst Forest with two brigades. Here the main worry had been the flooded Broembeke which lay astride the line of advance. However, the men, under cover of an efficient barrage, slowly waded across without using the planked bridges on hand and ready to be laid down if necessary. Then, behind a hail of machine-guns that unceasingly swept the swampland before them, the British sloshed through light opposition (the enemy made no more than token attempts to defend this . ground) and reached their 'red' objective about a mile away. It was still early in the morning. Casualties were 1,112.

Last of the participating British troops was the Guards Division. Their experience was similar to that of the adjacent 29th. Protected by an outstanding mortar barrage they too forded the Broembeke and advanced against token defences. Only the 1st Coldstream battalion on the extreme left flank was held up to any extent— this by a pill-box near Louvoir Farm. Eventually all forty of its occupants surrendered, except for one officer, whom it became necessary to bayonet. The Guards captured a mile and a half of ground in front of the forest; in so doing about one-third of its personnel were listed as killed, wounded, or missing.

And, finally, the French First Army to the left of the Guards also advanced about a mile to the edge of the forest.

By the end of the afternoon the French and the Fifth Army were occupying the bog they had captured, and were repelling without difficulty the slight counter-attacks of the enemy, who seemed to show little interest in the ground and possibly considered it more of a liability than an asset. It was in the dreary depths of blasted Houthulst Forest itself that the Germans would make their stand, as everybody well knew. It was there that pill-boxes studded the ground like hobnails on a boot, where other machine-gun emplacements had been built by hundreds, and where the enemy had stationed great masses of élite troops.

The advance of Gough's and Anthoine's troops, plus the tiny but more significant progress of Plumer's men up the Passchendaele ridge, had cost the allies over 13,000 men, of whom some 4,000 were dead. Possibly due to British artillery difficulties German casualties were unusually low that day—only about half those of their opponents. An official British historian refers years later to the battle as a 'comparative success'—for the Germans. But at the moment the latter did not entirely recognize the efficacy of their new defences (they had held forward positions lightly and forced the attackers to advance through shrapnel and harrassing fire in depth before reaching the main defence lines), and a comment added to their record complains that 'the sufferings of the troops bore no relation to the advantage gained'. One suspects that the day was no picnic for them either. Sir Douglas Haig in his Government Despatch refers to 'stiff fighting', 'unfavourable conditions' and the advance of the line by Gough and Anthoine. He has little to say concerning the virtual stalemating of Plumer's army against the ridge. And his entire diary entry for the day reads: '*Tuesday, 9 October*. A general attack was launched at 5.30 a.m. today from a point S.E. of Broodseinde on the right to St. Janshoek on the left (1 mile N.E. of Bixschoote). The results were very successful.'

In England and America the newspapers also described the attack as a victory. It is true that their correspondents (billeted in the old town of Cassel perched on a hill a few miles deep in the Salient) were in a difficult position, both for observing and reporting. Censorship was rigid. Negative attitudes were frowned upon. Military Intelligence officers headed by Brigadier-General Charteris exerted great pressure upon them. G.H.Q. resented aspersions upon its omniscience and efficiency, nor did most of these officers see any reason why the war had to be reported anyway. Measures were taken to keep the civilian writers in line. Top men like Perry Robinson of *The Times*, Philip Gibbs of the *Daily Chronicle*, Beach Thomas of the *Daily Mail*, all knew their jobs and what was happening. But the most they could do was refer to the patience and suffering of the men without implying that affairs were disgraceful or impossible. Yet behind the brave headlines these and other war reporters gave a fairly plain impression that, in the words of one officer attached to the Press corps, 'To fight the whole German army, on that narrow strip of land between the Belgian inundations (on the north) and the industrial valley of Lys (on the south) in torrents of rain, was almost hopeless.'

The *New York Times* headlines read:

BRITISH AND FRENCH SMASH THROUGH
WIDE GERMAN FRONT NORTH OF YPRES
All Haig's Objectives Gained . . .

———

Attack Launched at Dawn, with Allied Airplanes Co-operating Effectively in a Clear Sky.

And the London *Times* special correspondent at G.H.Q. reported as follows, beneath a headline referring to the joint British–French effort:

SIDE BY SIDE TO SUCCESS

. . . conditions of extraordinary difficulty and discouragement . . . seem to have made no difference. The blow has been struck as surely and with results as decisive, as any of the former blows. . . . The story is the same story I have had to tell so many times, the story of an attack pushed with perfect determination and gallantry to final and complete success. The Germans on the whole fought badly.

But in his memoirs, General Gough writes:

Still the guns churned this treacherous slime. Every day conditions grew worse. What had once been difficult now became impossible. . . . No battle in history was ever fought under such conditions. . . .

In the aftermath one correspondent wrote:

It was on the Menin Road that I first noticed the condition in which our men were coming back. A couple . . . passed us, going very slow. They were white and drawn and detached, and put one foot slowly in front of the other, as I had not seen men do since the Somme winter . . . but these men looked whiter.

There were hundreds of cases referred to, often contemptuously, as shell-shocks, which in later years would be diagnosed not wholly in terms of reaction to artillery fire but as serious neuropathic disorders resulting from a total experience beyond their capacity to assimilate. Such men, tramping stolidly back from No-Man's-Land along the ankle-deep duckboards, could not always be recognised as mental casualties unless they were crying uncontrollably, or giggling, or muttering under their breaths, or falling prone at every explosion or sharp command. Some were, in fact, outwardly quite normal. If you would ask one his name he knew it, and if you told him rations were down he might very well wander off to meet them, and if you asked him his outfit he might tell you plainly. He would know where he was

and did not seem too distressed. But he would be vaguely confused under more pointed questioning, and perhaps a little too
anxious to leave; and as for further fighting he would be plainly
far beyond that—perhaps even beyond defending himself.

In that war men in this condition were scarcely dignified by
the term casualty. Casualty meant a physical wound or a complete
emotional collapse. There was no doubt about the former when
the battle ended. They came streaming back soaked in blood and
carelessly plastered in field dressings (those who still lived, or
could walk, or were lucky enough to be picked up by stretcher-
bearers) by the thousands for the next three days. Wounded or
not, their eyes smouldered in faces that no longer seemed human.
They craved whisky—even those who had never touched it
before—as though by instinct. The bearers of British rum rations
were grabbed·as though they alone carried the flame of life, and
there was no satisfying the demand for their wares.

The stretcher-bearers first retrieved the seriously wounded
British; then the moderately wounded British; then the British
dead; then the German lightly wounded. The German seriously
wounded mostly had to be ignored, and enemy dead in No-
Man's-Land were never touched by British bearers except for
souvenirs. While on an individual basis the campaign was fought
by both armies with reasonable decency, sometimes hideously
wounded men found lying on the battleground were mercifully
shot by their opponents. In one reported instance a British officer
scouting the area came across an enemy soldier mangled but
still alive. 'Shoot him', he said unhappily to his runner, as the
German lay watching them in a stupor of agony. The runner
unslung his rifle but could not fire, nor could another soldier
in the little patrol. The officer drew his own pistol, stared in
gloom at the German writhing on the ground below; and could
do no more. Later he said savagely: 'Damn funny, wasn't it?
And we just left him there, so I suppose he'll die in the mud
tonight.'

One photograph shows six stretcher-bearers carrying one
wounded soldier back from the front. The bearers, up to mud

from one's ankles to another's hips, seem to be smiling almost apologetically. All day the walking wounded in their bandages drifted back, punctured and lacerated in the usual ways of war, trudging along the porridge-like roads in their heavy boots which resembled nothing but blobs of mud. (Some got lost at night and walked the wrong way—directly back into the wire.) At regimental-aid posts, only a few hundred feet rearward, doctors worked swiftly at routine first-aid or serious amputations required on the spot. Then the men were passed back to another dressing station, except for those still needing surgery, who were moved to a Casualty Clearing Station. At these collecting points the ambulances lined up by the hundreds like taxis at the Waldorf —waiting and loading and rattling through the area all day and night with their sodden cargoes. The men moaned or lay half-stunned during the clattery ride back to hospital, where they would variously find peace or permanent disability, or an anti-climatic death after all.

But many of the lightly wounded were more cheerful, and joked about small injuries which meant a soft life for months, perhaps a permanent assignment in 'Blighty'. Unlike these gay chaps were the majority of silent, brooding ones who sat covered with whitish clay, staring at charcoal stoves and waiting for ambulances. In some the spirit of soldiery sometimes still flickered, and at least one remarked sullenly, 'Only the mud beat us. We should have gone much further except for the mud.'

At the roadside dressing stations danger was not yet past, for still the Germans probed the roads and intersections with their long-range guns. Doctors themselves were killed there, and the wounded were sometimes wounded again, or finally finished off for good. At these collecting points around Broodseinde, Poelcapelle, along the Menin Road and beside the Ypres–Staden railway, the wounded congregated crying and moaning so that the sound rang in everyone's ears all day and destroyed many an appetite. And later in the day and evening some of the dead began to be hauled back in mummy-like blankets ready for burial. Pitifully small they seemed, hardly half the size of the cursing, burly fellows (four per corpse) that slid and stumbled down the tracks with their tolerant burdens.

In No-Man's-Land the wounded still lay in the mud. Their shouting and sobbing kept everyone's nerves on edge. Those in shell-holes generally drowned there. Slowly they slipped down the muddy banks into the water below, too weak to hold themselves up. Their feeble whispers often could not be heard by comrades passing by. As time went on No-Man's-Land thus became converted into a vast limbo of abandoned dead and dying. Each shell-hole with blood on its water usually meant another corpse entombed below.

Unfortunately the harried stretcher-bearers had encouraged the wounded to try to make their own way back. Hundreds started off, but could not keep going. Exhausted and losing blood they crawled into shell-holes, only to learn that this blunder would cost them their lives. Battlefield deaths of this kind are described by a survivor:

> . . . a khaki-clad leg, three heads in a row, the rest of the bodies submerged, giving one the idea that they had used their last ounce of strength to keep their heads above the rising water. In another miniature pond, a hand still gripping a rifle is all that is visible, while its next-door neighbour is occupied by a steel helmet and half a head, the staring eyes glaring icily at the green slime which floats on the surface almost at their level.

The drier portions of the battlefield held more orthodox collections of dead: one German was pinned to the ground by a bayonet around which his hands had stiffened as he tried to withdraw it. A corporal's trousers had been blown off and his belly ripped open up to the chest. The top of a machine-gunner's head was missing, and his shoulders and gun coated with blood. One corpse was so strangely battered that nobody could understand what had happened. Many hundreds bore tiny perforations not visible beneath their uniforms. Machine-gunners lay scarcely relaxed beside their machines—hard, grim fighting men still facing the enemy British. A few were fearfully butchered by near hits of large shells. The faces of the dead everywhere were brown and aghast, their white teeth always showing.

The action of 9 October (known as the battle of Poelcapelle, though the capture of the upper half of this town was a minor item) was over; but desultory shelling, machine-gun fire, and patrol work continued throughout the 10th and 11th. One Englishman scouting the area wrote before he died, '. . . I was lying out in No-Man's-Land. A little German dog trotted up and licked my British face. I pulled his German ears and stroked his German back. He wagged his German tail. My little friend abolished No-Man's-Land, and so in time can we.'

But at the moment it was necessary to prepare for the attack of 12 October. And as usual Sir Douglas Haig was plagued by the most abominable luck, for on Thursday night of the 11th it began to rain again after two dry days. Then the weather cleared for a few hours. But at exactly six the following morning, as the troops went over the top, showers began to fall. Soon torrents of rain were pelting the mud, the brimming craters, the planked roads, and the British infantrymen again advancing warily and half-crouched across the forward zone of the Salient.

14

Journey's End

IN London the ladies were agog, for the autumn fashion shows were the most exciting, the most fabulous, in generations. Outside the salons private motor-cars swarmed; within, closely packed throngs of women watched as gorgeously attired models toured the rooms. 'Is there a war?' inquired Lady Sarah Wilson pointedly in the *Tatler*. But it was the war which had created the craze. Middle- and lower-class women were earning more than ever before and had turned from the plain clothes of yesteryear to more thrilling modes—ninon and crêpe de chine blouses, taffeta and velveteen dresses, cobweb stockings, fancy shoes. It was regrettably true, as Colonel Repington had pointed out, that many people seemed to be enjoying the war. A new set of bureaucrats entrenched in minor power was fearful that peace might break out, and there were cries of treason when the *Nation* reported in October that five million pamphlets on peace negotiations had been dropped into letter boxes.

For millions the war was a provocative change and a huge game, as well as a source of profit—though the pound note had shrunk in value to the equivalent of ten shillings before the war. The aerial bombings went on. ('Don't you think our gun sounds jolly when fired in raids?' one woman asked a writer.) Waste-paper was diligently collected, and odd bits of wool and cotton, for they were said to be valuable in making shells. Everyone seemed to be gardening for victory: and potatoes and cabbages and peas grew where once there had been green lawns. Crystal gazers and palm readers were the rage; but the muffin man, tray on head and forlornly tinkli. g his little bell, was seen no more.

Society too was changing; the classes were at least superficially mixing. Even upper-class ladies busied themselves with war work, if only (it was whispered) to show off their clothes. So-called mixed marriages were vastly on the increase, and betrothals of young people 'above' or 'below' their station were causing much dismay among the titled stratum. It was practically bolshevism in action. Saturday-night crowds in the City were enormous; in restaurants, night clubs and theatres, earls and seamstresses, welders and landed gentry, intermingled with increasing naturalness. Perhaps the pleasures were nervous ones as 1917 waned, the laughter too brittle, wages and prices and fun equally inflated; and perhaps beneath the excitement, the self-conscious committees, the love-making, the proud headlines, the drinking, and the heavy spending there flowed a rip-tide of pain and disillusionment, anxiety and overwork.

Thus in London the days passed feverishly, and fewer and fewer could pretend to remember why the war went on. The populace worked and played blindly; and in the centre of this human beehive stood the symbolic Statesman who, as sketched by the *Nation*, directed it all:

He has a musical and sonorous voice . . . the unaggressive gesture of authority, a gaze of unquestioning but extremely well-bred confidence. . . . War and peace, kingdoms and dynasties, settlements, shrink to items in his notes. The fantastic shapes of struggling armies and the cries of dying men fade away. What remains solid, indisputable, contemporary, is that aristocratic figure, so free from any vulgarity or self-assertion, so practised, so confident, so traditional. . . . He has always stood just in that place between the Abbey and the Thames.

It was now that Siegfried Sassoon's case was angrily aired in Parliament and in the pubs, for this lieutenant, after receiving the Military Cross for gallantry, had decided that he would fight no longer: 'I believe that the war is being deliberately prolonged . . . has become a war of aggression and conquest. . . .' But *John Bull*

17

raved: 'The Huns—vicious in victory, cowards in defeat—deserve no more consideration than a mad dog or a venomous snake . . . to Hell with pacifists. . . . We're out for War—let it be War to the death!'

The internecine struggle between Easterners and Westerners reached a new pitch, the former emboldened by the bogging down of the Flanders campaign. From the War Office Robertson wrote to Haig:

> . . . I gather from Lord R. Cecil that you are perhaps a little disappointed with me in the way I have stood up for correct principles, but you must let me do my job in my own way. . . . He [Lloyd George] is out for my blood very much these days . . . intolerable conduct during the last week or two . . . he has got my Future Policy Paper and your Memo. A Cabinet is now sitting. He will be furious and probably matters will come to a head. I rather hope so. I am so sick of this d——d life.
>
> I can't help thinking he has got Painlevé and Co. here in his rushing way so as to carry me off my feet. But I have big feet!

Events moved along the road to Passchendaele. The Prime Minister told Sir William cruelly that 'the patient, after a three years' course of treatment not being yet cured, thinks it advisable to call in another couple of specialists'. At a meeting of the War Cabinet on 11 October he suggested turning to Lord French and Sir Henry Wilson for consultation at this 'turning-point of the war'. Robertson derided the medical analogy. The two new doctors were not to discuss symptoms with the old but were to stay severely apart from the latter. Furthermore, a rank layman in military medicine, Mr. David Lloyd George, would then take it upon himself to make a final diagnosis and decide what was to be prescribed. The idea was not only stupid but insulting, 'Wully' snorted. He wanted to resign, but Haig dissuaded him.

As for Sir Douglas, he had no intention of stepping down. His job was Commander-in-Chief in the West, and in his dour way he liked it. If the civilians wanted him out, they should sack him; he would never voluntarily abandon his plain duty to the King. But he was bitter, and wrote in his diary concerning Lord French,

'Never before, perhaps, has a Commander-in-Chief, who has been superseded on account of failure, been invited by his government to criticize his successor'. As for Wilson, he was a mere court jester 'busily ingratiating himself with the Prime Minister, who appreciates his vivid conversation and lively humour'.

The views of the two advisers ran along predictable lines. Haig calls French's paper 'a poor production . . . evidently the outcome of a jealous and disappointed mind'. It spent twenty out of twenty-six pages questioning Haig's strategy and recommended going on the defensive until the Americans arrived. Wilson's memorandum was similar, and like French he suggested that a supreme inter-Allied war council be put into motion to control strategy in general and, by implication, Haig and Robertson in particular.

The controversy dragged along for weeks, settling nothing, and creating even more strain between the two factions.

In Flanders the weather had improved during the 10th and 11th, worrying the troops, who were beginning to feel that they would be thrown back into heavy fighting whenever the rain ceased for an hour. Efforts were being made to clear No-Man's-Land of British wounded who had fallen during the Poelcapelle affair and still lay there famished and suffering. But a new attack was about to start almost immediately.

Those two days were cold and bleak; and as the assault brigades trudged forward they seemed, to observers, unusually depressed. When they arrived at the front the New Zealanders could see with sobering clarity great masses of unbroken wire facing them. A fine drizzle had commenced, greasing the upper inch of ground which had previously started to dry. One of this division's generals wrote in his diary: 'We all hope for the best tomorrow, but I do not feel as confident as usual. Things are being rushed too much. The weather is rotten, the roads very bad, and the objectives have not been properly bombarded. . . .'

Sir Douglas had tea at Château Loewe with General Gough,

who expressed concern whether the Second Army was not over-committing itself.

Next Haig had another irritating discussion, this time with the visiting M. Poincaré, President of France, who could only speak of the British taking over more line. Haig thought he was 'a humbug', trying to get as much as he could out of the British. He told the Frenchman that his only plan was to attack, and to keep on attacking.

On the morning of the 11th there were more dissonant developments:

Plumer, who had confidently expected to take Passchendaele next day in a brisk leap-frog operation, was told of the formidable wire entanglements facing both the New Zealand and 3rd Australian divisions. They were thirty yards in depth and could not possibly be cut by shell-fire within twenty hours.

Something simply had to be done, it was also suggested, about the hundreds of wounded men stranded in the mud between the lines, being leisurely sniped at by Germans on the slopes to the east. Could the attack really go on in spite of them? Pill-boxes up ahead were overflowing with casualties, and outside them the dead lay piled in heaps. The latter were no problem any longer, but what of the living? Sir Herbert was non-committal; he turned his face aside; the attack would go on.

Then, too, the present line, it turned out, was not at all where the generals had thought it was. After Poelcapelle it had been assumed that the 66th Division had reached the fringe of Augustus Wood. The new barrage plan had been based on that under-standing. Now, it was learned, Lawrence's people were precisely where they had started from the morning of the 9th. What now? It was decided, somewhat negligently, to work out a minor change in the rate of advance of the barrage and to make the best of it.

Next artillery officers of the New Zealand Division reported that they could not get their batteries across the Steenbeke— which was no great surprise—nor could they promise artillery support in any event, due to the instability of their gun platforms and the excessive range. The announcement was an unpleasant one. If the history of warfare on the stalemated Western Front had proved anything it was that troops attacking without surprise, and without the heaviest possible barrage, had no chance.

Haig called for Charteris, who could always be depended upon for an encouraging word; and one suspects that as usual he delivered it; but that evening the Intelligence chief had a different story for his diary:

> He was still trying to find some grounds for hope that we might still win through this year . . . but there is none. . . . Moving about close behind a battle . . . when one is all keyed up with the hope of great results, one passes without much thought all the horrible part of it. . . . But when one knows that the great purpose one has been working for has escaped, somehow one sees and thinks of nothing but the awfulness of it all. . . .

It was a remarkable and distraught admission coming from Charteris, even though made privately. But the time had come for Haig, too, to make some veiled concessions. Before a meeting of Press correspondents that afternoon at G.H.Q. he first asserted that 'we are practically through the enemy's defences' and that there were no more block-houses in his army's path—this despite the fact that they could be clearly seen by front-line soldiers— and then proceeded: 'It was simply the mud which defeated us on Tuesday. The men did splendidly to get through it as they did. But the Flanders mud, as you know, is not a new invention. It has a name in history—it has defeated other armies before this one.'

That evening Gough telephoned Plumer and asked him to postpone the attack. Sir Herbert declined to do so. It took place after the following dawn along a six-mile front and gained an average of 400 yards. For lack of a better name it was called 'The First Battle of Passchendaele', though in that direction the crater front was pushed forward only 100 yards. The New Zealanders were badly mauled. The 2nd Brigade, especially, had been trapped astride the Gravenstafel Road as they pressed on to the entanglements, under a torrent of small-arms and machine-gun fire. This wire was totally unbreached except for a single lane along the sunken road. Through it the men poured, desperate at the sight of their comrades caught and yelling on both sides; but as they shambled down the road they were cut down by concealed machine-guns, and not one escaped.

So thin had been the barrage that the men could hardly believe that this brief, almost casual shelling of the Ridge actually constituted their artillery support. After the war an official historian coldly asked whether 'any of the higher commanders [were] aware that in these operations their infantry attacked virtually without protection'. The episode had, in fact, almost crossed the line which divides war from murder. Thirteen thousand men were lost in a few hours, and the New Zealand brigadier who had been so pessimistic before the event now wrote:

> My opinion is that the senior generals who direct these operations are not conversant with the conditions, mud, cold, rain, and no shelter for the men. Finally, the Germans are not so played out as they make out. All the attacks recently lack preparation, and the whole history of the war is that when thorough preparation is not made, we fail . . . you cannot afford to take liberties with the Germans. . . .

Very few rations arrived up front that day and next. It was still raining and supply difficulties had reached the breaking point. Darkness and chaos on the duckboards forced the carrying parties to work at day—a risky procedure, in plain view of enemy field gunners. Horses and mules were in desperate shape. Exhausted and balky, they were showing signs of panic. Yukon packs were tried—a Canadian invention which had worked at the Somme—frames of wood and canvas supposed to hold over 100 lb.; but here in Flanders they failed, for the weight simply dragged the animals down into the mire. The scene along the Steenbeke was an incredible one. That stream, once only a few feet across, had overflowed to a width of 100 yards. The gentle slope leading down to it was now packed with abandoned guns and a weird collection of floating and embedded equipment. The road stopped 150 yards from the front. Supply animals had to attempt this interval in saturated clay, and few of them made it.

By now most of the wounded from 9 October were dead, but some still lingered, and a new crop had blossomed. On the 14th an informal truce took place. The Germans allowed British stretcher-bearers to clear the area in peace, and for hours they moved about the battleground bringing back those who were still alive. The enemy watched from the nearby heights and shot any man carrying a gun. An Australian officer reconnoitring the line near the Ravebeke reported:

> The slope . . . was littered with dead, both theirs and ours. I got to one pill-box to find it just a mass of dead, and so I passed on carefully to the one ahead. Here I found about fifty men alive, of the Manchesters. Never have I seen men so broken or demoralized. They were huddled up close behind the box in the last stages of exhaustion and fear. Fritz had been sniping them off all day, and had accounted for fifty-seven that day—the dead and dying lay in piles. The wounded were numerous—unattended and weak, they groaned and moaned all over the place . . . some had been there four days already. . . .

And later:

> . . . I shifted to an abandoned pill-box. There were twenty-four wounded men inside, two dead Huns on the floor and six outside, in various stages of decomposition. The stench was dreadful. . . . When day broke I looked over the position. Over forty dead lay within twenty yards of where I stood and the whole valley was full of them.

And finally:

> Anyway we are out now and I don't mind much. Only I'd like to have a talk with some war correspondents—liars they are.

Thus ended 'another fine bit of work by our gallant men'. The *Spectator* reported 'a great week for the Allies in Flanders. They have dealt two more hammer strokes.' On the morning of

15 October Haig and his staff met at Second Army headquarters in Cassel and decided to halt all further attacks pending an improvement in the weather which would, at a minimum, allow the artillery to co-operate properly. Whether this resolution, which was beginning to have a familiar and empty ring, would be adhered to remained to be seen. In a bizarre development never thoroughly understood, Lloyd George took this unfortunate occasion to send an ardently false telegram to Sir Douglas congratulating him on his achievements since 31 July. 'I am personally glad', he concluded, 'to be the means of transmitting this message to you . . . of renewing my assurance of confidence in your leadership. . . .' The field-marshal was astounded, if not convinced, and laboriously copied in his diary the entire message—the first of its type he had received from the new Prime Minister since taking command.

On the 22nd there followed a curious, half-hearted attack by the French and elements of the Fifth Army, in which almost 1,000 Allied troops were lost. A few yards were gained, some of which were retaken later in the day by enemy counter-attack. Next day the Canadians, making their first appearance in the Salient, demonstrated briefly in the direction of Passchendaele. It was their turn now. They had relieved the utterly spent II Anzac Corps five days previously; and until the end of the campaign the sputtering torch would be carried by these brawny youngsters from the farms and forests of the northlands across the sea.

Germany had made a habit of crushing one of her lesser opponents each autumn—in 1915 Serbia, in 1916 Rumania. Now it was Italy's turn. On the morning of 24 October the Austrians, reinforced by six German divisions brought down from the Russian and Flanders fronts, struck at Caporetto. Completely surprised, enfeebled by endless attacks on the Isonzo which throughout the years had accomplished nothing, the Italian army melted away in twelve hours. Winston Churchill was relaxing at his home in Kent when Lloyd George telephoned and asked that he drive at once to Walton Heath. There he was shown telegrams which cautiously indicated that the worst disaster yet to overtake the Allies was in progress. The Prime Minister was palpably shaken. The two men discussed the situation quietly and sketched out a plan of action to salvage whatever might be left of the wreckage.

Sir Douglas had claimed that Italy could hold her own unaided, had not conceded that an attack was coming, and had refused to reinforce Cadorna's front—not that it really mattered; for under the autocratic mishandling of Cadorna the Italian army had long been a shell in all but numbers. By 27 October even this vast quantity was seriously reduced. When the headlong eighty-mile rush for safety had ended 800,000 Italians were out of the war through wounds, death, capture and desertion. A defensive front was hastily rigged up behind the River Piave. Cadorna, before being sacked, sent out a melancholy cry for help.

Haig's published diaries omit any mention of Caporetto. When requested on the 27th to send two divisions to Italy he merely noted, 'If the Italian Army is demoralized we cannot spare enough troops to fight their battles for them.' The military demise of both Italy and Russia had, it seemed, less effect upon him emotionally than the loss of a mile of mud in Belgium. But others were not so ready to write off the Italian army. Sir William Robertson immediately left for talks with the Italian General Staff. Sir Henry Wilson insisted that more than two divisions be sent, and quickly. In his diary he wrote, 'We may lose this war yet if we try', and next day after a talk with Winston Churchill: 'I quoted also my example of the different strategies—ours and the Boches': 1, We take Bullecourt, they take Rumania; 2, we take Messines, they take Russia; 3, we don't take Passchendaele, they take Italy.'

The War Cabinet was alarmed at the genuine possibility that Italy might ask for peace and decided to dispatch not two but five of Haig's divisions to the River Piave. This was a blow to Sir Douglas. He rushed General Kiggell to London to protest—a poor choice, for Lloyd George despised the man—but it was a heaven-sent chance for the Prime Minister to cut Haig down to size. He would have snatched twenty divisions away if he could. Within a few weeks the 23rd, 41st, 7th, 48th and 5th divisions, in that order, had been trundled through the tunnels under the Alps and were standing beside the remnants of the Italian army on the plains north of Venice.

If nothing else, Caporetto had proved that the Allies could not go on much longer without co-ordinating their war efforts. The idea of each nation's general staff fighting its own war in something resembling jealous secrecy, telling each other what they were doing the day they did it, ignorant of each other's Intelligence data, free to formulate local strategy of any dimension without regard for the others, made no sense at all; and practically everyone but Haig and Robertson was now ready to agree that a supreme control had to be set up for 1918. No doubt Lloyd George hoped that an inter-Allied control council would also control Sir Douglas Haig—something the Prime Minister freely admitted he was unable to do. For even as the Central Powers were smashing through at Caporetto and driving the Italians southward like leaves before a winter wind, General Headquarters on the Western Front had completed plans for yet another attack in Flanders 26 October.

In wars of other days, troops attacking at daybreak knew they would win or lose by nightfall. In Flanders there was no such expectation. Each day was like the one before, and the pattern of hopeless suffering seemed to have no end. Old-timers wondered how long their luck would hold. Replacements, many of them boys in their teens who had never seen a German soldier, tried to put on a casual show; but their spirits were quickly deadened by the unnatural atmosphere in which they found themselves. Apathy and a large measure of cynicism hung heavily in the air. There had never been such a silent army. Too morose even to complain, the men masked their emotions and seemed to wait with equal indifference for death or deliverance; and their frequent sullenness chilled the new men, who had expected to be received with traditionally coarse but friendly banter. After one hour under shell-fire in a watery shell-hole or a shallow trench of pure mud, among filthy, unshaven men who resembled the living dead, each neophyte knew the Salient well, and was gripped by nameless fears.

But there was little tension left among the veterans who had been in and out of the line constantly since Messines and were fairly accustomed to the never-ending battles and cannonade. When a signaller called out, 'Raid a complete success, fifty casualties', their reply was at best, 'Success my bloody backside' —at worst, they neither reacted nor replied. Stolidly they formed up for each attack or raid, and carried it out as best men could who found it more tolerable to fight than to desert, or feign illness, or self-inflict a minor wound, or allow themselves to be slightly gassed. Casualties had become so astronomical that most old friends were gone and they fought beside strangers. Only among fresh units like the Canadians was there at least a sense of familiar unity. Yet the dogged courage of the British infantrymen persisted; a phenomenon almost beyond the understanding of neutral observers separated from the event by a long span of years. With no remaining hope for the success of the campaign, they none the less advanced on schedule and to the limit of their abilities. Long ago they had written off the glamour of war as a fairy story for the ears of children; yet in hand-to-hand encounters they fought ferociously. By and large what gains they carved out they held, as though the gains were precious; by and large they faced death obstinately, if not cheerily. Sir Douglas Haig was to a degree fortunate in possessing this army; and one is entitled to doubt whether any other would have demonstrated such dour bravery in the fields of Flanders that appalling year.

Mustard gas thrown nightly into the back areas and the valley of the Steenbeke had, in the words of Lord Birdwood 'virtually finished off the Australian attempts on Passchendaele Ridge'. Casualties from trench-foot were rising alarmingly, and while the ailment was no joke it was welcomed by many as a way out. Dysentery was commonplace. Almost everyone was sniffling and sneezing; colds and influenza were practically endemic and were accentuated by respiratory irritations caused by gas, which had settled everywhere in the shallow basin of the Salient and had affected every trooper to some degree.

Half the terrain was so flooded that it resembled a natural lake. By late October this water had become icy cold. While it was only a few inches deep it was impossible to traverse, for nobody knew when he would step into a submerged shell-hole. On the broad surface of these pools floated the débris and filth of the battlefield. Calling for the Royal Navy to come and take up the fight had become a standard quip.

In most sections of No-Man's-Land, where wooden tracks did not exist, even the strongest men could barely move. During raids and larger attacks they were easily picked off by snipers. Bogged down, they could not out-manœuvre the pill-boxes. Gough wrote that 'the state of the ground had been frightful since the 1st of August, but by now it was getting absolutely impossible'. Shells exploded three feet below the surface of the mud. Instead of steel splinters, only clay and water whipped through the air, and to kill a German or knock out a machine-gun an almost direct hit was needed.

The demoralization and growing callousness of the men were reflected in their treatment of the dead. After each attack the souvenir hunters got to work. Gradually the corpses were picked over, the whites of their pockets turned out, their tunics and shirts undone. Revolvers were the best prizes; but money, watches, rings and the crosses of Catholics were also in demand. An artilleryman examining German corpses for revolvers was observed (by a writer at the front) giving one a vicious kick and snarling, 'The dirty barsted, somebody's bin 'ere before me.' Front-line soldiers were quickest in the pursuit of loot; artillery and labour troops slower and more methodical. Letters and photos were ignored; these fluttered limply in the mud or floated away on the water.

By that week there were some British shell-holes on the western slopes of the Ridge. Though dangerously exposed, they were not entirely flooded, and by the pathetic standards of the time and place were considered fairly habitable. The men who huddled there, and some who attacked, kept their rifles and Lewis guns wrapped in cloth; and many a soldier too late in unwrapping his weapon paid a severe penalty.

It was that week in mid-October that the *Spectator* performed another of its many services to morale by reprinting the poem 'Christ in Flanders' in leaflet form and offering to send out copies post free at a price of 1s. per hundred.

Sir Douglas Haig decided that the campaign had proceeded almost far enough for the time being, though he still hoped to capture Passchendaele and the Westroosebeke ridge. In the letters, diaries and communiqués of the German defenders, written as October slipped by and winter approached (when not even Haig could dream of attacking), one senses a new confidence and calmness. A Bavarian officer wrote typically that 'although the battle rages constantly in incomprehensible confusion round Poelcapelle and Passchendaele, there is nothing frightening about that. We have been fighting the last summer flies, which attack one so unkindly, almost as much as the English. The morale of the men appears to be excellent. . . .' And General Sixt von Armin had this to say when interviewed by a representative of *Korrespondenz Norden* on the 24th:

> They occupy the southern part of the heights which encircle Ypres, while we are in possession of the northern part . . . a dozen kilometres from the acknowledged goal of the English—namely Ostend, Ghent, and Zeebrugge—without the possession of which the battles of Flanders, in spite of their partial successes, remain bloody defeats for the English. Thanks to the tenacious bravery of the English, they have succeeded in pressing us back further in the Ypres bend, and have driven a wedge in the centre of that bend, but that is all. There is no danger in this because, so long as the enemy continues his pressure at this point, he is exposed to our flanking fire and to the danger of being threatened from all sides in the rear, and he would be brought into the same sort of position that we were in when holding the Wytschaete bend.

Lloyd George could not have put it better.

The 25th of October had been a beautiful day, but at midnight a continuous rain began to fall. At 2.30 in the morning General Gough phoned 'Tim' Harington to ask Plumer to stop the attack. At that moment Sir Herbert walked into Harington's smoky little room, packed with corps commanders and members of their staffs. He waited until Harington put the telephone down, listened to the message, and then turned to each general for his opinion. Morland and Currie, of X Corps and the Canadian Corps respectively, stated that in their opinion three hours was not enough time to get cancellation orders through. Plumer picked up the telephone and put through a call. 'Is that you, Gough?' he shouted.

The reply came almost inaudibly over the crackling wire. 'Yes, this is Gough.'

'The attack must go on. I am responsible, not you. Good night and good luck.'

It began at 5.40, and by nightfall the Canadian Corps had won 500 yards. X Corps gained nothing. Two French divisions moved about a tenth of a mile closer to Houthulst Forest. In the Fifth Army, XIV Corps got nowhere; and as for XVIII Corps the official history says, 'Here, too, the mud, knee-deep, checked progress to a crawl of rather less than a yard a minute.' The barrage was lost, rifles became quickly clogged, and the men fell back, if they could, to the starting line, or were cut off. In this caricature of a military engagement 12,000 British and French were lost.

Though Haig confessed in a dispatch to the King that 'the persistent continuation of wet weather had left no further room for hope . . .' he continued mysteriously that 'in view of other projects which I had in view it was desirable to maintain the pressure on the Flanders front for a few weeks longer'. He intended to halt only for the winter and to pick up the offensive again next spring, and said so quite frankly to Colonel Repington, who was touring the front. The sense of his divine mission continued to envelop the commander-in-chief. Conceding momentary set-backs, he knew that in the long run God was with him. With the sure instinct of a sleep-walker (to use the later phrase of a German of note) he ignored circumstances and advice which would have given pause to another man. His cause was just, his plan the only one which led to victory. He pitied those who were less inspired, for he was God's middleman and it was his task alone to enact the plain will of the Maker. He beseeched Robertson to temper certain frank statements rendered to the Press by the War Office: 'They do, I feel sure, much harm, and may cause many in authority to take a pessimistic outlook, when a contrary view, based on equally good information, would go far to help the nation on to victory.'

Perhaps General Charteris was somewhat cleverer than his chief, but he was more disliked, and the despair of all who tried to impress upon him the misery and futility of the waning campaign. His habit of remarking absently that war was an ugly thing—whatever the plea or complaint—was infuriating to those who had to deal with him. Even Plumer was reported (by the ubiquitous Repington) 'rather sarcastic about Charteris' optimism', and as for the disillusioned General Gough he had made it a point not to talk to the man at all, if he could help it.

The outlook of General Davidson, Chief of Operations, during these hard times continued to be a replica of Haig's, except that he favoured more deliberate methods.

Rounding out the foursome of inspired gentlemen who currently directed the British Expeditionary Force in France and Belgium, was Haig's Chief of Staff, General Kiggell, whose attitude had just been recapitulated in a luncheon talk with Colonel Repington. The Huns must stand in Flanders, he had said; 'therefore' the British would beat them there. He was not in favour of taking over one yard of front from the French. It would be 'fatal' to abandon Haig's plan. This winter they would capture the rest of the Ridge, next April the Channel ports and the rest of the Belgian coastline. The campaign would take two months at the most and would, for all practical purposes, end the war. The Germans were already so weakened that they might give way at any moment. All he needed was half a million more men.

Repington was startled, could not agree with these impetuous conclusions, and told Kiggell so. Another who hitherto had been unswerving in his support of the campaign was the Jewish general, Sir John Monash, commanding the 3rd Australians, but by October even he had become distressed over the conduct of affairs, and wrote his wife, 'It is bad to cultivate the habit of criticism of higher authority, and, therefore, I do so now with some hesitation. . . . Our men are being put into the hottest fighting and are being sacrificed in hare-brained ventures, like Bullecourt and Passchendaele, and there is no one in the War Cabinet to lift a voice in protest.'

After the loss of Broodseinde, Crown Prince Rupprecht had decided to revert to the earlier technique of holding his front almost exclusively by machine-gunners—a handpicked collection of hard, murderous veterans—with the bulk of his infantry further back in position to counter-attack. The policy had largely accounted for British defeats during the balance of October, and would continue to prove its worth. The Germans had learned that a new attack was coming on the 30th, and five minutes before zero hour their own bombardment fell heavily upon the narrow Canadian front athwart the Ravebeke. The weather had been cold but dry for three days, and, for a change, rain was not falling when the 3rd and 4th Canadians jumped off, supported on their left by XVIII Corps under Sir Ivor Maxse. It was 5.50 a.m. and pitch dark. Rain had been forecast, and torrents began to fall before noon. Again pill-boxes held up the advance. By afternoon many of those furthest forward were still holding out, spitting flame, surrounded by piles of dead Canadians. But the slow advance continued, and gradually some dominion troops moving north-east found themselves on sandier, drier soil. They were now 500 yards from the centre of Passchendaele. Further attempts to push on were thwarted by a series of enemy counter-attacks. On the left flank, XVIII Corps suffered severe casualties and was unable to make headway. Knee-deep in mud, splashing and struggling in the ponds of various streams, they tried all morning to penetrate the enemy zone near Lekkerboterbeke, but could not follow their barrage and were cut down by German guns operating from high ground near Westroosebeke. At dusk, it was still pouring. It was of this period that Ludendorff later wrote in a famous passage:

> The horror of the shell-hole area of Verdun was surpassed. It was no longer life at all. It was mere unspeakable suffering. And through this world of mud the attackers dragged themselves, slowly but steadily, and in dense masses. Caught in the advance zone of our hail of fire they often collapsed, and the lonely man in the shell-hole breathed again. Rifle and machine-gun jammed with the mud. Man fought against man and only too often the mass was successful. . . . The enemy charged like a wild bull against the iron wall. . . . He dented it in many places, and it seemed as if he must knock it down. But it held, although a faint tremor ran through its foundations.

From far-away Russia Major-General Max Hoffmann noted approvingly: 'There is heavy fighting in the west, the English mean to win a victory at all costs; which is a good sign.' And at 10 Downing Street Lloyd George's mood turned even more wrathful. In meetings of the War Cabinet he paced the floor and startled his listeners with violent comments concerning Sir Douglas. It was easy for Haig and his staff to continue attacking, he exclaimed; *they* did not have to fight; and in his memoirs he writes of 'the pencil which marched with ease across swamps and marked lines of triumphant progress without the loss of a single point. As for the mud, it never incommoded the movements of this irresistible pencil.'

He received Charteris, who 'treated me as a stupid civilian who knew nothing of war'. He spoke of the casualties and was told that 'you could not expect to make war without death and wounds'. He alluded to the weather and the resultant terrain, and Charteris replied, 'Battles could not be stopped like tennis matches for a shower.'

The views of the French had turned sardonic. From the beginning neither Foch nor Pétain had expected the campaign to

18

succeed—they always would have been satisfied with limited, inexpensive demonstrations and with the British taking over more of their line—and by now they were expressing themselves quite derisively. Lord Rawlinson, wild for something to do, had been sent to Pétain to discuss various matters; in a letter to a friend he quoted the Frenchman as saying that 'once the Boche has been given time to bring up reinforcements, the moment has arrived to stop and try elsewhere'. Since this point had been reached months ago, Rawlinson had to agree that the Flanders scheme was in a bad way.

Many newspapers had begun to turn against Haig and the General Staff. The *Manchester Guardian* and the *Evening Standard* were especially critical, though David Davies had started it two weeks previously in *The Times*. Haig and Robertson were sure that the Prime Minister was the instigator. Colonel Repington agreed that the attacks were ignorant and unjust, 'display a common origin', and were a despicable attempt on the part of the politicians to turn public opinion against the top Westerners.

Early in November plans for a Supreme War Council finally crystallized. France, England and Italy agreed to subordinate their war effort to the Council (Foch was appointed Allied Commander-in-Chief the following spring), by each nation sending to Versailles a Military Member. In turn, these gentlemen would then constitute a group empowered to make and change plans without referring to the respective chiefs of staff. 'Wully' walked out on the meeting at which this was decided. 'I wash my hands of this present business', he grunted, and asked to be summoned when something new was ready for discussion.

Haig hated the decision too, but his reaction was more subtle. By what channel, he asked mildly, was he to receive his orders? And this new Allied Central Reserve. Where would it come from? Where would it exist? Surely its components would not be controlled by an external agency. Was such a concept possible, or even legal? There was no question in the minds of the field-marshal and the C.I.G.S. that the Supreme War Council would drastically downgrade them to foreigners and civilians. Of course it was too late to affect the Flanders campaign, but by next year (and with the Americans added to it) it was bound to clip their wings.

They were especially annoyed, for Wilson, of all people, was to be the British Military Member. 'The whole future of the war rests on your shoulders,' Lloyd George told him. 'You must get us out of the awful rut we are in.' General Kiggell, that luckless emissary, arrived and pleaded for another eight days of fighting in Flanders to make Haig secure for the winter. He also hinted darkly at another secret operation Haig had in mind 'which promised satisfactory results provided no more troops were sent to Italy'. But at 10 Downing Street the stock of Haig's staff had fallen very low indeed, and Kiggell was treated with indifference.

On Sunday, 4 November, Haig himself travelled to Paris and spoke to the Prime Minister in his room at the Hôtel Crillon. It was the civilian's turn to be incensed at attacks against him in the *Morning Post*, *Spectator*, *Nation*, and *Globe*. He felt that the military brass were the instigators, and in particular complained of Mr. Spender of the *Westminster Gazette*, who had returned from Haig's headquarters with an article to the effect that the field-marshal was upset over Lloyd George's interfering tactics. The general and the civilian exchanged a few sharp words. In his diary that evening, in his usual neat small handwriting where never a word was added or scratched out, Sir Douglas wrote:

I thought L.G. is like our German enemy who, whenever he proposes to do something extra frightful, first of all complains that the British or French have committed the enormity which he is meditating. L.G. is feeling that his position as P.M. is shaky and means to try and vindicate his conduct of the war in the eyes of the public and try and put the people against the soldiers. In fact, to pose as the saviour of his country, who has been hampered by bad advice given by the General Staff!

At 12 o'clock he asked me to go out for a walk, and I went with him up the Champs Elysees to the Arc de Triomphe. Quite a pleasant little man when one had him alone, but I should think most unreliable.

That week Ramsay MacDonald moved again for a peace by
negotiation. He was supported by only twenty-one Members.
The man was almost a lunatic, it was felt. Feared and hated, he
was held at arm's length even by his own Labour Party colleagues.

On 6 November, as if in reply, the final attack on Passchendaele
took place. By 7.10 a.m. the 6th Brigade (Brigadier-General H. D.
B. Ketchen) of the 2nd Canadian Division (Major-General H. E.
Burstall) was in and around the town and the members thereof
were bayoneting German diehards along the main street. Thus
(in a typical cold rain) fell Passchendaele, or Passion Dale, or
Easter Valley, as it was sometimes called by the English after the
event. And of this final 500-yard lunge the Canadian official
historian found a new way to associate God with war:

> It is not too much to compare the Canadian troops struggling
> forward, the pangs of hell racking their bodies, up the Ridge, their
> dying eyes set upon the summit, with a Man who once crept up
> another hill, with agony in soul and body, to redeem the world and
> give Passchendaele its glorious name.

It had once been an archaic little cross-roads village, like so
many others in Belgium or Sussex or Vermont: a few dozen
cottages and shops clustered along the main road that straggled
north to Westroosebeke. Years ago another narrow country
road had intersected it. At the north-east corner a simple church
had stood, built of white stone and reddish brick. For three years
British soldiers had watched Passchendaele gradually vanish
under shell-fire. In time nothing stood but the church, and this
too was half ruined when the Third Battle of Ypres began. Now
Passchendaele was shelled anew, and as time passed, and as the
British army inched sluggishly up the slopes of the Ridge, it was
shelled with increasing ferocity. Soon the only distinguishable
ruins became blurred; but the soldiers staring upward through the
drizzle and mist could still identify a vague scribble of stones
several feet high. This they continued to call the church.

The Canadians, smoking cigarettes and trailing their rifles as they walked over the site, could hardly grasp that it had once been a town. The cobblestone and dirt roads had disappeared, and in their place was a muddy maze of German army trails. Not one building remained, other than the feeble remnant of the church. Not one brick stood on another. Sand and mud had drifted over the remains. In a later war atomic bombs wrecked two Japanese cities; but Passchendaele was effaced from the earth. An aerial photograph shows not a ruined town but only pill-boxes and shell-holes, the latter in such numbers that (from the airman's altitude) it is hard to discern any bit of ground which is not part of a crater.

From the ex-village, fifty feet above the Flanders plain, the Canadians looked down dully at thousands of ant-like men on both sides—British troops below the western slope near Gravenstafel, Germans in the lowland near Moorslede to the east—and watched the flash and smoke of field guns still pounding the Ridge and both fronts, as daylight dimmed.

The following day Lieutenant-General Sir Launcelot Kiggell paid his first visit to the fighting zone. As his staff car lurched through the swampland and neared the battleground he became more and more agitated. Finally he burst into tears and muttered, 'Good God, did we really send men to fight in that?'

The man beside him, who had been through the campaign, replied tonelessly, 'It's worse further on up.'

War and Peace

THE situation that now existed was not a comfortable one. Haig had correctly stressed that a good winter line would have to include possession of the high ground running north to Westroosebeke; since this had not proved possible, the capture of Passchendaele had only created a worse salient, a sore little semi-circular thumb a mile and a half across the base and about the same distance to the apex. So it was a miniature Ypres projection into which the entire Canadian Corps was now jammed, facing the prospect of spending several months under German guns ranging an arc of 180 degrees from Goudberg Copse to Moorslede.

G.H.Q. recognized that the position would be vulnerable in the event of a strong enemy attack, and that it was more exposed than the original Salient had been; and, even as the newspapers were exulting in the capture of the town, staff-officers were considering the likelihood of abandoning it. Instead, the field-marshal, still probing almost instinctively toward Westroosebeke, called for another attack. In a rainstorm, the 1st Canadian Division lunged northwards another 500 yards on the 10th. This gain made matters worse, for the new tongue of ground jutted out even more awkwardly and now could be fired into not only from three sides but slightly from the rear as well. A few more costly minor actions took place the following week, and on 20 November Haig decided to close down the Flanders campaign. 'It had served its purpose.'

One final episode concluded the British operations on the

Western Front—a most significant one, for it proved after all that
Haig held a trump card irrelevant of head-on assaults and attrition.
It will be recalled that the Tank Corps people had been searching
for a likely place in which to prove themselves, and this they had
found at Cambrai, some forty miles to the south-east. Here the
terrain was relatively dry, had not been torn up by shell-fire, and

The Passchendaele Salient: 11 November, 1917

presented an ideal downslope. Sir Julian Byng, commanding the
Third Army, risked his professional career and (against Haig's
judgment) authorized a mass tank attack without the firing of a
single preparatory artillery shell. Out of the morning mists on
20 November, 381 tanks lumbered without warning against the
Hindenburg Line and cracked it open like an egg-shell. In one
day an average gain of four miles was registered (not much less
than the entire Ypres campaign over a period of four months),

10,000 prisoners and 200 guns captured, all this against the loss of 1,500 British troops. It was one of the most startling and one-sided successes of the war, but since the Flanders fighting had depleted Haig's reserves, Byng had none with which to exploit it, other than a few cavalry battalions, notoriously helpless against machine-guns and snipers. The attack petered out quickly. On 30 November the Germans counter-attacked in strength, won back most of their previous loss in ground, and recaptured the same number of men and guns which had been wrested from them ten days earlier. The score was even. The momentary thrill of an outstanding victory had led to an even greater reaction, and the military year closed in despondency, while an official court of inquiry delved bitterly into the reasons for this final and most embarrassing débâcle.

It is now time to summarize the British effort in France and Flanders during 1917.

The purely tactical situation is readily evaluated by quoting G.H.Q.'s special instructions for dealing with the Passchendaele sector and the new bulge created after Cambrai, dated 13 December, and withheld from the War Cabinet:

> These salients are unsuitable to fight a decisive battle in. It is, however, desirable to retain possession of them if they are not attacked in great force; and in the event of attack in great force to use them to wear out and break up the enemy's advancing troops as much as possible before these can reach our battle zone of defence, which will be sited approximately as a chord across the base of each salient.

And, in the event, the Passchendaele salient did furnish target practice for German guns for the rest of the winter, and the men in it suffered heavy losses for no advantage.

There has never been any argument about the worthlessness of the few miles of muddy ground captured. Nine thousand yards was the largest gain. The average was about four miles of terrain which was to have been occupied three or four days after the main attack started on 31 July. The Channel ports were out of sight and out of mind. Less than half the Ridge was in British hands—not even enough to make Passchendaele heights defensible, and this by Haig's own admission. The northern end of the Messines–Passchendaele ridge, eastern wall of the Ypres bastion, was still in German hands. The line of the Yser, flooded from Ypres to Nieuport, had been captured, but by the enemy, and if there had ever been any possibility of a turning movement it had ended long ago.

The Western Front

Excluding the dubious achievement at Passchendaele, we find no gains of value on the flanks. To the south there had been small and meaningless advances around Gheluvelt. On the north, most divisions wound up crouching and drenched in or near the icy mud of Houthulst Forest, shelled night and day throughout 600 acres of broken tree stumps, wreckage and swamps—'the acme of hideousness, a Calvary of misery'.

Since the campaign had degenerated into a swamp battle, '... nothing can be said', in the words of the tank expert on the War Committee, 'in defence of the fatuous employment of

machines, weighing over thirty tons, in the liquid mud. . . .'
And Baker-Carr, sharp-tongued to the end, remarked that 'the
tanks had failed in common with all other arms. . . . The cavalry
did not even have the melancholy satisfaction of failing.'

As the summer and autumn dragged on, Haig, as we have seen,
turned more and more to the concept of attrition and the need for
shielding the French army as justifications for his campaign. There
is nothing that can be said conclusively about the latter argument.
Demoralization cannot be weighed, measured or counted. The
anti-Haig faction claims that the French were at least capable of
self-defence a month or two after the Nivelle fiasco and that they
were virtually back to normal military morale by October.
Major-General J. F. C. Fuller in his *Military History of the Western
World* dismisses the entire campaign in one paragraph which
ends: 'To persist after the close of August in this tactically impossible battle was an inexcusable piece of pigheadedness on the part
of Haig, because on the 20th of that month the French had recovered sufficiently to mount an attack at Verdun, which was
continued until 15 September with the usual heavy losses.' And
the French had also fought normally at Malmaison in October
and at the northern end of the Flanders line under General
Anthoine for four solid months. Winston Churchill considered
Haig's argument mythical: 'The French Army was no doubt
saving its strength as much as possible, but the casualty tables
show that during 1917 they inflicted nearly as many losses on
the Germans as did our own troops.'

On the other hand, there are those who feel that the Flanders
campaign saved France. General Davidson, of Haig's staff, flatly
says that if and when the Germans had learned fully of the French
weakness they would have immediately attacked and would have
had 'no difficulty in destroying their army and compelling its
surrender'. The Australian historian, Bean, is more moderate, but
on this issue (if on few others) takes Haig's side:

> It is not sufficient to show that French resentment at British inaction
> *might* not have had fatal consequences, or that the Germans *might* not

have attacked the French Army, or that, if relieved by the British on part of its front, that army *might* have shattered a German offensive. The situation was such that Great Britain could not afford to take a risk.

Haig himself, in a later letter to Charteris, stated his case bluntly: '... the possibility of the French army breaking up in 1917 *compelled me to go on attacking* ... on account of the *awful* state of the French troops!' And still later he maintained that he had fearfully kept many facts about the French decay even from Charteris.

Today the consensus is that the French argument was an afterthought with Haig, that his plan to attack in the Salient was complete long before Nivelle's episode, and that his insistence on continuing the campaign after its initial bogging down was based, at the time, almost entirely upon the theme of attrition.

Since the debate is endless and by its nature cannot lead to a conclusion, let us turn to the repellent but more tangible process of 'counting heads'. At once a curious problem arises, for it turns out that there are two sets of figures.

In March 1922 the British War Office published its *Statistics of the Military Effort of the British Empire during the Great War*. Released as soon as possible after the event, it flatly lists British casualties between July and December 1917 (the Flanders campaign and Cambrai) at 448,614. This does not include French losses on the north flank, which may be conservatively reckoned at 50,000 for the same period. Thus the total Allied loss comes to half a million. The Flanders campaign was normal for the Western Front, in which the proportion of dead to other casualties almost always ran about 30 per cent; therefore, 150,000 approximately were killed.

In the same report German casualties are listed as 270,710.

The figures are not questioned by the Australian official historian, who remarks that 'the balance of loss was still strongly against the British', though not as badly as at the Somme in 1916, where British casualties were 481,842 against the German

236,194. In other words, the proportion against the attacker had been greater than two to one at the Somme, and only 1.6 to one in the 1917 campaign. The writer then suggests that both sides were in error; cautiously re-figuring the losses, he allocates 52,000 more to the British than to the enemy. Haig, of course, thought it was the other way around; and in all these figures French losses are disregarded. In any event, the arithmetic is in line with experiences on the Western Front throughout the war: the attacker suffers more than the attacked. There seems no reason why the ratio that held good at the Somme should not roughly apply to Flanders. Both campaigns were similar. They were fought approximately the same length of time. The terrain was similar—though the mud was worse in Flanders and hampered the attackers more. The tactics were similar: pure and simple bludgeoning. The ratio of artillery and infantry was much the same. It is hard to escape the conclusion that the ratio of casualties must also have been similar, and the 1922 report bears this out.

But now comes new arithmetic. In Volume 4 of his *War Memoirs* Lloyd George noted: 'I learn that an elaborate effort is being made to gerrymander the casualty returns—both British and German—so as to present a more favourable balance sheet for this adventure.' In 1948 the British official history, admitting that 'the clerk-power to investigate the exact losses was not available', totals the British casualties at 244,897. Then follows a series of assumptions ending with this sentence: 'There seems every probability that the Germans lost about 400,000.' So the ratio was 1.6 to 1 against the defender, rather than in his favour, a rather incredible reversal.

The case for Haig is further weakened by the statement that British casualties of 244,897 included 'normal wastage'. Normal wastage in the Salient, before the campaign started, was running around 7,000 weekly. The Flanders campaign lasted about fourteen weeks, during which time wastage would have totalled almost 100,000, leaving battle losses at less than 150,000. This figure is far less than reported day by day, and implies that the attackers lost about half as many troops as the defenders. Logic points toward the original 1922 statistics as substantially correct, rather than those announced twenty-six years later by a general officer admittedly on Haig's side of the argument.

But even though the 1922 figures seem correct it remains true that the Germans had been badly mauled, that they could less afford their losses than the Allies, and that pragmatically the campaign hurt them more than the British. Let us assume that Tommie has thirteen pennies, and that Fritz has eight. Tommie throws three pennies into the lake each time that Fritz throws two. Soon Tommie, despite his profligacy, will be solvent while Fritz is bankrupt. While in terms of warfare this may be a revolting process, the Germans recognized its effectiveness. General von Kuhl writes: 'On this point Field-Marshal Haig was right in his judgment—even if he did not break through the German Front, the Flanders Battle wore down the German strength to a degree at which the damage could no longer be repaired. The German sword, heretofore sharp, was blunted.'

The German official history says: 'Divisions disappeared by dozens into the turmoil of the battle, only to emerge from the witches' cauldron after a short period, thinned and exhausted, often reduced to a miserable remnant.'

In his diary, Crown Prince Rupprecht of Bavaria states: 'Most perturbing is the fact that our troops are steadily deteriorating.'

And the German official history concludes: 'Above all, the battle had led to an excessive expenditure of German forces. The casualties were so great that they could no longer be covered, and the already reduced battle strength of battalions sank significantly lower.'

It may be observed that these and similar quotations might also have been uttered by British authorities.

The life expectancy of a machine-gunner in battle on the Western Front has been computed at thirty minutes. Since the Germans defended their Flanders line largely with machine-gunners their losses in these élite troops were enormous. But the flower of the British army had also withered away: its junior officers. The 1922 report shows that 22,316 of them became battle casualties in the west between July and December, as against only 6,913 Germans. Again this reflects the lethal risks taken by men proceeding slowly through mud, led by lieutenants and captains, against barricaded machine-guns manned by non-commissioned officers and privates. Sir Douglas Haig claimed that his men 'advanced every time with absolute confidence in their power to overcome the enemy even though they sometimes had to struggle through mud up to their waists to reach him'. Whether or not they had such confidence, their inability to evade hostile small-arms fire under such conditions is clear.

What Lloyd George thought of the Flanders campaign from the standpoint of casualties can well be imagined. An excerpt from his memoirs will suffice:

> During the whole battle we recovered less ground, we took fewer prisoners, we captured fewer guns (about one-quarter) than we did in the despised Nivelle offensive, and that with nearly three times the casualties we sustained in that operation, which was always alluded to by the Staff as a 'failure'. . . . So much for the bovine and brutal game of attrition on the Western Front.

And in speaking at a Paris luncheon he said, concerning the Passchendaele phase, 'When we advance a kilometre into the enemy's lines, snatch a small shattered village out of his cruel grasp, capture a few hundred of his soldiers, we shout with unfeigned joy . . .', and he went on to compare this kind of thing with the tremendous Austro-German triumph at Caporetto. The quoted sentence was given a bad Press in London, for it came quite close to saying publicly that the British army was being incompetently led and that the entire Third Battle of Ypres had been a needless blood bath; nor did the remark sit well with the masses in the army who had fought desperately and suffered much, nor was it much solace for those back home who had lost their young men in Flanders. The newspapers were not happy, and in Parliament many spoke up bitterly against Lloyd George. Sir Edward Carson, for one, regretted that his chief had seen fit

to hold up the High Command 'to the odium of their countrymen, as though in some way or other they were betraying their
country, if not by their corruption, at least by their incompetence'.

Gough came in for the major share of blame, and defended
himself thus in his book, *The Fifth Army*: 'But these battles were
not fought on my initiative, nor was I responsible for their
continuance, nor was the Fifth Army the only participant. . . .'
Harington admitted that perhaps the campaign should have
started and ended with Messines, and that perhaps there was no
place where his army could have reasonably stopped for the
winter, once the fighting had bogged down. General Davidson
regretted that Plumer had not been given charge from the very
beginning, and implied that Gough ran the offensive into the
ground scarcely before it had time to get under way. The
Australian historian pointed out that since the enemy artillery
could never be dislocated by the snail-like nature of the advance,
Haig's far-reaching strategic aims were impossible of achievement. Churchill derided the false god of attrition, in view of the
official figures: 'If we lose three or four times as many officers
and nearly twice as many men in our attack as the enemy in his
defence, how are we wearing him down?'

An Army Commanders' conference at Doullens on 7 December appears to have been a morose affair. Sir Douglas pointed out
that the manpower problem was extremely serious; he had little
hope of bringing his divisions up to strength by next spring,
whereas it was now an open secret that German divisions were
coming down from the Russian front at the rate of ten per month,
Russia having signed an armistice with the Central Powers
several days previously. General Rawlinson, who attended the
meeting, was grim over the turn of events but blamed it on the
civilians:

. . . by the end of February we are likely to have a lively time.
Anyhow, we shall be thrown on the defensive, and shall have to
fight for our lives as we did at the first battle of Ypres. We have had

no luck this year. There is something radically wrong with the general management of the war by the Allies. The politicians insist on butting in just at the wrong time. . . .

General Plumer was assigned to take charge of British forces in Italy, and left remarking that he was glad to be out of the mud and blood of Flanders. His Second Army was handed over to Rawlinson. By this time Gough, a hard-luck commander virtually in disgrace, was in command of only one corps. At the suggestion of General Kiggell, Haig removed Charteris from G.H.Q.; at once a torrent of abuse rained down on the Intelligence officer's head. In turn, Kiggell was replaced by the commander-in-chief, on grounds of ill-health. The old order of command and power in France and Belgium was fast disintegrating. Who would be next?

Long had 'Wully', Chief of the Imperial General Staff, been railing over the mechanics of the Versailles Supreme War Council. Not only did he consider that body unworkable, but he insisted that the C.I.G.S. could not be made the errand-boy of General Wilson and a pack of foreigners. As far as Lloyd George was concerned, Robertson could resign if he wished. Everybody was in step but him—even Sir Douglas, who, to the Prime Minister's surprise, would not fight for his old friend in a personal talk with Lloyd George at Walton Heath. In fact, Haig remarked, he himself had no interest in all these petty quarrels; he would 'play up all he could' with the decisions of the War Cabinet. Since the same could not be said of Sir William, his finish was plainly in sight. But Haig continued to stand apart, and to his wife wrote that Robertson, after all, had never resolutely adhered to the Western Front philosophy. So the only man who might have saved Robertson turned his face away. It was a stunning disappointment for the burly, grumpy, popularly loved chief of staff, and this after years of playing Haig's game. On 8 February the War Cabinet decided that he and Sir Henry Wilson should switch jobs.

A distasteful episode followed. In a ferocious temper at this stage, and almost impossible to talk to, 'Wully' refused to resign and flatly declined the Versailles appointment. Haig visited him at the War Office, where he was still moodily holding on, and tried to persuade him to work on the Supreme War Council. 'Wully' refused, and in his diary Sir Douglas wrote: 'I am afraid that in the back of his mind he resents Henry Wilson replacing him in London, and means to embarrass the Government to the utmost of his power.' On 18 February Robertson read in the newspapers that he had 'resigned', that Wilson was the new C.I.G.S., and that he—Sir William—had been given the Eastern Command, an incongruous assignment for one of the most traditional bulwarks of the Western Front.

Subordinated to a war council which generally opposed him, the strange bed-fellow of a new chief of staff who had gone on record as disagreeing with his Flanders campaign (which he expected to start up again next spring), almost alone against the animosity and plots of the Prime Minister, mistrusted by the War Cabinet after the failure of his 1917 plan, Douglas Haig too seemed to be at the cross-roads. Would it be his turn next to leave the paths of glory?

December ended and another cheerless New Year's Day dawned on the Western Front, as rigid and granite-like as ever. The stalemate still held; despairingly the vast armies continued to face each other, and peace seemed all too familiarly remote. America was in but Russia was out, and so, for all practical purposes, was Italy. Many in the War Committee had come to realize that Haig's promises had led to nothing; one by one his assurances delivered in the spring had proved empty. Many newspapers formerly sympathetic to Sir Douglas now turned against him. Even Lord Northcliffe underwent a sudden revulsion and demanded a 'prompt, searching and complete' inquiry into what had happened, and *The Times* roared: 'We can no longer rest satisfied with the fatuous estimates, e.g. of German losses in men and morale, which have inspired too many of the published messages from France.'

But the dissatisfaction did not spring merely from distorted communiqués. Behind it was a feeling that the campaign had

19

been botched and that countless young men had been butchered for nothing. A new and nagging realization arose that the generalship on the Western Front had been something less than inspired. In the words of Mr. H. G. Wells:

> ... the professional military mind is by necessity an inferior and unimaginative mind; no man of high intellectual quality would willingly imprison his gifts in such a calling ... this war after fifty years of militarism was a hopelessly professional war; from first to last it was impossible to get it out of the hands of the regular generals....

Tactics had been on a rather low level, and if there were those who said that nothing else was possible on the Western Front there were others who replied that Napoleon would have found a way. But the British in Flanders had no Napoleon. Planning could not have been more routine. Except at Messines and Cambrai, surprise and deception were neglected. A date for each attack was decided upon. The staffs glanced at their maps and decided which divisions would participate. These were assembled at the front. Guns and supplies were brought forward. Zero Hour was set. Lines were traced on the map showing the objectives. A bombardment softened up the defences and completed the job of tipping the attacker's hand. Finally the assault brigades went over the top and walked directly at the prepared, entrenched enemy. Thus France and England had fought the war for three years on the Western Front; and as to which leadership of the two allies was the more inept, Hindenburg writes: 'The Englishman was undoubtedly a less skilful opponent than his brother in arms. He did not understand how to control rapid changes in the situation. His methods were too rigid.' But, he admits, they were indeed obstinate.

Essentially it is Haig that the German describes, and despite his continual attacks Haig must be regarded as more attuned psychologically for defence. 'He had not a critical mind', writes Charteris, nor was his imagination appropriate for the dash and subtlety of successful offensive operations. Like General Ulysses

Grant, his nature was best suited to a calculated process of attrition; and there is a remarkable parallel between the 1917 Flanders campaign and Grant's operations in 1864 from the Rapidan to Petersburg.

Both Haig's supporters and detractors agree on one thing: the timing had been unfortunate. To start the Flanders campaign just before the rains was to invite calamity. If it had to take place at all, spring was the time. Given dry ground and acknowledged superiority in artillery and shells, Haig might have accomplished much more than he did. When Nivelle's plan was given precedence, and when subsequent delays began to pile up, it might have been best to wait for the Americans, for the tanks, and for 1918. Haig had come to the well once too often—at the Somme for 500,000 men, at Ypres for 400,000. And the Australian historian writes:

> When in the near future he pressed for still more men, the War Cabinet felt, not without reason, that, if given another 100,000, he would stake them to gain the next shell-shattered hilltop; he would use up all he had, and his side would not be appreciably nearer to victory. To political leaders, forced to accept his plans but shocked with the result, the obvious moral was: 'Keep back the men.'

As a result, incidentally, of this policy of keeping back the men, Haig's skeleton armies were less able to withstand the German offensive that burst upon them in 1918.

The argument that started when the campaign ended has never been settled with finality. Should it have taken place at all? Should it have been stopped after Messines, after the August breakdown, after Broodseinde? Was the gain in ground in any sense meaningful? Were the Germans hurt more—relatively or absolutely or both—than the Allies? Did the campaign save France, and how weak *was* that nation's army when 31 July dawned? A small but determined minority, mostly army officers, believes that Haig was right from start to finish. But an equal or larger number of military personnel, and almost all civilians, have always felt (in varying degrees) that Haig blundered, or was irrationally stubborn, or was at least misled by his Intelligence advisers.

The controversy is strikingly similar to that which later revolved around Truman and MacArthur. In both cases the general's side was taken by a violent and highly articulate minority. In both cases there seemed to be no neutrals. In both cases the general was looked upon almost as a god by his followers. In Haig's case, the last is hardest to explain. Few men in public service have been more plagued by an unattractive personality than he. His inarticulateness was so severe as to give circulation to a host of anecdotes—some affectionate, some malicious—such as the one concerning his speech when presenting trophies to an Aldershot cross-country team: 'I congratulate you on your running. You have run well. I hope you run as well in the presence of the enemy.' At mess the field-marshal ate silently. He had no nickname, no small talk, no sense of humour, no warmth in his dealings with other men. His public speeches were hardly of the sort to arouse idolatry; written out meticulously in advance, they dealt always with 'Sacrifice' or 'Duty' or 'Endeavour'. Yet the devotion to the man and to his 1917 campaign has always been inversely proportional to the number of devotees, and probably will always be so.

The analyses of those who have written of Haig and Flanders naturally reflect their own prejudices. At one extreme is Brigadier-General J. E. Edmonds, the British official historian, in whose eyes Haig could do no wrong, German casualties almost doubled the British, the military victory was substantial, Flanders was the best place to attack, the bad weather was exaggerated, the mud was routine and not as bad as at the Somme, the tanks co-operated successfully until October, and so on.

At the other stands David Lloyd George. In his *War Memoirs*, Volume 4, 116 pages are devoted to the 'Campaign of the Mud: Passchendaele', later widely circulated as a separate pamphlet. These are vitriolic pages, hard to answer but intemperate in language (some of which has been quoted in this narrative), in which Haig emerges as a stubborn, fame-hungry, cold-blooded, deceiving oaf, and his campaign a military abortion unparalleled in the history of the Western world.

Between these lies Volume 4 of the Australian official history, admirably written by Dr. C. E. W. Bean, in which blame and credit are so evenly apportioned that one cannot enter the result on one side of the ledger or the other.

Haig never wrote his memoirs, but several of his followers later took up the war of words on his behalf. Dewar and Boraston, formerly of his staff, issued their appraisal in 1922—an unfortunate effort showing considerable bias; it was received badly, and even Haig was not pleased by it. His official biography, by Duff Cooper, paints 'the conventional picture of a soldier without flaw'; and his life as interpreted by General Charteris is scarcely less idealistic. General Davidson's book is largely a resumé of the official history.

On the other hand, the biographies of Lloyd George by Thomas Jones and Frank Owen are laudatory of the Prime Minister, especially the latter; and the various works of Captain Liddell Hart show little sympathy for the field-marshal. Hart's books are by far the most widely read, and his point of view has deeply permeated the public consciousness. It is no surprise to learn that he advised Lloyd George militarily throughout the preparation of his memoirs, and that it is his voice which is heard in the many definitive articles concerning the First World War in the *Encyclopaedia Britannica*.

Sir William Robertson's *Soldiers and Statesmen* summarizes his expected attitudes with icy restraint. The official histories of Canada and New Zealand are critical of Haig to a degree, but generally noncommittal. Almost all the worm's-eye views of the campaign, such as those written by Charles Edmonds, Reginald Farrer, Robert Graves, Stephen Graham, Thomas Hope and Ralph Mottram, plus a thousand others in this vein, are shockingly bitter. Sir Arthur Conan Doyle's fourth volume in his microscopic history of the course of battles on the Western Front is, perhaps, the most uninhibited apologia for the tactics pursued by G.H.Q.

and, since it has been superseded by later and more authoritative technical accounts, may be considered of meagre value. Haig's own published *Despatches* to the King are somewhat coloured by a tinge of propaganda and self-justification. These, along with his edited *Private Papers*, however, present an ardent case for the policy he pursued so inflexibly to Passchendaele's bitter end. The writings of Sir Philip Gibbs vary radically between praise for Sir Douglas and his wise leadership, horror at the conditions of warfare and at the concept of warfare itself, admiration for British valour, hatred for the ineptitude of certain British generals, and sheer propaganda to bolster public opinion. It is hard to classify this distinguished writer, though in public speech and after the war he showed himself to be in opposition to the Flanders plan and execution.

One may turn, therefore, to these and innumerable other sources to arrive at an opinion, or to justify one's preconceived opinion. The face of history is, as usual, blank and imperturbable. This is war, it says; this is life as twentieth-century man chose to conduct it. The third battle of Ypres was fought thus and so, and human judgment is inadequate to categorize its ultimate meaning, if, indeed, it has any meaning within the larger surge of life. Broad and turgid, the river of time flows toward an unnamed sea. On it the Flanders campaign survives for only a moment, an eddy of muddy water that convulsively twists and turns and then disappears.

On 21 March, 1918, the long-anticipated German onslaught crashed against the British Third and Fifth Armies and within two weeks had penetrated to a maximum of forty miles. The second phase began on 9 April. In a matter of hours the little strip of Ridge won at such cost by Haig's troops the previous year was wiped out. Soon the entire Salient was obliterated and twelve more miles gained. In May Ludendorff struck another heavy blow, this time at the French in Champagne; after four days the Marne was reached, thirty miles further away, and again Paris was threatened. But the sands had run out for Germany. The

Allies had fumbled and almost panicked, but they had held. The Americans were on the scene in considerable force. All surprise was now gone. The last great German attack (in July) fell against a thoroughly prepared and determined opponent; it failed, and three days later Foch counter-attacked, using masses of tanks and 100,000 feverishly combative American troops as spearheads.

Throughout all these titanic experiences Haig remained cool, and surprisingly prudent of human life. He, like Gough, had learned much from Flanders. It was a sadder and wiser man who met the enemy juggernaut, skilful in defence, methodical in his dispositions, ready and willing to work with the Supreme Commander, Marshal Ferdinand Foch.

With this offensive the German war machine committed suicide, for in thirteen weeks 688,000 of its men were lost. 'They were worn down', says Churchill, 'not by Joffre, Nivelle and Haig, but by Ludendorff.' On 8 August, 'the black day of the German army in the history of the War', Haig smashed through on the Somme. There followed a series of sharp punches all along the line, ending with the American victory at St. Mihiel on 12 September. On the 29th Haig broke through the Hindenburg Line. Bulgaria, then Turkey, then Austria capitulated. German peace overtures were proffered when revolution was sweeping over the land. When her admirals tried to send the fleet on a death-or-glory ride, the sailors mutinied. More alert to impending bolshevism than to military defeat, the German government rushed a peace delegation to Foch on 6 November.

It remains to be said, as usual, that the war ended at the eleventh hour of the eleventh day of the eleventh month of 1918. It had meant nothing, solved nothing, and proved nothing; and in so doing had killed 8,538,315 men and variously wounded 21,219,452. Of 7,750,919 others taken prisoner or missing, well over a million were later presumed dead; thus the total deaths (not counting civilians) approach ten million. The moral and mental defects of the leaders of the human race had been demonstrated with some exactitude. One of them (Woodrow Wilson) later admitted that the war had been fought for business interests;

another (David Lloyd George) had told a newspaperman: 'If people really knew, the war would be stopped tomorrow, but of course they don't—and can't know. The correspondents don't write and the censorship wouldn't pass the truth. The thing is horrible, and beyond human nature to bear, and I feel I can't go any longer with the bloody business. . . .'

But now the thing was over. After a few final shells thrown into enemy lines at eleven o'clock by cannoneers who shall be for ever nameless, an uncanny silence enveloped the Western Front. Cautiously, unbelievingly, the men raised themselves above their trenches, shell-holes, and dug-outs, and stared at the opposing lines. Soon they became very excited, and often regrettably drunk; and, as the once-hostile armies merged, the men exchanged cigarettes, wine, embraces and souvenirs. Then came the stern, inevitable order forbidding fraternization.

In London madness reigned, a mixture of joy and sorrow almost too poignant to be endured. At the first stroke of Big Ben's chimes thousands poured out into the streets. Now all the bells of the city began to clang. Drivers of buses and military lorries careened in all directions with loads of screaming passengers. Hordes flocked to Buckingham Palace and sang 'God Save the King' until His Majesty appeared on the balcony and tried to speak through the cheers, the singing, the sputtering of fire-crackers. Flags appeared from countless shops and houses. One crowd hauled out a captured German gun from the Mall and burned its carriage in Trafalgar Square. Soon all traffic choked to a stop. It began to rain, but few noticed, and dancing and singing continued in the open air. Some people climbed into the arms of Queen Victoria's statue. Under an archway in a tiny street near Charing Cross two old women in capes and bonnets danced primly to the music of a barrel organ. That night all the previously darkened streets were lit up like a carnival, and the merry-making went on—in restaurants (where the food soon ran out), in pubs, on the streets, in night-clubs—and there was no end to the confetti throwing. To the shout, 'Have we won the war?' the answer came back in a roar, 'Yes, we've won the war!'

Clerks, factory workers in caps and overalls, a stout colonel beating a dinner gong on top of a taxi, wounded soldiers in hospital blue, girl messengers, sailors, government officials, and many a child—all were caught up in the maelstrom. And that day a new song was often heard:

> 'What shall we be
> When we aren't what we are? . . .'

A rollicking little thing it was, but there were those who found it vaguely disquieting.

Sequel

AFTER the war the famous generals were allotted great tasks at the seven corners of the earth. Sir Herbert Plumer became Governor of Malta and later High Commissioner for Palestine. In 1920 Sir Henry Rawlinson was assigned to India as Commander-in-Chief. As military adviser of the Government, Sir Henry Wilson was active at Versailles, and subsequently entered Parliament as Member for North Down. Sir Hubert Gough was named head of the British Mission to the Baltic States, General Byng became Governor-General of Canada, General Allenby High Commissioner for Egypt. Thus all but one were honoured by a grateful Empire for services rendered. Only Sir Douglas Haig was given nothing to do. At the age of fifty-eight, in perfect health, a handsome figure of a man, after stepping ashore at Dover in 1919 he found that his official life was over; he was in effect unemployed.

Innumerable titles and decorations were conferred upon him by France, the United States, Italy, Belgium, Portugal, Japan, Serbia, Rumania, even China. He was raised to the peerage as Earl Haig and Baron Haig of Bemersyde. Parliament granted him £100,000 and he remained on the active list as a field-marshal. Talk of appointing him Viceroy of India came to nothing. He concealed his emotions behind a mask of stone, toured the land and made speeches concerning duty, sacrifice and service, became active in veterans' affairs, unveiled any number of war memorials, went to Edinburgh to live, and toiled daily on the grounds and gardens of his estate. He entered the local social life, hunted foxes with his neighbours, and lived quietly with his wife and the son who had been born in the month of Ludendorff's 1918 offensive. All letters—and they poured in like a stream—he answered in his own hand. He joined the boards of several great companies, cultivated an interest in business, attended their meetings and studied the details of their operations. In connection with the British Legion he did much charity work for the survivors, the wounded, and the relatives of those killed in the war. Always religious, he became active in the Church of Scotland. But still Lloyd George and the Government spurned him.

He golfed at St. Andrews, and one may unearth delightful pictures of him in several old golf volumes, stiffly dressed, a ghost of a smile on his lips as he struggles with the maddening game. We find him in Andra Kirkaldy's book photographed while teeing off as Captain of the Royal and Ancient. The ball is on its way, the crowd peers down the fairway, and one learns sadly that his drive was the Flanders campaign in microcosm—very short but very straight; and one may also observe that the field-marshal's grip is, typically, far too rigid, his weight piled back on the wrong foot somewhat in the manner of a later distinguished soldier, President Eisenhower.

As the years passed, Earl Haig became somewhat more talkative, less abrupt, more tolerant in his judgments. He began to speak humorously of what he would do when the infirmities of age beset him. Always pathetically addicted to weird diets, he now concentrated on oranges. Over and over he re-lived the war before his fireside, and welcomed people with whom he could discuss it—especially old comrades in arms. On trains he asked the Railway Transport Officer for the names of the passengers; if he recognized one he would seek him out.

The 1920s waned, and Earl Haig aged quickly in the way of those who have nothing to do. Ignored by the authorities, he turned to dreams of the past and to his family, making no attempt to defend himself against attacks on his war leadership that had sprung up when the censorship was lifted. The official history would vindicate him, he assured his wife and friends; nothing else mattered. So the people of Britain gradually forgot him and less and less wondered why he was not to be found in the spheres of power and prestige. One winter evening he played cards with his wife and sister, and went up to his room. A cry was heard. He had suffered a heart attack; and on 29 January, 1928, the old soldier passed away.

The long road followed by David Lloyd George after the end of hostilities is a familiar one and may be briefly summarized. In 1918 he was returned overwhelmingly to power and at Versailles tried without much success to weaken Clemenceau's ferocious demands on the defeated enemy. In a lukewarm way he took President Wilson's side on the League of Nations issue, but never attended any of its meetings. The general election of 1922 returned the Conservatives to leadership and Lloyd George to the Opposition. From here to the end his political fortunes declined while the Labour Party grew in numbers. In 1929 the Liberals under his ostensible leadership were able to win only fifty-nine seats in the Commons.

Increasingly he stayed aloof from the national scene and spent three full years (1931–34) writing his *War Memoirs*. He became one of the earliest appeasers of Hitler, a phase which continued almost until the start of the new war. As Germany went from victory to victory Lloyd George waited for a nod from Churchill that would bring him back into the Cabinet. It never came, while the elder statesman brooded and fretted and almost seemed to welcome some shattering crisis that would cause those in the inner circles to seek out his aid and prestige. This, too, never developed, whereupon he predicted disaster for the Allies under Churchill's leadership. In 1941 the death of his wife, Dame Margaret, left him even more pessimistic, lonely, detached from the new war that he did not quite understand—its origin, its strategy, the aims of its belligerents. His attitude towards Russia alternated throughout the years; at first he welcomed the revolution; then for a long period he fancied Herr Hitler as the man who might mercifully throttle that revolution; but his last speech in Parliament (11 June, 1942) was to congratulate the government on its treaty with the Soviets. Next year, at eighty, he married his secretary, Frances Louise Stevenson, and returned to his farm in Wales. By now the old fighter was failing fast, hardly even aware of the war. Each morning he awakened late, strolled down to the village, came back for luncheon, napped, smoked, supped, and talked to old friends. He could no longer run actively for office; yet to make no speeches and conduct no campaign, and then to be defeated by some glib youngster, would be tragic. While debating whether to evade the contest, he was asked by Winston Churchill to have his name submitted to the King for an earldom. He wired the Prime Minister: 'Gratefully accept', and became free, in theory, to speak in the Lords. The Great Commoner, to the amusement and resentment of many, thus was named on New Year's Day, 1945, the Right Honourable Earl Lloyd-George of Dwyfor.

For three months the wizened, senile Welshman held on, very weak and seldom rational. Occasionally his mind cleared, and, for a wonderful hour or two, operated with its old speed and acid clarity; then on 26 March he died in the presence of his wife and two daughters. During his funeral several aircraft roared by, and the villagers asked each other if Mr. Churchill had finally arrived; but they were war-planes bent on other business that cold and foggy afternoon.

It had cost Sir William Robertson dearly to hitch his wagon to Haig during the war years. After being removed as Chief of the Imperial General Staff, the whipping boy of those who had not found it possible to sack Sir Douglas, he never again attained his former glory. In 1919, after receiving a baronetcy and a grant of £10,000, he was given command of British troops on the Rhine, an appointment he soon relinquished when the forces under him dwindled. His military career ended in 1921 and he turned to writing his autobiography and his classic work, *Soldiers and Statesmen*. Later, somewhat surprisingly, he immersed himself in peace propaganda—'a role', in the words of Liddell Hart, 'which seemed to some who knew him well as due more to disappointment than to conviction'. After receiving many honours of the Empire and foreign nations he died, irascible and shrewd to the end, in 1933, at the age of seventy-three.

After the war Ypres was rebuilt in elaborate mediaeval style, with only the ruins of the Cloth Hall allowed to lie and moulder as the war had created them. The venture was an astounding *tour de force* but an unsuccessful one; today the town seems too precious, too self-conscious, and its old-world curiosity-shop flavour is for ever gone. It thrives on the tourist trade.

No longer does the Menin Road, dreary and squalid, a tragedy of mud, weeds and shell-craters, lead to the Western Front. Now it is a trim provincial highway; and the sweating, heavy laden, sleepy-eyed men are wraiths of the past. The Menin Gate, too, has been reconstructed: a gigantic memorial of marble, broad, vaulted, Roman in design. Facing the former enemy, a stone lion crouches; his paw holds his prey, and he does not intend to let go. 56,000 names are engraved in gold on the walls, all British dead whose graves or bodies were never found in the Salient during or after the war. It was of this that Siegfried Sassoon wrote his biting sonnet, 'On Passing the Menin Gate', which begins:

'Who will remember, passing through this Gate,
The unheroic Dead who fed the guns? . . .'

The remaining British missing are recorded in Tyne Cot Cemetery, Passchendaele, largest British cemetery in the world. And, among others, there is the Canadian Memorial near St. Julien. Here the colossal head and shoulders of an ordinary soldier rises from a tall column and seems to grieve for all soldiers of all lands since time began.

In all, 174 British cemeteries cram the one-time Salient, tended by a small army of British subjects under the employment of the Imperial War Graves Commission. All crosses are white and scrupulously neat in arrangement, and brilliantly green is the grass between them, the rows only interrupted here and there by the sawn-off propellers of fliers who fell to their death in Flanders. These cemeteries, land 'that is for ever England', were conceded in perpetuity to Great Britain by the Belgian government in 1917: they contain in the Ypres area 40,000 British graves, while untold thousands still lie under unmarked soil. All are bounded by a low wall or fence. Within them trees and flowers grow. The orderly rows are marked by headstones showing the deceased's name, rank, unit, date of death, regimental crest, religious symbol, and any simple inscription that his friends might have cared to add. Officers and other ranks lie side by side. There is a Cross of Sacrifice at the entrance of each cemetery, and a Stone of Remembrance inscribed with the words: 'Their name liveth for evermore.' One registers at each entrance gate. Visitors may learn in advance at 32 Grosvenor Gardens, S.W.1, the location of the deceased, the name of his cemetery, the row, the number in the row. There is a Graves Enquiry Bureau in Ypres where an official map may be consulted. It is all extremely efficient.

Long were the fields of the Salient littered with the débris of war, especially near the Menin Road. In the 'Tank Graveyard' seventeen machines lay embedded where they had been struck down. Tours were conducted around Ypres; the most popular was Number 7, which led through St. Julien, Poelcapelle and Houthulst Forest. For years the Ridge was too trenched, cratered and mined to be of any value, and nothing grew on it but the coarsest of weeds. On Hill 60 the peasants dug up vast quantities of souvenirs—buttons, badges, pistols, boots, the bones of soldiers, holsters, wooden pipes, cartridges, shell fragments, and the like—and sold their wares out of little boxes to tourists who flowed like battalions across the ex-battlefield. Everything was priced quite methodically: twenty francs for a Smith and Wesson revolver, one penny for a brass button, and so on.

A former soldier became caretaker of one portion of the Ridge maintained as a memorial in its original state. He lived in an army hut, talked to visitors, and for one franc conducted them on his little tour to Death Trench. Each day after tea the caretaker and his dog walked down the communications trench (Princes Street) to the support line (Paradise Alley), up International Trench to the mine crater, through formless Schenken Redoubt, and returned by way of the sap that entered the German dug-outs (Piccadilly Buildings). He mended the duckboards, noted where the imitation concrete sandbags were split by frost, and kept the shallow trenches at the summit boarded up; and as he walked his heavy boots rasped against the remnants of rusty barbed wire and occasionally jostled a helmet, or a rifle barrel from which the wood had long since decayed. Only this, and sometimes the barking of his dog, disturbed the death-like silence where once men had screamed in fear and agony amid the clamour of the guns.

In time the caretaker disappeared, along with his bit of Western Front. Only along the coast, near Nieuport, does another such replica still exist, and this too, it is said, is soon to be abandoned. Time reclaimed the Ridge and what was once the Salient. But in 1940 war rolled again through Poelcapelle, Passchendaele, Ypres, Poperinghe, Messines. Again this weary land and these familiar towns, soaked with the blood of centuries, were occupied by new armies; and later other legions passed through and drove their enemy back, as the Duke of Parma did in 1584, as the French did in the seventeenth century, as Austria did in the next, as a hundred armies did before them. And again the Salient reverted to farmland. Yet today the millions of shell-holes have never quite levelled out, and anyone who walks through the fields south and west of the Ridge can still sense the undulations caused by shells that blasted this ground in the First World War.

In *Sartor Resartus*, a hundred years earlier, Carlyle wrote:
... there dwell and toil, in the British village of Dumdrudge, usually some five hundred souls. From these ... there are successively selected, during the French War, say thirty able-bodied men: Dumdrudge, at her own expense, has suckled and nursed them; she has, not without difficulty and sorrow, fed them up to manhood, and even trained them to crafts, so that one can weave, another build, another hammer, and the weakest can stand under thirty stone avoirdupois. Nevertheless, amid much weeping and swearing, they are selected; all dressed in red; and shipped away, at the public charges, some two thousand miles, or say only to the south of Spain; and fed there till wanted. And now to that same spot in the south of Spain, are thirty similar French artisans, from a French Dumdrudge, in like manner wending: Till at length, after infinite effort, the two parties come into actual juxtaposition; and Thirty

stands fronting Thirty, each with a gun in his hand. Straightway the word 'Fire!' is given: and they blow the souls out of one another; and in the place of sixty brisk useful craftsmen, the world has sixty dead carcasses, which it must bury, and anew shed tears for. Had these men any quarrel? Busy as the Devil is, not the smallest! . . . their Governors had fallen out: and, instead of shooting one another, had the cunning to make these poor blockheads shoot.—Alas, so it is in Deutschland, and hitherto in all other lands . . .

Reference Notes

THE majority of direct and indirect quotations in this book are accompanied by their sources, and since the sequence is fairly chronological it has not seemed necessary in most cases to relate them to exact dates and page numbers. The following notes will substantiate other quotations not identified in the narrative, as well as factual statements requiring verification. Except where indicated, references are to the bibliography.

Chapter 1, The Deadlock

The episode of the seventeen shells was derived from Gibbs' *Struggle in Flanders*, p. 39. For my portrait of the Western Front I drew heavily on Mottram, Williamson, Charles Edmonds, James Edmonds, the Mottram–Easton–Partridge volume, Graves, Purdom, and from a multitude of other accounts of this kind—especially the two books by Gibbs, who was far and away the most gifted lay reporter of the war. Stallings' pictures were also extremely useful in their way. The various quotations by Foch, Napoleon, etc., appear in the introduction to Hart's *Fog of War*.

Chapter 2, The Home Front

Curzon was quoted in *The Times*, 1 January; the peace rebuff and Pankhurst uproar are also reported on that date. While I collected many fragments from many places concerning the home islands during the war, the majority in this and later chapters may be credited to Peel, Playne and Willis; Peel, for example, quotes the child's plaintive 'Mummy . . .' phrase. The conversation with the worker is recounted by Playne, who also writes of the rush-hour jam. Sylvia Pankhurst tells of Conan Doyle's suggestion concerning fallen women. See Peel, p. 58, for the German lady's letter. Strachey is discussed by Graves, p. 249, second revised edition. I discovered the Smuts remark in Playne. Lloyd George's gloomy greeting to Lord Hankey in November is quoted by Thomas Jones, p. 78. Primarily I leaned on Thomas Jones,

Owen, Robertson, Churchill's *The World Crisis*, and Bernard Shaw for the general political background of the day, and on these plus Hart's books, Callwell, and Bean for summaries of the East-West controversy. Duff Cooper tells of newspaper attitudes and the 'twenty-three ropes' placards. Mr. Asquith's comment appears in Beaverbrook. See Charteris for a summary of Haig's post-Somme memorandum. Bean, p. 12, and Thomas Jones, p. 76, refer to Lord Lansdowne's letter, and Duff Cooper quotes Robertson in reply. Mostly I used Bean, James Edmonds, and Owen on the Chantilly conference.

Chapter 3, *The Overture*

Charteris, Duff Cooper's official biography, and Hart's *Reputations* and *Fog of War* tell of Haig's life and character to date. See Duff Cooper and *Fog of War* (p. 36) for excerpts from the marshal's early correspondence, and the latter p. 37, for the comment on his operations in the Boer war, plus the subsequent phrases and quotations. The quotation ('The British cavalry officer seems to be impressed . . .') was reported by Gronow from the Frenchman, Excelmann; I extracted it fom Cecil Woodham-Smith's *The Reason Why*. Shaw's opinion appears on page 216. Haig's spiritual and religious attitudes are noted in Hart's *Fog of War*, p. 43. The Churchill extract appears in *Great Contemporaries*; this essay has also been reprinted in *Famous British Generals* (Barrett Parker, Ed., Nicholson & Watson, 1951). I followed Duff Cooper, Thomas Jones, and Robertson, among others, for details of the Rome conference. Thomas Jones, Owen, and Hart's *Fog of War* tell of Lloyd George's career and nature. See Thomas Jones, p. 15, for Gladstone's plea 28 April, 1892. From Duff Cooper I extracted Lloyd George's monologue in the train after the Rome meeting, and Kiggell's letter to Haig. The various Nivelle assurances may be found in Churchill's *The World Crisis*, pp. 712 *et seq.*, and Hart's *Outline*, pp. 173–4. See diary entries of 16 January for Haig's counter-views. Wilson's entry ('an amazing speech') was written on 24 January. Lloyd George's argument in favour of a single army command is quoted by Owen, p. 392. Haig's reaction appears in his diary 26 February; and the letter to his wife was derived from Duff Cooper. Again, Duff Cooper provides the reference for Robertson's comment on the Prime Minister ('I can't believe that a man such as he . . .'), for Haig's next diary entry, and for his letter to Nivelle concerning 'unity of effort'.

The dialogue between Sir Douglas and Gough is recounted by the latter in *The Fifth Army*. See Haig's published diaries 28 February for the letter to Robertson: 'Briefly it is the type of letter . . .' The technicality over the Haig-Nivelle grade differential is commented upon by Hart in his *Outline*, p. 171. Repington in his diary 13 April tells of Sir William's sour views on the Russians. I have borrowed from Willis concerning the various quotations by Haig, by the *Daily News* and by Lloyd George prior to America's entry. The beautiful poem, 'I hear a noise of breaking chains . . .', appeared 9 April and was written by James Douglas. This, too, is from Willis, as well as the report on the Savoy luncheon.

Chapter 4, *L'Affaire Nivelle*

Winston Churchill in *The World Crisis*, pp. 705 *et seq.*, has written a fascinating appreciation of the inception and unfolding of the French spring offensive. This, and Owen and Duff Cooper are my major sources for the present chapter. See the first, p. 724, for the quotation beginning, 'So Nivelle and Painlevé, these two men . . .', and pp. 718-9 for Rupprecht's words. The increase in German divisions from nine to forty is verified here, p. 720. See various sections of Bean and James Edmonds *re* facts and figures on the German withdrawal. Ludendorff's 'decision to retreat' was taken from Gibbs' *Now It Can Be Told*, p. 454, and the statements of the villagers from the page following. See *The World Crisis*, p. 717, for the text of Nivelle's 6 March directive. The astounding claims of Nivelle prior to the attack are derived also from Churchill's chapter, and from Hart's *Outline*, pp. 173-4. Again see Churchill, pp. 721-2, for Nivelle's order to Micheler, and the next page for an account of the meeting 3 April. Wilson's diary excerpt, a typically lively one, is dated 8 April. 'The effect of the Nivelle alterations . . .' is on p. 713 of *The World Crisis*. Another absorbing account of the Nivelle episode appears in Pierrefeu's volume; the conversation between d'Alenson and the general is reported here. I found Hart's summary in *The Real War*, pp. 321-9, sufficient for telling briefly the Arras story. The bitter passage concerning Bullecourt was written by Bean, pp. 349-50, as well as the phrase about Haig and Gough (p. 352) which follows. See Haig's *Private Papers* under date of 18 April for the excerpt from Wilson's letter, and Callwell for Wilson's diary note of the day before, which begins, 'Nivelle will fall. . . .' By far the best source for what little is known about the French mutinies is the famous article, 'The Bent Sword', by A.M.G., published in *Blackwood's Magazine*, January, 1944. It is, by the way, reprinted in its entirety as Appendix I, pp. 139 *et seq.*, by Davidson. I have used it liberally, as well as similar related material in Churchill's above-mentioned chapter on Nivelle. Quotations from the French troops, however, were uncovered in Hart, *The Real War*, pp. 300–1. Concerning Lloyd George's note to Haig after the imbroglio, Painlevé's visit to the latter, and Haig's replies, see Duff Cooper. The occurrence at French G.H.Q. is recited by Pierrefeu. The final quotations from Haig's papers, dealing with Nivelle, Ribot, and Robertson, are dated 3 May, 26 April, and 29 April respectively.

Chapter 5, The Interlude

I am indebted to Bean and James Edmonds for their recapitulations of the gradual evolution of Haig's Flanders plan. Broadly speaking, these appear in Edmonds, pp. 1–32, and in Bean, pp. 546–60, although there are many other references to its theory and growth: for example, in James Edmonds' final chapter: 'Retrospect'. Simonds, pp. 194–217, concisely reviews the U-boat problem. Henry Wilson's 'case for Haig' will be found in Callwell; this is a diary entry dated 22 April. See Dewar and Boraston for the means by which Ypres was selected 'by a process of exclusion'. Lloyd George quotes Asquith's memo to Robertson on p. 327, and Robertson's letter to Joffre on pp. 325–6. See Callwell for the 1 May conference, p. 345. The meeting held 4 May was more important and is reviewed in many books. Thomas Jones, among others, reports Lloyd George's statement, 'We must go on hitting . . .', pp. 117–8. See also Bean, pp. 547–53, from which the next quotation ('it is no longer a question') is derived. Lloyd George, p. 335, mentions his exchange with Pétain. I used Maurice for the following week's conference at Doullens, and James Edmonds, p. 26, for Robertson's warning to Haig concerning the unlikelihood of French co-operation. Pétain's fateful prediction to Wilson about Haig's certain failure appears in Callwell, Vol. 1, p. 355. The fragment from Hoffmann's diary is dated 1 June. In describing the Flanders terrain I made much use of Johnson and Muirhead. The pregnant reference of Charteris: 'Careful investigation of the records . . .' appears in his published diaries, p. 272. Johnson is also the background for the sundry quoted remarks about the Flanders mud. Poignant pictures of Ypres itself have been sketched by many a wartime writer. From our bibliography I refer the reader to Beatrice Brice, Farrer, Hurst, and especially Mottram. From these sources I have done my best to reconstruct the pathetic, almost fabulous reality of 1917.

Chapter 6, Triumph at Messines

The best sketch of General Plumer is perhaps to be found in Harington's *Plumer of Messines*; and as for the general background of Messines I have consulted Bean, James Edmonds, and Johnson. The conversation concerning the mines at Hill 60 is reported by Harington in *Tim Harington Looks Back*. Bean, p. 599, verifies von Kuhl's suggestion for a withdrawal, and on the same page quotes the XIX Army Group's order to stand fast. See this reference, also, for the long excerpt concerning the drama of 9 May. It appears on pp. 958–9. In the same section appears the sections about Captain Woodward and Sapper Sneddon. I secured the next bit ('. . . he had been working underground . . .') from Gibbs' *Struggle in Flanders* (which was earlier entitled *From Bapaume to Passchendaele*), p. 214. The details and technicalities that follow, prior to the attack at Messines, are mostly drawn from James Edmonds, pp. 32 *et seq*. Bean on p. 579 relates the detail about Monash and his circular. The quotations in the next paragraph have been taken from Gibbs, *Struggle in Flanders*, p. 193. Consult Lytton for the trials and tribulations of war correspondents of the day, including the statement made to them by Harington, 6 June. Fox's small volume tells of the attack in journalistic terms; and James Edmonds, pp. 54 *et seq*., follows it through in his usual style. But see Bean, pp. 588 *et seq*., for a more dramatic account, including the Australian lieutenant's quotation. *The Real War*, Hart, p. 330, calls Messines a 'siege-war masterpiece', and is also responsible for the phrase which follows.

Chapter 7, The Signed Contract

Sir William's pungent letter to Haig is reprinted in the latter's *Private Papers* on the same date. The latter's reaction was developed piecemeal from his diary entries. The fact that the War Office disagreed with the optimistic views of Haig and Charteris concerning Germany's weakness is documented in James Edmonds, p. 98. Here we find that the Director of Military Intelligence, Brigadier-General

G. M. W. Macdonogh, opposed G.H.Q. Intelligence right down the line. It is also noteworthy that Robertson cautioned Haig to avoid contradicting the War Office on this vital point, writing, 'It would be very regrettable at this juncture if different estimates of Germany's resources were presented to the War Cabinet.' See the marshal's diary 7 June for Pétain's quoted assurances. Lytton is one of many who, at the time, wondered whether the time element would not work against Haig's projected campaign. German awareness of the impending assault is noted in Bean, p. 699. The following page of the Australian History tells of Rupprecht's preparation, his reaction to the Lens feint, etc. Footnoted on p. 699 (Bean) one may locate the diary entry of the Australian on leave. Lloyd George tells, p. 390, of encountering the *Frankfurter Zeitung* story. It would not be useful to document the entire proceedings in London during the momentous days of 19–21 June. These three conferences are dealt with in Davidson, Haig's published diary, Lloyd George, James Edmonds, Robertson (Vol. 2), Thomas Jones, and Duff Cooper; however, the more arresting quotations will be cited. Haig's demonstration at the conference map is described by Lloyd George, p. 359. James Edmonds' admission ('the outline of the campaign may seem super-optimistic') is on p. 101. See Lloyd George, p. 359, for 'the aerial tower' phrase. Churchill's labelling of Jellicoe's claim as 'wholly fallacious', and his reasons, appear in *The World Crisis*, p. 734. Lloyd George's summary, after the 19 June meeting, is in turn summarized in his volume, pp. 363 *et seq*. For Robertson's 20 June memo see Lloyd George, pp. 581–5, and pp. 586–90 for Haig's memo of the same date. The entire exchange that day is outlined in brief by Lloyd George, pp. 379–81. His long speech of 21 June is recapitulated on pp. 387–97. I derived the detail of the Germans shelling Dunkirk from Leugenboom from Dewar and Boraston. J. Edmonds, p. 132, records Anthoine's tardiness on 2 July. See Robertson, Vol. 2, p. 247, for his 6 July letter to Haig. Gough's request for a five-day delay is substantiated by James Edmonds, p. 132. See Robertson, Vol. 2, p. 248, and the British historian, p. 105, *re* Sir William's 19 July letter to Haig, the latter's reply, and the War Cabinet's long-delayed approval of his Flanders attack.

Chapter 8, *On the Brink*

Much of interest concerning the Eastern Front from the bolshevik point of view exists in Leon Trotsky's *History of the Russian Revolution*.

See Vol. 1, p. 356, for his reference in the second paragraph of this
chapter, and page 387 for the phrase reported by the Russian 11th
Army. The incompetence of Gough's staff was known to many. Haig's
later diary entry 10 September is a typical source. Gibbs' *Now It Can Be
Told*, pp. 476–7, is another, vastly more forceful. Lytton refers to the
matter, and the Australian Official History often does the same. Haig
himself comments (diary, 5 October) rather mildly, 'I think Gough's
Staff Officer (Malcolm) is partly the cause of this feeling.' As for the
dubious composition of the Fifth Army, Gough appraises it frankly
in *The Fifth Army*. I consulted James Edmonds, pp. 126–8, for Gough's
intention to advance to the theoretical limit, and Haig's approval of
same. Davidson's objections are aired in his own book, pp. 28 *et seq.*,
and his record of Plumer's outburst en route to the conference is found
on p. 31. I extracted Churchill's suggestion to Lloyd George ('It is
clear however that no human power . . .') from *The World Crisis*,
p. 735. Bean is credited on p. 698 for the 'mixture of motives' phrase;
and there is much more concerning the ambiguous planning, lack of
surprise, and the German side of the coin in pp. 685–701 of his history.
Regarding Uniacke's warning, see Hart's *Outline*, p. 193. Baker-Carr
comments dryly on the cavalry preparations. The aerial background is
discussed in immense detail by H. A. Jones. Haig's instructions to
Rawlinson were dated 5 July and may be verified in Maurice, who also
describes Fourth Army training. See James Edmonds generally concerning the German defensive dispositions, and p. 142 for von Lossberg's role. Nichols' is one of the better divisional histories, and I have
drawn upon it for the situation 'during the latter half of July'. Rupprecht's notation, 'My mind is quite at rest . . .' is derived from Hart's
The Real War, p. 340. The sentence about 'ridiculous maps' is
mentioned by Lloyd George, p. 385. I have quoted Arthur Conan
Doyle concerning 'a tract of ground which was difficult when
dry . . .'. See Repington's diary for 24 June concerning his talk with
Sir Douglas. The 'sunny days before the attack' are portrayed by
Hope, by Gibbs in both his books used in the present narrative, and by
Bean. I am in debt to these sources in my attempt to recapture this
wistful phase. See MacDonagh for the 7 July air raid, Playne for the
Swift and *Broke* naval episode. I derived Mr. Pringle's protest from
The War Magazine, 21 June. Note Haig's diary for his 30 July visit
with Gough. See the account by Alfred Willcox in Purdom's book
concerning the firing just before the 31 July dawn assault.

Chapter 9, The Opening Phase

The problem of the 30th Division is discussed by James Edmonds, p. 153, and German defences on pp. 141-6. Churchill's caustic phrase, 'the hopes of decisive victory . . .' derives from *The World Crisis*, p. 733. See Vol. 2 of Hindenburg's memoirs for his quoted paragraph. I acquired the background for the attack itself almost entirely from Conan Doyle, Gibbs' *Struggle in Flanders*, and the British Official History. Baker-Carr is the source for the two messages concerning tanks; the following paragraph, also having to do with the tank failure, is a composite of the narrative in Ralph Jones and Nichols. The 10.40 message was sent by Major-General W. de L. Williams and is noted by James Edmonds, p. 155. The officer who found himself 'suddenly threatening a sergeant-major' was Edmund Blunden, who on p. 223 describes the state of affairs at this juncture. The death of artillery Lieutenant Shelley of the 18th Division near Zillebeke is reported by Nichols. I secured facts about Haig's visit with Gough that afternoon from Duff Cooper and Haig's diary of the 31st. Gough's instructions to his two corps commanders are summarized in *The Fifth Army*. See James Edmonds, p. 177, for Haig's 4 August note to the War Cabinet, and p. 181 for Rupprecht's opposite views. I located Gough's appraisal of Charteris in the former's *Soldiering On*, and Lloyd George's similar estimate in his own memoirs, p. 413. The date of Charteris' diary entry, 'Every brook is swollen', is 4 August; it is quoted in Hart's *Outline*, p. 193. The description of the terrain forwarded by Haig to the King emanates from Boraston, p. 116. At this time Colonel J. F. C. Fuller was Chief General Staff Officer of the Tank Corps, and it was he who wrote the memorandum ('From a tank point of view . . .') quoted in Hart's *Reputations*, p. 135. The German burial scene appears in Binding. Father Doyle's first passage is dated 5 August. I am indebted to Miss Luard for her various diary entries of 1 and 2 August, and for other items concerning the handling of casualties. Father Doyle's next note is to be found in the 7 August issue of *The Dublin Review*. For James Edmonds' summary see pp. 177-80. The *Spectator's* paean of praise is dated 4 August. I discovered Charteris' revealing protest ('D.H. has not only accepted . . .') footnoted on p. 724 of Bean. Lloyd George, pp. 410-3, requotes the various allegations as to German weakness, and there comments further on Haig ('It naturally pleased Haig . . .') and Kiggell. Robertson's letter to Haig is reproduced at length in the latter's *Private Papers*, pp. 251-2. I extracted Haig's comment ('I could not have believed . . .') from Hart's *Fog of War*, p. 47. My primary source for the section concerning the switch to attrition, and Rawlinson's paper in this connection, was Bean, pp. 725-6. In *Soldiering On* Gough relates his suggestion to close down the campaign in August, and in *The Fifth Army* he also tells how and why Plumer was handed the key assignment on the 25th. More about this may be noted in James Edmonds, p. 206. See Gibbs' *Now It Can Be Told*, p. 477, for his conversation with the officer leaving Flanders. The continuation of the attacks in August, the phrase 'these strokes . . .', the reports received by Rupprecht, and Ludendorff's transfer of nine divisions away from the Salient are all recorded by Bean, p. 728. Baker-Carr's book substantiates the passages which follow. Again I have quoted from Vol. 2, Ludendorff, regarding his reaction to the August fighting. The *Daily News* carries the full text of H. G. Wells' plea in its 14 August issue; and Lloyd George uses much of the Pope's note two days later on p. 278. Gibbs' dispatch concerning Inverness Copse was dated 30 August, and is reprinted in *The Struggle in Flanders*, pp. 310-5.

Chapter 10, *The Intermission*

Sir Douglas Haig's 2 September report is on record; for a brief summary see James Edmonds, pp. 232-3. I derived Lloyd George's 'blood and mud' citation from Spears, as well as Joffre's 'nibbling' phrase. Playne has furnished the background for the section concerning the flood of rumours and the young ladies from the East End. Carson's warning about peace talk is cited in the *Evening Express*, and Thomas Jones (pp. 121-2) tells of the whispering about changes at the helm. Robertson's remarks to Repington may be noted in the latter's diary, 20 August; his 3 September wire to Haig appears in the field-marshal's *Private Papers* of the same day. For my account of the conference 4 September I have used Haig's diary of that date, James Edmonds, pp. 233-4, and Davidson, pp. 42-3. The quotation from Sir Henry Wilson ('This is unfortunate . . .') is a combination of his diary entries 4 and 5 September. At this time the military was complaining incessantly about manpower shortages on the Western Front; for one of many examples in dozens of sources, the reader may note James Edmonds, p. 234. In this vein, and for Wilson's remark ('to take troops away from France . . .') check his diary 15 September. Pétain's specious argument which follows is discussed by Davidson, pp. 42–3, who also outlines reprovingly (pp. 22–3) the weird episode of the Russian division which mutinied in France. I borrowed from several passages in Bean, such as the one on p. 748, to write of the dry September interim. See also pp. 757–8. James Edmonds cites von Kuhl's 'inmost conviction', p. 244. I unearthed the 'Admiral' sketch from Williamson, and the paragraph about the Hôtel du Sauvage from Gibbs' *Now It Can Be Told*, pp. 482–3. See Witkop for Corporal Zschutte's letter, and Bean, pp. 730–1, concerning the Australians for whom 'time was running out'. Many parts of Reynold's book furnish the background for my aerial material. Richthofen's report is quoted by Gibbons; I used James Edmonds, pp. 236–9, for the analysis of Plumer's scheme. and p. 251 for von Armin's view on the 17th. Bonar Law's letter to Lloyd George was used by Owen, p. 401. See Bean, pp. 753–4, for 'the usual comments from onlookers'. James Edmonds verifies, pp. 250–1, that Gough wanted the impending attack stopped. The capture of the Australian officer is detailed by Bean, pp. 758–9.

Chapter 11, *The Menin Road*

I have referred mostly to Bean, Edmonds, and Conan Doyle for my description of the attack on the 20th. The various heroisms sketchily noted are indexed in Bean and Edmonds. It was J. D. Rogers who reported, 'I have just returned . . .' as per Bean, p. 767. Again, see Bean, pp. 788–9, for the comment on casualties, the German re-quote ('The new English method . . .'), and on p. 790 the words of Lord Bertie. Robertson, who 'had to knock out a scheme . . .', writes of it on pp. 253–4, Vol. 2. Regarding Lloyd George's dilemma *re* dismissing Haig, note Owen, pp. 399–400, and the Prime Minister's own memoirs, pp. 446–55. He tells on pp. 412–4 of his visit to the front; Gough also writes of it in *The Fifth Army*. 'The usual stuff' from Charteris is derived from Lloyd George, pp. 415–6, and on the latter page also appears the quote: 'G.H.Q. could not capture the Passchendaele ridge . . .'. Rupprecht's expression ('It is to be hoped . . .') is used by Bean, p. 803. Ludendorff's words which follow were picked up in James Edmonds, p. 294. Shaw, p. 240, writes how 'the war dragged on . . .'. Robertson's well-known and revealing admission to Haig—'My views are known to you'—have been noted in many sources; *i.e.*, his own work, Vol. 2, p. 255. The essay 'Two Appreciations' is in Captain Hart's *Fog of War*. Churchill's attitude toward attrition is reprinted from *The World Crisis*, p. 563, and Lloyd George's similar view from his memoirs, p. 408. I used Gibbs' *Now It Can Be Told*, p. 485, for the episode about the officer sentenced to death. Four sources were consulted for the 28 September conference: Gough's *Fifth Army*; James Edmonds, pp. 296–8; Davidson, p. 51; Bean, pp. 878–80. See Bean for Haig's ebullient estimate *re* German casualties, p. 943. As for the meeting held 2 October, I went to Haig's diary of that date; Davidson, p. 51; and Bean, p. 880. I am under obligation to Caroline Playne for my material on the home front. Finally, see Haig's diary 3 October for the 'great bombshell' about taking over more of the French line.

Chapter 12, *Haig's Decision*

All the German quotations in the first paragraph are in Davidson, p. 55, except the last, which was taken from Bean, p. 876. For Charteris' exclamation, see Bean, p. 908. 'An overwhelming blow' is claimed by Bean, p. 875; and Gibbs' sentence is from *The Struggle in Flanders*, p. 379. I used Stewart for the passage, 'Long ere now . . .'. Haig's dispatch may be examined fully in Boraston, p. 127. Duff Cooper reports the congratulations from Pershing and Lord Derby. Repington's diary entry—'nations counted money no more than pebbles'—is dated 4 October. The Charteris note of the 7th is from his own published diary. I hesitated about using Foch's almost too-familiar warning ('*Boche* is bad . . .'), but succumbed; it may be noted in Churchill's *The World Crisis*, p. 739. Davidson, p. 58, has summed up the 7 October conference. The need to 'tranquilise public opinion' is stated by Stewart. For Haig's memo to Sir William and the politicians, see his *Private Papers* under date of 8 October, and Hart's *Fog of War*, pp. 264 *et. seq.* 'Still another smashing triumph . . .' is quoted from Lloyd George, p. 417. Check *The Struggle in Flanders*, p. 386, for the Gibbs excerpt. Pétain's remark to Repington about Charteris was confided to the colonel's diary 7 October, along with the one about British generals. Shipping losses were derived from Simonds. Lloyd George has written at length, pp. 262 *et seq.*, concerning Baron von Kuhlmann's peace overture. I also derived some material about it from Thomas Jones, pp. 129–30. Churchill's appraisal of Haig, who 'acted from conviction', and Robertson appears in *The World Crisis*, p. 739. The almost unbelievable statement by Charteris ('With a great success tomorrow . . .') causes one to wonder if, after all, this otherwise brilliant officer was quite balanced; it is drawn from Bean, p. 908. Also see Bean for an account of Harington's press conference: pp. 884-5.

Chapter 13, *The Slough of Despond*

The section 'through what might have been a porthole' has been re-quoted from Housman. All military details about the attack 9 October may be verified in Bean and James Edmonds. See Davidson, p. xix of his Foreword, for the little formula $D = W/2$. The remarks of the Australian subaltern ('Ah doan' know what our brigade was doin'') are chronicled by Bean, p. 887, and the recollections of soldiers struggling to reach the jump-off line appear in Gibbs' *Struggle in Flanders*, p. 399. The officer who remarked, 'Our turn now', was quoted by George W. Wear, whose story is published in Purdom's invaluable volume. Again see Purdom, quoting George Brame, as to the corporal who failed. The phrase 'there was no curtain of fire at all' is Bean's, p. 888. Two pages later this historian comments on the pre-battle decimation of the 6th and 7th brigades, 2nd Australian Division. I used Hope's description of an attack on a pill-box ('Suddenly his helmet seems to be knocked off . . .'). The forlorn encounter of the eighty-five men who raided Celtic Wood is told by Bean, pp. 899-900. The admission that the Germans won a 'comparative success' that day is James Edmonds', p. 337, where one also finds the German complaint concerning 'the sufferings of the troops'. My reference for the paragraph beginning, 'In England and the U.S. the newspapers . . .' is Lytton. Gough's expressive and much-quoted passage ('Still the guns churned this treacherous slime . . .') is from *The Fifth Army*, and the citation immediately thereafter was taken from Bean, p. 890. See Charles Edmonds for the episode about the British officer and his men who could not bring themselves to shoot the wounded German. There is much in both Gibbs books which deals with casualties after the battle; for example, see *Now It Can Be Told*, p. 482. Hope, p. 138, depicts those who died in shell-holes; and Housman tells of the little German dog.

Chapter 14, *Journey's End*

The artificial aspect of life in the metropolis during the war years is recalled in many a contemporary account; generally I referred to Playne and Peel. Lady Sarah Wilson's query is dated 20 October. I was also aided by Sylvia Pankhurst's classic autobiography of the embattled pacifist. See the *Nation*, 25 August, for the incantation on the 'symbolic Statesman'. Robertson's letter to Haig is published in the latter's papers 9 October. Lloyd George's quote ('the patient . . .') appears in Callwell, Vol. 2, p. 17, and Sir William states his reaction in *Soldiers and Statesmen*, Vol. 2, pp. 256–8. Haig's comment on Lord French ('Never before, perhaps . . .') was derived from Duff Cooper, as well as the next sentence about Wilson. 'A poor production . . .' comes from the commander-in-chief's diary 31 October. See Stewart's fine account of the menacing phase 10 and 11 October, including the passage, 'We all hope for the best . . .'. I used Haig's diary 10 and 11 October for his meetings with Gough and Poincaré respectively, and James Edmonds, pp. 338–9, concerning Plumer's problems with German wire and British wounded. Note Bean, pp. 906–7, for the misapprehension as to the 66th Division's front. The state of New Zealand artillery is conveyed by James Edmonds, p. 339. I found Charteris' quotation ('He was still trying to find some grounds . . .') in Bean, p. 908, on which page one may also find Haig's interview with the newspapermen. Gough's telephone call to Plumer that evening is cited by Bean, p. 910; and it is Bean, p. 912, who observes that the infantry 'attacked virtually without protection'. The diary entry, 'My opinion is . . .', was dated 12 October and appears in Stewart. The Australian who patrolled the line near the Ravebeke was Lieutenant W. G. Fisher; his reports are given by Bean, pp. 906–7, 927, 931. Refer to Haig's diary 16 October for Lloyd George's message of praise. I used Churchill's *The World Crisis*, pp. 739–40, anent Caporetto. Sir Henry Wilson's diary entries: 'We may lose . . .' and 'I quoted also . . .' are dated 29 and 30 October; see Callwell's Vol. 2, p. 19. Birdwood, p. 318, tells of the effect of mustard gas on his men. I extracted Gough's words about 'the state of the ground' from *The Fifth Army*. See Graham, *A Private in the Guards*, re souvenir hunting. The *Spectator* note is under the date of 20 October. Binding is the Bavarian officer who deprecated the British effort; this is in his diary 18 October. I learned of General von Armin's press interview via *The Times' History of the War*, Vol. 16. The last in Gough's long series of pleas 'to stop the attack' is verified in *Tim Harington Looks Back*. It is James Edmonds, pp. 351–2, who writes, 'Here, too, the mud . . .'. Haig's dispatch 'The persistent continuation of wet weather . . .' is reproduced in Boraston, p. 130. Duff Cooper cites the marshal's request that Robertson's people issue more optimistic reports. See Lytton for his rebuke of Charteris, Repington (14 October) for Plumer's related opinion, Repington (15 October) concerning his talk with Kiggell. The citation from Monash combines his letters of 15 and 18 October. Ludendorff's 'horror of the shell hole area' derives from Vol. 2. See Hoffman, 28 October, for his extract. Turning to Lloyd George on 'the pencil' and Charteris, we find these comments on pp. 424–5. Maurice quotes Rawlinson *re* Pétain: '. . . once the Boche has been given time . . .'. The press revolt against the military is noted by Repington, 2 and 3 November. I drew upon Callwell, Vol. 2, p. 20, for the paragraph about the Superior War Council and Kiggell. The meeting between Haig and Lloyd George on 4 November is described in the former's diary of that date. I referred to MacDonagh concerning Ramsay MacDonald's peace move. The final passage on Kiggell tells again the incident related by Owen, p. 402; Hart in his *Outline*, p. 199; and Hart in *The Real War*, p. 343, where an expanded version is given.

Chapter 15, *War and Peace*

The new difficulties inherent in the Passchendaele salient are pointed out by Bean, p. 936. See Lloyd George, p. 427, for G.H.Q.'s 13 December instructions: 'These salients are unsuitable . . .'. Nichols writes mordantly about conditions in and near the Houthulst Forest. The quotation ('Nothing can be said . . .') is by Ernest Swinton, tank expert on the War Committee, and is taken from *Eyewitness*. I next used Fuller's *Military History*, Vol. 3. Churchill's statement *re* the French army in 1917 appears in *The World Crisis*, pp. 733–4. Davidson's estimate is on p. 19. Bean, p. 938, writes, 'It is not sufficient . . .'. Haig's reason why he had 'to go on attacking' appears in Duff Cooper. See Churchill's *The World Crisis*, p. 567, for casualty statistics, and Bean, p. 943. Lloyd George, p. 421, alleges that the figures may in time be gerrymandered. James Edmonds, pp. 360–3, enunciates the new statistics. I quote Bean, p. 941: 'On this point Field-Marshal Haig was right . . .'. The following three German complaints may be checked in Davidson, pp. 71–2. Haig's phrase about men advancing 'through mud up to their waists' is from a dispatch to the King; see Boraston, p. 133. The Prime Minister's comparison between Haig's offensive and Nivelle's is on pp. 420–1. Charteris is one of many sources for

Lloyd George's rather unfortunate speech: 'When we advance a kilometre . . .', and this general also quotes Carson in rebuttal. The retrospective views in the next paragraph emanate respectively from *Tim Harington Looks Back*; Davidson, pp. 72–3; Bean, p. 941; *The World Crisis*, p. 569. I consulted Maurice for the Doullens conference and Rawlinson's cited passage. For a broad picture of the fall of 'Wully', see Hart's *Fog of War*, pp. 108–10. Owen verifies (p. 462) that Haig virtually abandoned his C.I.G.S. The marshal's diary entry, 'I am afraid that in the back of his mind . . .' was inscribed 11 February, 1918. Owen, p. 401, tells of Northcliffe's 'sudden revulsion'. Note Wells' *Outline of History*, Vol. 2, p. 1087, for his views on the military mentality. Hindenburg's appraisal of British generalship appears in Vol. 2. Charteris *re* Haig's uncritical mind is quoted by Hart, *Fog of War*, p. 48. See Bean, p. 946, for the excerpt, 'When in the near future . . .'. The tale of Haig's presentation at Aldershot was derived from Hart's *The Real War*, p. 388. I found Churchill's remark ('They were worn down . . .'), referring to the German spring 1918 offensive, in *The World Crisis*, p. 571. My figures on total war casualties were acquired from *The Encyclopaedia Britannica*, 1953 edition, Vol. 23, p. 775. Owen, p. 442, has recorded Lloyd George's words ('If people really knew . . .') to the newspaperman. My sketch of London at the Armistice was drawn from material in *The World Crisis*, H. G. Wells' *Outline*, and especially Mrs. C. S. Peel's published recollections.

Sequel

The facts about Haig's declining years were culled from Charteris, Duff Cooper, and Churchill's *Great Contemporaries*. My references for Lloyd George's 'long road' are Owen and Thomas Jones. See Hart's *Fog of War* and the *Britannica* concerning my passage on Sir William Robertson. Finally, I owe much to Brice, Farrer, Hurst, Mottram, Muirhead, Pulteney, and Williamson, from whom I composed the medley on Ypres, the cemeteries of Belgium, and the former battleground.

Bibliography

ASTON, GEORGE, *Marshal Foch* (Hutchinson, 1929).

BAKER-CARR, C. D., *From Chauffeur to Brigadier* (Benn, 1930).

BEAN, C. E. W., *Australian Official History of the War of 1914–18*, Volume 4 (Sydney: Angus & Robertson, 1935).

BEAVERBROOK, LORD, *Politicians and the War* (Butterworth, 1928).

B.E.F. *Times: A Facsimile Reprint of the Trench Magazine* (Jenkins, 1918).

BINDING, RUDOLPH, *A Fatalist at War* (Allen & Unwin, 1928).

BIRDWOOD, FIELD-MARSHAL LORD, *Khaki and Gown* (Ward Lock, 1944).

BLUNDEN, EDMUND, *Undertones of War* (Cobden-Sanderson, 1930).

BORASTON, J. H., *Haig's Despatches 1915–1919* (Dent, 1919).

BRICE, BEATRIX, *Ypres* (Murray, 1929).

CALLWELL, C. E., *Field-Marshal Sir Henry Wilson: His Life and Diaries* (Cassell, 1927).

CHARTERIS, JOHN, *Field-Marshal Earl Haig* (Cassell, 1929).

CHURCHILL, WINSTON, *Great Contemporaries* (Cassell, 1935).

—— *The World Crisis* (Butterworth, 1927).

COOPER, ALFRED DUFF, *Haig* (Faber & Faber, 1936).

DAVIDSON, JOHN H., *Haig, Master of the Field* (Peter Nevill, 1953).

DEWAR AND BORASTON, *Haig's Command* (Constable, 1922).

DEWEERD, H. A., *Great Soldiers of World War I* (New York: Norton, 1941).

DOYLE, SIR ARTHUR CONAN, *The British Campaign in France and Flanders*, Volume 4 (Hodder & Stoughton, 1920).

DREW, H. T. B., *The War Effort of New Zealand* (Whitcombe & Tombs, 1924).

EDMONDS, CHARLES, *A Subaltern's War* (Peter Davies, 1929).

EDMONDS, J. E., *British Official History of the War: Military Operations, France and Belgium, 1917.* Volume 2 (H.M. Stationery Office, 1948).

FARRER, REGINALD, *The Void of War* (Constable, 1918).

FEILDING, ROWLAND, *War and Letters to a Wife* (The Medici Society, 1929).

FOCH, MARSHAL FERDINAND, *Memoirs* (Heinemann, 1931).

FOX, FRANK, *Battle of the Ridges* (C. A. Pearson, 1918).

GIBBONS, FLOYD, *The Red Knight of Germany* (Cassell, 1931).

GIBBS, PHILIP, *The Struggle in Flanders* (Heinemann, 1919).

—— *Now It Can Be Told* (Heinemann, 1920).

GOUGH, HUBERT, *Soldiering On* (Arthur Barker, 1954).

—— *The Fifth Army* (Hodder & Stoughton, 1931).

GRAHAM, STEPHEN, *A Private in the Guards* (Macmillan, 1919).

—— *The Challenge of the Dead* (Cassell, 1921).

GRAVES, ROBERT, *Goodbye to All That* (Cape, 1929).

GREY, CHARLES, *History of Combat Airplanes* (U.S.A., Norwich, Vt.: Norwich University, 1941).

GUEDALLA, PHILIP, *The Two Marshals* (Hodder & Stoughton, 1943).

HAIG, DOUGLAS (ed. by Robert Blake), *Private Papers* (Eyre & Spottiswoode, 1952).

HARINGTON, CHARLES, *Plumer of Messines* (John Murray, 1935).

—— *Tim Harington Looks Back* (John Murray, 1940).

HART, LIDDELL, *Reputations Ten Years After* (John Murray, 1928).

—— *The Real War* (Faber, 1930).

—— *The War in Outline* (Faber, 1936).

—— *Through the Fog of War* (Faber, 1938).

HOFFMANN, MAX, *War Diaries and Other Papers*, Volume I (Secker, 1929).

HOPE, THOMAS, *The Winding Road Unfolds* (Putnam, 1937).

HORNE, CHARLES (Ed.), *Source Records of the Great War*, Volume 5 (U.S.A., Indianapolis: The American Legion, 1930).

HOUSMAN, L. (Ed.), *War Letters of Fallen Englishmen* (Gollancz, 1930).

HURST, L. C., *The Silent Cities: Illustrated Guide to War Cemeteries in France and Flanders* (Methuen, 1929).

JOHNSON, DOUGLAS, *Battlefields of the World War* (Oxford, 1921).

JONES, H. A., *The War in the Air*, Volume 4 (Oxford, 1928).

JONES, RALPH E., *Fighting Tanks since 1916* (U.S.A., Harrisburg, Pa.: Military Service Publishing Co., 1933).

JONES, THOMAS, *Lloyd George* (Oxford, 1951).

JUNGER, ERNST, *The Storm of Steel* (Chatto & Windus, 1939).

LLOYD GEORGE, DAVID, *War Memoirs*, Volume 4 (Nicholson and Watson, 1934).

LUARD, K. E., *Unknown Warriors* (Chatto & Windus, 1930).

LUDENDORFF, ERICH, *Ludendorff's Own Story*, Volume 2 (Hutchinson, 1919).

LYTTON, NEVILLE, *The Press and the General Staff* (Collins, 1921).

MACDONAGH, MICHAEL, *In London During the Great War* (Eyre & Spottiswoode, 1935).

MAURICE, F., *Life of Lord Rawlinson of Trent* (Cassell, 1928).

MONASH, JOHN, *War Letters* (Sydney, Angus & Robertson, 1935).

MOTTRAM, RALPH, *Through the Menin Gate* (Chatto & Windus, 1932).

MOTTRAM, RALPH; EASTON, JOHN; PARTRIDGE, ERIC, *Three Personal Records of the War* (Scholartis Press, 1929).

MUIRHEAD, FINDAY, *Belgium* (Macmillan, 1924).

NICHOLS, G. F. H., *The 18th Division in the Great War* (Blackwood, 1922).

OWEN, FRANK, *Tempestuous Journey: Lloyd George, His Life and Times* (Hutchinson, 1954).

PANKHURST, SYLVIA, *The Home Front* (Hutchinson, 1933).

PEEL, MRS. C. S., *How We Lived Then* (The Bodley Head, 1929).

PIERREFEU, JEAN DE, *French Headquarters, 1915–1918* (Bles, 1924).

PLAYNE, CAROLINE, *Britain Holds On* (Allen & Unwin, 1933).

PULTENEY, WILLIAM, *The Immortal Salient* (John Murray, 1925).

PURDOM, C. B. (Ed.), *Everyman at War* (Dent, 1930).

QUIGLEY, HUGH, *Passchendaele and the Somme* (Methuen, 1928).

REPINGTON, CHARLES A'COURT, *The First World War* (Constable, 1920).

REYNOLDS, QUENTIN, *They Fought for the Sky* (New York: Rinehart, 1957).

ROBERTSON, WILLIAM, *Soldiers and Statesmen* (Cassell, 1926).

RUPPRECHT, CROWN PRINCE, *Memoirs of the Crown Prince of Germany* (Butterworth, 1922).

SHAW, GEORGE BERNARD, *What I Really Wrote about the War* (Constable, 1931).

SIMONDS, FRANK H., *History of the World War*, Volume 4 (New York: Doubleday Page, 1919).

SPEARS, EDWARD, *Prelude to Victory* (Cape, 1939).

STALLINGS, LAURENCE, *The First World War: A Photographic History* (Heinemann, 1935).

STEELE, HARWOOD, *The Canadians in France 1915–1918* (T. Fisher Unwin, 1920).

STEWART, H., *The New Zealand Division* (Whitcombe and Tombs, 1922).

Times, The, History of the War, Volumes 15 and 16.

VON HINDENBURG, PAUL, *Out of My Life*, Volume 2 (Cassell, 1920).

VON KURENBERG, JOACHIM, *The Kaiser* (Cassell, 1954).

WILLIAMSON, HENRY, *The Wet Flanders Plain* (Beaumont, 1929).

WILLIS, IRENE COOPER, *How We Got on with the War* (National Labour Press, 1919).

WITKOP, PHILIP (Ed.), *German Students' War Diaries* (Methuen, 1929).

Index

'Admiral', the, 171

Alberich operation, 56–8

Allenby, Field-Marshal Edmund (later Viscount), 60–1, 74, 97, 188, 274

Alsace-Lorraine, 205–6

Anthoine, General François, 105, 121, 122, 132, 144, 165, 197, 207, 212, 223, 225, 258

Armies, British: Second, 75, 87, 95, 101ff, 128–9, 131–2, 144, 158, 172ff, 210ff, 264; Third, 62, 254–6, 270; Fourth, 86, 107, 131–2, 205; Fifth, 55, 61, 62, 127–8, 131, 134–5, 138–9, 158, 159, 172, 180–1, 184, 192, 208, 225–6, 240, 246, 263, 270

Armin, General Sixt von, 132, 175–6, 245

Armistice, 272–3

Arras, battle of, 60–1, 96, 140, 188

Asquith, Herbert H. (later Earl of Oxford and Asquith), 23, 28, 38, 75

Augustus, Philip, 82

Australian Official Historian, *see* Bean

Austerlitz, battle of, 174

Austria, 4, 27, 39, 104, 113–4, 271, 280

Avery, Captain, 93

Bacon, Admiral Reginald, 25, 131–2, 187

Baker-Carr, Colonel C. D., 134, 159–60, 258

Balfour, Arthur (later Earl of Balfour), 27

Ball, Albert, 173

Barrie, Sir James, 193

Bean, C. E. W. (Australian Historian), 194, 220–1, 258–60, 263, 267–8

B.E.F. Times, 161–2

Benedict XV, Pope, 161

Bertie, Francis, Viscount, 181

Birdwood, Field-Marshal William (later Lord), 171, 176, 207, 210, 243

Birks, Lieutenant, 180

Bishop, Billy, 173

Boer War, 31

Borch, Count de, 193

Bottomley, Horatio, 18

Briand, Aristide, 28, 39, 41, 52

British Official Historian, *see* J. Edmonds

Broke (destroyer), 137

Broodseinde, battle of, 192, 194–6, 203–4, 248, 267

Brusilov, A., 124

Bulgaria, 23, 27, 114, 271

Bullecourt, battle of, 61, 96, 127, 241, 248

Burstall, Major-General H. E., 252

Byng, Field-Marshal Julian (later Viscount), 274

Cadorna, General Luigi, 39, 105, 114, 166, 169, 182, 201, 241

Calais conference (26 February 1917), 45–7

Cambrai, battle of, 255–6, 259, 266

Canadian Memorial, 278

Caporetto, battle of, 203, 240–2, 262

Carlyle, Thomas, 280–1

Carson, Sir Edward (later Lord), 163–4, 165, 166, 262–3

Castelnau, General de, 43, 52

Casualties, summaries of, 5, 11, 102, 147–8, 153, 161, 172, 181, 186, 194–5, 200, 223, 225, 246, 259–62, 271

Cavan, Earl of, 207, 212, 216–7, 224

Cecil, Lord Robert, 166, 234

Cemeteries, Belgian, 278–9

Chantilly conference (15 November 1916), 28, 40, 69, 71

Charteris, General John, on Flanders weather, 81; on weakness of German army, 120, 155; distorts news, 149–50; appraised by Gough and Lloyd George, 150; on Flanders terrain, 150; protests against Haig's report, 21 August, 155–6; and 20 September attack, 181–2; his September estimates, 184; comments on Broodseinde fight, 197; on rain, 7 October, 198; his remarks, 8 October, 207; his pressure on correspondents, 226; his admission, 11 October, 237; his seeming indifference, 247; and Lloyd George, 249; removed from Intelligence post, 264; on Haig, 155, 264, 269; mentioned elsewhere, 60, 105, 154, 184, 188, 203, 259

China, 274

Churchill, Winston, opposes frontal strategy, 24; and Dardanelles expedition, 24–5; appraises Haig, 34–5; on Nivelle and Painlevé, 53, 58, 59; on checking Haig, 130; opposes attrition, 189, 263; and convoy system, 204; on Haig and and Robertson, 207; learns of

Churchill, Winston (*contd.*)
Caporetto, 240–1; on French army, 258; mentioned elsewhere, 27, 37, 69–70, 112, 141, 163, 240, 271, 276, 277

Clausewitz, Carl von, 4

Clemenceau, Georges, 276

Clinton, Lieutenant, 92–3

Colvin, Lieutenant, 179

Committee on War Policy, 109ff

Convoy system, 204

Currie, Arthur W., 246

Curzon, George (later Marquess), 13, 109, 110, 116–7, 120, 122, 156

Daily Chronicle, 16, 226

Daily Mail, 25, 226

Daily News, 49, 137, 161, 183

d'Alenson, Colonel, 60, 66, 149

Dardanelles expedition, 24

David, Lieut.-Colonel T. Edgeworth, 88

Davidson, Brigadier-General John H., 129–30, 160, 203, 247, 258, 263, 269

Davies, David, 250

Defence of the Realm Act, 21

Derby, 17th Earl of, 197

Divisions, British: 1st Australian, 84, 96, 99, 132, 236, 248; 4th Australian, 61; 1st Canadian, 254; 2nd Canadian, 252; 3rd Canadian, 248; 4th Canadian, 248; New Zealand, 100, 132, 194–5, 235–8; Guards, 212, 224; 1st, 133; 4th, 212, 224; 7th, 242; 8th, 142–3; 11th, 211, 224; 16th, 152; 18th, 142, 153; 19th, 174; 21st, 195; 23rd, 242; 24th, 142–3; 29th, 212, 224–5; 30th, 142–3; 33rd, 185; 41st, 242; 48th, 211, 223, 242; 49th, 210, 213,

Divisions, British (*contd.*)
215, 221-2; 55th, 144, 147-8;
66th, 210, 213-4, 217-22, 236
Doullens conference (7 December
1917), 263
Doyle, Sir Arthur Conan, 20,
269
Doyle, Fr. William, 152, 162
Dublin Review, 152
Duff Cooper, Alfred (later Viscount
Norwich), 269

Earl, Sapper, 92
Edmonds, Charles, 269
Edmonds, Brigadier - General Sir
James (British Historian), 34, 111,
153, 225, 246, 260, 268
Edward VII, 18, 30, 32, 46, 73, 196,
246, 272
Egerton, Corporal, 180
Eisenhower, President Dwight, 275
Evening Standard, 250
Fanshawe, Major-General R., 223
Farrer, Reginald, 269
Flanders, 80, 86, 122-3, 134-6, 140,
190-1
Foch, Marshal Ferdinand, 3-5, 43,
52, 63, 73, 79, 114, 156, 165-6, 199,
249, 250, 271
Fowke, Brigadier-General G. H., 88
France, 44, 205
Franco-Prussian war, 3
Frankfurter Zeitung, 108
French Army, during first months of
war, 3-5; weakness of, 39, 110, 113,
144, 168, 201; Sixth, 60, 62; and
Nivelle, 62-7, 121-2, 168; attack
on Bruges by First, 132; and
Italians, 166; and Gheluvelt Plateau
attack, 174; under Pétain, 204;
Haig and, 258-9, 267

French, Field-Marshal Sir John (later
Earl of Ypres), 31, 33, 234-5
Fuller, Major-General J. F. C., 258

Gardiner, A. G., 183
Gaulois, French battleship, 19
Geddes, Sir Eric, 163, 167-8
German Army, on Swiss-Belgian
border, 5-6; at Salonika, 27;
retreat from France, 55; in *Alberich*
operation, 56-8, and Belgium, 72;
fraternizing with Russians, 76;
and Messines Ridge, 81, 83,
96-103; and mining of British
front line, 89-92; and British
shelling, 97-8; Robertson and, 106;
casualties, 155, 161, 191, 262
Germany, *The Times* and, 13; Crown
Prince on conditions in, 20; and
United States, 43-4; and Russian
Revolution, 48; end of German-
American diplomatic relations, 48-
9; and Nivelle plan, 54-5; Philip
Gibbs and, 203; and her opponents,
240
Gibbs, Sir Philip, 103, 158, 162, 190,
203, 226, 270
Gladstone, W. E., 36
Glanville, Lieutenant, 179-80
Globe, 251
Godley, Lieut.-General Sir Alexander
210
Goering, Hermann, 173
Gough, General Sir Hubert, at
Rollincourt, 3 January, 36; and
rumour of replacing Haig, 46;
and Bullecourt operation, 61; at
Doullens conference, 7 May, 78;
asks Haig for delay, 7 July, 122;
appraised as commander, 126-7;
his staff and army, 127-8, 141; his

Gough, General Sir Hubert (*contd.*)
part in 31 July attack, 128–33;
expands 31 July plan, 129–31; sees
Haig, 30 July, 138; sees Haig,
31 July, 145, 148; delays further
attacks, 148–9, 151; appraises Charteris, 149–50, 247; attacks, 9
August, 153; suggests ending campaign in August, 157; attacks
22 August, 157; replaced by
Plumer, 158; and Baker-Carr,
159–60; and early September operations, 172; and Plumer's September
plan, 173–4; suggests cancelling
20 September attack, 176; and
Lloyd George's visit to front, 184;
at September 28 conference, 191;
at 2 October conference, 192;
rejects break-through idea, 191–2;
and Broodseinde operation, 195;
and 7 October Army meeting, 200;
his role in 9 October attack,
207ff; writes of bad ground conditions, 227, 244; and Haig's visit,
10 October, 235–6; suggests cancelling 12 October attack, 237;
suggests cancelling 26 October
attack, 246; blamed for generalship,
263; his later years, 274
Graham, Stephen, 269
Grant, General Ulysses, 266–7
Graves, Robert, 269
Guynemer, Georges, 173

Haig, Field-Marshal Sir Douglas
(later Earl), in command at Somme,
5; promoted Field-Marshal, 18;
favours Western Front pressure,
1916, 24–6; his post-Somme memorandum, 256; on Lansdowne's
letter, 27; at Chantilly conference,

Haig, Field-Marshal (*contd.*)
28; his life to 1917, 30–5; on
cavalry, 33–4; at Rollincourt,
3 January, 36; resents entry of
Nivelle, 42–3; and German naval
policy, 44; at Calais conference,
45–6; opinion of Lloyd George,
46, 156; fears replacement by
Gough, 46; plan for Flanders
offensive, 51, 69–75; on Nivelle,
50, 57, 62, 67; writes War Cabinet,
1 May, 67; at Paris conference,
4 May, 76; at Doullens conference,
7 May, 78; sees Pétain, 18 May, 78,
79; worries about Messines attack,
90–1; cautioned by Robertson,
104–6; at London conference,
19–21 June, 108–20; awaits Cabinet
approval, 121–3 delays attack, 122;
writes War Cabinet, 20 July,
122; receives Cabinet approval,
123; and 31 July attack, 129, 131,
132, 134, 137, 140, 154; accepts
Gough's views, 129–30; further
instructs Rawlinson, 131–2; fears
rain, 135, 162; visits Gough,
30 July, 138; awaits 31 July attack,
139; visits Gough, 31 July, 145,
148–9; writes War Cabinet, 4
August, 148; and Charteris, 149,
237; on bad terrain, 150–1, 196;
urges Pétain to attack, 150–1; and
August attacks, 157; gives Plumer
main role, 158; reports to War
Cabinet, 2 September, 163–4;
wired by Robertson, 3 September,
165; at 4 September conference,
165–8; on French army weakness,
168–9; demands additional drafts,
167–8; and early September operations, 172; and 20 September
attack, 175, 180–1; and Gardiner's

Haig, Field-Marshal (*contd.*)
visit, 183; reports to Lloyd George in September, 183–4; and Polygon Wood operation, 185; on attrition 187–8; appraised by Liddell Hart, 189; at conference 28 September, 191; at 2 October conference, 192; and importance of 4 October attack, 194; writes King of difficulties, 196; tries to hurry next October attack, 197; and 7 October meeting, 200–1; decides to continue offensive, 200ff; his 8 October memoranda, 201–2; and his offensive to date (8 October), 203–5; ignores U.S. entry, 50, 204; on peace terms, 206; Churchill and, 206–7; on Anthoine, 207–8; reports on 9 October fight, 226; and ensuing rain, 231; on Generals French and Wilson, 234–5; visits Gough, 10 October, 235–6; and Poincaré, 236; sees correspondents, 11 October, 237; and 15 October decision, 239; accepts Lloyd George's congratulations, 240; and Caporetto, 240–1; protests against sending divisions to Italy, 241; resists supreme War Council, 242, 250–1; considers ending campaign, 245; his continuing sense of mission, 246–7; attacked by Press, 250, 265; sees Lloyd George, 4 November, 251; and the new front line, 254; calls for attack, 10 November, 254; ends campaign, 20 November, 256; and Cambrai battle, 254–5; his views in retrospect, 257, 258–67; and ensuing controversy, 258ff; at Doullens conference, 7 December, 263; removes Charteris and Kiggell,

Haig, Field-Marshal (*contd.*)
264; abandons Robertson, 264; his character appraised, 266–8; biographies of, 269–70; his *Despatches* and *Private Papers*, 270; and remainder of war, 270–1; raised to peerage, 274; his later years, 274–6

Harington, Major - General Sir Charles, 87–8, 89, 127, 174, 194, 208, 213, 246, 263

Harmsworth, Alfred, *see* Northcliffe

Hart, Captain Liddell, 102, 189, 269, 277

Henry, Major, 93

Hindenburg, Field-Marshal Paul von, 103, 141–2, 266

Hindenburg Line, 55, 56, 255, 271

Hitler, Adolf, 276

Hoffmann, Major-General Max, 80, 115, 134, 168, 186, 202, 249

Hope, Thomas, 269

Imperial War Graves Commission, 278

Inflation, 17, 232–3

Inverness Copse, battles of, 158–9, 162

Inwood, Private, 179

Isonzo River, battles of, 105, 166, 240

Italy, 28, 44, 105, 114–5, 120, 165, 182, 201, 205, 241, 265, 274

Izvolsky, Alexander, 28

Jacob, Field-Marshal Sir Claud, 140, 142, 144, 148, 153, 157

Japan, 206, 274

Jellicoe, Admiral Sir John (later Earl), 76, 79, 112, 116–7

Joffre, Marshal Joseph, 5, 28, 29, 35, 39, 41, 52, 73, 75, 164, 168, 201, 271

John Bull, 18, 233–4
Jones, Henry Arthur, 193
Jones, Thomas, 269
Jutland, naval battle of, 23, 112

Kerenski, Alexander, 121, 124, 169
Ketchen, Brigadier-General H. D. B., 252
Kiggell, Lieut.-General Sir Launcelot, 40–1, 75, 155–6, 167, 241, 248, 251, 253, 264
Kirkaldy, Andrew, 275
Kitchener, Earl, 31, 32, 33
Korrespondenz Norden, 245
Kuhl, General von, 90, 170, 261
Kuhlmann, Richard von, 205–6

Langemarck, battle of, 154–5
Lansdowne, 5th Marquess of, 27
Law, Andrew Bonar, 110, 116–7, 137, 156, 166, 175
Lawrence, Major-General H. A., 220, 236
League of Nations, 43, 276
Lens, battle of, 107
Lloyd George, David (later Earl), claims war lost, 22; character of, 23; and War Office, 23–4; his opinion of Haig, 24, 206, 268–9; opposes (1916) Western Front operations, 24; on Lansdowne letter, 26–7; at Chantilly conference, 28–9, 35; his life to 1917, 36–7, 163; at Rome conference, 38–40; his views after the Rome conference, 40; meets Nivelle, 41; underestimates new German submarine policy, 44; and Calais conference, 45–6; on U.S. entry, 50; queries Haig on Nivelle, 65;

Lloyd George, David (*contd.*)
at 1 May Cabinet meeting, 76; at 4 May Paris meeting, 76–7; and Messines plan, 80; his Italian scheme, 104, 122, 156; at London conference, 108–20, 129; appraises Charteris, 120, 149; derides optimism of generals, 155–6; at Birkenhead, 161; mistrusts Haig's 2 September report, 164; at 4 September conference, 165–8; withholds drafts from Haig, 167–8; on French army, 168; and Supreme War Council, 169, 242, 250; and Law's letter, 18 September, 175; doubts 20 September victory, 182; on Cadorna, 182; on removing Haig and Robertson, 183, 264; visits Haig in September, 183; and German prisoners episode, 183–4; on GHQ "propaganda", 184–5; on hopeless attacks, 189; states views of Broodseinde fight, 203; rebuffs von Kuhlmann, 205–6; sponsors Palestine offensive, 206; and advice from Generals Wilson and French, 234–5; congratulates Haig, 240; and Caporetto, 240–1; berates Haig and Charteris, 249–50; sees Haig, 4 November, 251; on casualty figures, 260, 262; compares campaign to Nivelle's, 262; on capturing Passchendaele, 262; his *War Memoirs*, 117–8, 260, 269, 276; biographies of, 269; on stopping the war, 271; his later years, 276–7
Lloyd George, Dame Margaret, 276
London, 14ff, 24, 136–7, 192–3, 232–4, 272
London conference (19–21 June), 108–20

Lossberg, Colonel von, 132–3
Luard, Nurse K. E., 153, 162
Ludendorff, General Erich von, 44,
 55, 56, 80, 96, 150, 159, 186–8, 194,
 201–2, 249, 270–1, 274
Lyautey, Louis (later Marshal), 52

MacDonald, Ramsay, 252
Malcolm, Lieutenant, 193
Malmaison, battle of, 201, 258
Manchester Guardian, 250
Mangin, General Charles, 60, 62, 66
Mannock, Mick, 173
Marlborough, Duke of, 82
Maxse, Lieut-General Sir Ivor, 207,
 211, 223–4, 248
McCudden, James, 173
Menin Gate, 85, 192, 278
Menin Road, battle of, 174ff
Messines, battle of, 75, 77, 80, 86,
 99ff, 106–7, 111, 113, 121, 133, 174,
 176, 186, 241–2, 263, 266–7
Micheler, General, 57, 66
Milner, Viscount, 109, 110, 116–7;
 122, 156
Mine warfare, 88–94
Monash, General Sir John, 84, 96, 99,
 248
Morland, T. L. N., 246
Morning Post, 192–3, 251
Mottram, Ralph, 269

Napoleon Bonaparte, 4, 37, 121, 214,
 266
Nation, The, 161, 193, 232–3, 251
National News, 137
New York Times, 226
Nivelle, General Robert, meets Lloyd
 George, 41; his plan, 42; and
 British War Cabinet, 15 January,

Nivelle, General Robert (*contd.*)
 42; and Calais conference, 44–6;
 his dealings with Haig, 46–7;
 yearns to attack, 52–3; and Painlevé, 52, 108; his problems and
 preparations, 53–4; his plans known
 to enemy, 54–5; and German
 withdrawal, 55–60; refuses to
 change plan, 56; influenced by
 subordinates, 60, 149; finally
 attacks, 62–4; replacement of,
 65–7; talks with Painlevé, 108–9
Northcliffe, Viscount (Alfred C.
 Harmsworth), 23, 73, 185, 265

Owen, Frank, 269

Painlevé, Paul, 52–3, 57, 58, 63,
 76–7, 108–9, 169, 205, 234
Palestine, 29, 105, 274
Pankhurst, Sylvia, 15–16
Paris conferences: (4 May), 76–7;
 (8 October), 206
Parma, Duke of, 280
Passchendaele, 86, 128, 200, 210, 220,
 236, 240, 243–4, 252, 278, 280;
 battles of, 237–8, 240, 248–9, 252–3
Perceval, Major-General E. M., 222
Pershing, General John J., 197
Pétain, Marshal Henri, as Nivelle's
 rival, 52; questions Nivelle's plan,
 53, 57, 58; considered as Nivelle's
 successor, 63, 66; named French
 Chief of General Staff, 66; calms
 French mutinies, 66–7, 204; at
 Paris conference, 4 May, 76–7;
 sees Wilson, 11 May, 78; sees
 Haig, 18 May, 78, 79; sees Wilson,
 19 May, 78; and co-operation with
 Haig, 105; reassures Haig in June,

Pétain Marshal, Henri (*contd.*)
110; on Russian army, 124; promises August diversion, 151–2; deprecates French army, 168; and Malmaison attack, 201; on Charteris, 203–4; on British generalship, 203–4; and Haig's campaign, 204, 249–50; talks to Rawlinson in October, 250

Pilckem Ridge, battle of (31 July), 138ff

Plumer, Field-Marshal Sir Herbert (later Viscount), at Rollincourt, 3 January, 36; and Flanders plan, 75–6; at Doullens, 7 May, 78; character and career to 1917, 87–8; and Harington, 87–8; prepares Messines attack, 80, 86, 88ff; and Messines attack, 101, 104; and 31 July role, 128ff, 132; agrees to Gough's objectives, 129–30; and August fighting, 157; takes over from Gough, 157–8; and September planning, 172–5; overrules Gough, 20 September, 176; and Polygon Wood operation, 185–6; at 28 September conference, 191; rejects breakthrough idea, 191–2; and 2 October conference, 192; and Broodseinde attack, 195–6; his views after Broodseinde, 195, 197; and 7 October army meeting, 200; his role in 9 October attack, 207, 210ff; and problems 11 October, 236–7; determines to attack 12 October, 237; determines to attack 26 October, 246; on Charteris, 247; leaves for Italy, 264; his later years, 274

Poelcapelle, battle of, 210ff, 235–6

Poincaré, Raymond, 236

Polygon Wood, battle of, 185–6

Portugal, 274

Punch, 156

Rawlinson, General Sir Henry (later Lord), at Rollincourt, 3 January, 36; at Doullens, 7 May, 78; his army surprised in July, 107; and 31 July role, 128; further instructed by Haig, 131–2; on attrition, 157; on Haig's campaign, 250; and Doullens conference, 7 December, 263; his later years, 274; mentioned elsewhere, 86, 126, 165, 187, 205, 264

Reichstag, the German, 122

Repington, Colonel A'Court, on Russia, 48; warns Robertson, 21 May, 78–9; warns Haig, 135; hears guns 28 July, 137; interviews Robertson in August, 165; on continuing the war, 197–8, 232; sees Pétain, 7 October, 204; talks to British commanders in October, 246–7; deplores Press attacks on Haig, 250

Review of Exemptions Act, 137

Ribot, Alexandre, 66, 67, 76

Richthofen, Captain Manfred von, 172–3

Robertson, Field-Marshal Sir William, favours Western Front operations, 1916, 24; on Lansdowne's letter, 26; at the Chantilly conference, 28–9; at the Rome conference, 38–9; doubts Nivelle will succeed, 43, 57; at the Calais conference, 45–7; his opinion of Lloyd George, 46; on Russian situation, 48; and Flanders plan,

Robertson, Field-Marshal Sir William (*contd.*)

73–5, 79; writes Joffre, 1 December, 1916, 75; at Paris conference, 4 May, 76; writes Haig, 13 June, 104; cautions Haig 104–5; at London conference, 108–20; writes Haig, 6 July, 122; writes Haig, 19 July, 122; deprecates War Cabinet, 156; his conversation with Repington, 20 August, 165; wires Haig, 3 September, 165; at 4 September conference, 165–8; and Bonar Law, 175; and shortage of drafts, 167–8; blocks Lloyd George, 24 September, 182; writes Haig, 27 September, 188; questions Western Front theory, 188; writes Haig, 3 October, 193; irritates politicians, 207; writes Haig, 9 October, 234; on Generals Wilson and French, 234–5; and Caporetto, 241; resists Supreme War Council, 250, 264–5; his decline and fall, 183, 264–5; and *Soldiers and Statesmen*, 269–70, 277; his later years, 277

Robinson, Perry, 226

Rome conference, 5–7 January, 35, 38–40

Royal Flying Corps, 84, 94, 131, 145, 172–3, 196

Royal Navy, 72, 86, 205, 244

Rumania, 19, 23, 26, 240, 241, 274

Rupprecht, Crown Prince, 16, 20, 54, 80, 90–1, 97, 99, 107, 133, 147–8, 159, 160, 170, 185–6, 194, 202, 261

Russia, troops of in Rumania, 19; decline of, 23, 47–8; Hoffmann on revolution in, 80; 1917 offensive, 109, 121, 124–5, 137; troops and revolution, 169; collapse of, 202,

Russia (*contd.*)

241; ambassador in Paris, 8 October, 206; armistice with Central Powers, 263, 265; Lloyd George and, 276

St. Andrews Bay, golf links at, 30, 181, 275

St. Mihiel, battle of, 271

Salonika, 27, 105

Sassoon, Siegfried, 233–4, 278

Schulenberg, Graf von, 54

Serbia, 205, 240, 274

Shaw, George Bernard, 34, 47, 187

Shell scandal (1915), 163

Smith-Dorrien, General Sir Horace, 33

Smuts, General (later Field-Marshal) J. C., 22, 109, 110, 111, 116–7, 122, 156, 166

Sneddon, Sapper, 93

Somme, battle of, and Foch's army, 5; losses in, 5; casualties in, 11–12; Press and, 23; Haig's views on 25–6, 34; Franco-British campaign considered, 71; compared with battle of Messines, 121; and shell shortage, 163; Joffre and, 201; mule packs used at, 238

Spectator, The, 154–5, 158, 239–40, 245, 251

Spender, J. A., 251

Strachey, Lytton, 21

Submarine warfare, 16, 23, 72, 110, 204

Supreme War Council, 250–1, 264

Swift (destroyer), 137

Tank warfare, 25, 94–5, 134–5, 142–3, 151, 159–60, 199, 212, 255, 257–8

Tatler, The, 232

Thomas, Albert (French Minister of Munitions), 16

Thomas, Sir William Beach, 226

Times, The, and German peace proposals, 13; and food shortage, 16; and travelling conditions, 17; and New Year 1917, 17; and enemy's progress, 19; and German U-boat commander, 19; and politicians, 23; and Ypres Salient, 148–9; and gains at Ypres, 151; and falsification of battle news, 155; and Pope's note to belligerent governments, 161; and Polygon Wood incident, 190; and Haig's success, 203; and Passchendaele battle, 227; turns against Haig, 250, 265

Trotsky, Leon, 124

Turkey, 16, 24, 27, 114, 271

Udet, Ernst, 173

Uniacke, Major-General H. C. C., 131

United States, the, and rumours concerning entry into war, 16, 48; President Wilson and 'peace without victory', 43–4; entry into war, 49–50; Haig's reference to U.S. power, 204–5; Press and Broodseinde attack, 225–6; and Supreme War Council, 251; and Marne battle, 271; victory at St. Mihiel, 271; and Haig, 274

Verdun, battle of, 41, 69, 71, 74

Versailles conference, 276

Vimy Ridge, capture of, 61, 113

Vivian, Dorothy, 32

Voss, Werner, 173

War Cabinet, 23, 26, 35, 67, 72, 73–4, 76, 112, 113, 121–3, 149, 156, 163–4, 165–8, 169, 183, 193, 202–3, 207, 241, 264, 267

Wells, H. G., 161, 266

Westminster Gazette, 251

Wilson, Field-Marshal Sir Henry, on Woodrow Wilson, 26, 43; at Rome conference, 39; on Nivelle, 59; his opinions after Nivelle's failure, 63; and Flanders plan, 74, 77, 80; quotes Pétain, 11 May, 78; quotes Pétain, 19 May, 78; doubts French will co-operate, 79, 80; quotes Foch, 2 June, 79; on French mutinies, 80; comments on 4 September conference, 166–7; on fighting Turkey, 168; visits Lloyd George, 5 October, 206; on Haig's strategy, 234–5; his comments after Caporetto, 241; named to Supreme War Council, 251; appointed C.I.G.S., 265; his later years, 274; mentioned elsewhere, 45, 116, 264

Wilson, Lady Sarah, 232

Wilson, President Woodrow, 26, 43–4, 48–9, 169, 271, 276

Woodward, Captain, 92–3

Ypres, 83–7, 134–5, 245, 278–80

Yser, battle of, 107, 131–2, 257

Zeppelin raids, 16

Zschutte, Corporal Helmut, 171

PENGUIN ONLINE